D1601710

CRITICAL ISSUES IN CROSS-NATIONAL PUBLIC ADMINISTRATION

CRITICAL ISSUES IN CROSS-NATIONAL PUBLIC ADMINISTRATION

Privatization, Democratization, Decentralization

Edited by Stuart S. Nagel

QUORUM BOOKS
Westport, Connecticut • London

Library of Congress Cataloging-in-Publication Data

Critical issues in cross-national public administration :
    privatization, democratization, decentralization / edited by Stuart
    S. Nagel.
        p.   cm.
    Includes bibliographical references and index.
    ISBN 1–56720–299–3 (alk. paper)
    1. Public administration.   2. Comparative government.
    3. Privatization.   4. Democratization.   5. Decentralization in
    government.   I. Nagel, Stuart S., 1934– .
    JF1351.C75   2000
    352.2'83—dc21   99–40350

British Library Cataloguing in Publication Data is available.

Library of Congress Catalog Card Number: 99–40350
ISBN: 1–56720–299–3

First published in 2000

Quorum Books, 88 Post Road West, Westport, CT 06881
An imprint of Greenwood Publishing Group, Inc.
www.quorumbooks.com

Printed in the United States of America

The paper used in this book complies with the
Permanent Paper Standard issued by the National
Information Standards Organization (Z39.48–1984).

10   9   8   7   6   5   4   3   2   1

To people who stimulated my values regarding
Privatization, such as David Wright and Paul Sweezy
Democracy, such as Robert Dixon and Roland Pennock
Decentralization, such as William Anderson and Harold Zink

Contents

Introduction

Stuart S. Nagel

This volume deals with the most contemporary issues in running a modern government. Those issues include (1) the allocation of authority between the public sector and the private sector, (2) the allocation of authority between the government and the people, and (3) the allocation of authority between the national government and the provincial and local governments. These issues are referred to as the issues of privatization, democratization, and decentralization. A key aspect of this book is to try to provide solutions to these controversies or conflicts of authority in such a way that both sides or all major sides can come out ahead of their best initial expectations. That is referred to as win–win policy. We can now give a brief example from each of the three issues.

PRIVATIZATION

The changes that are occurring in many regions and nations of the world provide an excellent opportunity to apply systematic policy analysis to determining such basic matters as how to organize the economy, the government, and other social institutions. Population control and land reform are highly important problems, but they may not be as basic as reconstituting a society.

Ownership

Figure I.1 analyzes the fundamental issue of socialism versus capitalism in the context of government versus private ownership

Figure I.1
Government versus Private Ownership and Operation

GOALS	C	L
	High productivity	1. Equity 2. Workplace quality 3. Environmental protection 4. Consumer protection
C Private ownership and operation	+	−
L Government ownership and operation	−	+
N Some government and some private	0	0
SOS or Win-Win 100-percent government owned and 100-percent private operation	++	++

Key: C = Conservative; L = Liberal; N = Neutral; + = relatively conducive to the goal (the best of the alternatives on the goal *before* the SOS alternative is considered); 0 = neither conducive nor adverse; − = relatively adverse; ++ = the best of the alternatives on the goal *after* the SOS alternative is considered.

and operation of the basic means of producing industrial and agricultural products. The essence of socialism in this context is government ownership and operation of factories and farms, or at least those larger than the handicraft or garden size, as in the Soviet Union of 1960. The essence of capitalism is private ownership and operation of both factories and farms, as in the United States of 1960. The neutral position or middle way is to have some government and some private ownership–operation, as in the Sweden of 1960. The year 1960 is used because that is approximately when the Soviet Union began to change with the advent of Nikita Khruschev. The United States also underwent big changes in the 1960s with the advent of John F. Kennedy.

Figure I.1 refers to government ownership–operation as the liberal or left-wing alternative, as it is in the United States and in world history at least since the time of Karl Marx. The figure refers to private ownership–operation as the conservative or right-wing alternative, as it is in the United States and elsewhere at least since the time of Adam Smith. In recent years in the Soviet Union and China, those favoring privatization have been referred to as liberals, and those favoring retention of government ownership–operation have been referred to as conservatives. The labels make no difference in this context. The object of Figure I.1 is to find a super-optimum solution (SOS) that more than satisfies the goals of both ideologies or groups, regardless of their labels.

The key capitalistic goal is high productivity in terms of income-producing goods substantially above what it costs to produce them. The key socialistic goal is equity in terms of the sharing of ownership, operation, wealth, and income. Other goals that tend to be more socialistic than capitalistic but are less fundamental consist of (1) workplace quality, including wages, hours, safety, hiring by merit, and worker input; (2) environmental pollution; and (3) consumer protection, including low prices and goods that are durable, safe, and high quality.

Going down the productivity column, the liberal socialistic alternative does not score so high on productivity for a lack of profit-making incentives and a surplus of bureaucratic interference in comparison to the capitalistic alternative, assuming the level of technology is held constant. The empirical validity of that statement is at least partially confirmed by noting that the capitalistic countries of Japan and West Germany are more productive than their socialistic counterparts of East Germany and China, although they began at approximately the same level in 1945 at the end of World War II. Going down the equity column, the liberal socialistic alternative does score relatively high. By definition, it involves at least a nominal collective sharing in the ownership and operation of industry and agriculture, which generally leads to less inequality in wealth and income than capitalism does.

On the goals that relate to the workplace, the environment, and consumers, the socialists traditionally argue that government ownership–operation is more sensitive to those matters because it is less profit oriented. The capitalists traditionally argue that private ownership–operation is more sensitive in competitive marketplaces in order to find quality workers and to increase the quantity of one's consumers. The reality (as contrasted to the theory) is that without alternative incentives or regulations, both government managers and private managers of factories and farms are motivated by the expenses of providing workplace quality, environmental protection, and consumer protection. The government-factory manager in the state factories of China may be just as insensitive to consumer safety and durability as their monopolistic counterparts in the American automobile industry.

As for how the super-optimum solution operates, it involves government ownership, but all the factories and farms are rented to private entrepreneurs to develop productive and profitable manufacturing and farming. Each lease is renewable every year, or longer if necessary to get productive tenants. A renewal can be refused if the factory or farm is not being productively developed, or if the entrepreneur is not showing adequate sensitivity to workers, the environment, and consumers.

As for some of the advantages of such an SOS system, it is easier to not renew a lease than it is to issue injunctions, fines, jail sentences, or other negative sanctions. It is also much less expensive than subsidies. The money received for rent can be an important source of tax revenue for the government to provide productive subsidies elsewhere in the economy. Those subsidies can especially be used for encouraging technological innovation–diffusion, the upgrading of skills, and stimulating competition for market share, which can be much more beneficial to society than either socialistic or capitalistic monopolies. The government can more easily demand sensitivity to workers, the environment, and consumers from its renters of factories and farms than it can from itself. There is a conflict of interest in regulating oneself.

This SOS alternative is mainly available to socialistic countries like Russia, China, Cuba, North Korea, and others, since they already own the factories and land. It would not be economically or politically feasible for capitalistic countries to move from the conservative capitalistic alternative to the SOS solution by acquiring ownership through payment or confiscation. This is an example where socialistic countries are in a position to decide between socialism and capitalism by compromising and winding up with the worst of both possible worlds: the relative unproductivity of socialism and the relative inequity of capitalism. The socialistic countries are also in a position to decide between the two basic alternatives by winding up with the best of both possible worlds: retaining the equities and social sensitivities of government ownership while having the high productivity that is associated with profit-seeking entrepreneurial capitalism. It would be difficult to find a better example of compromising versus super-optimizing than the current debate over socialism versus capitalism.

Competition

The conservative alternative of an unregulated marketplace may lead to only one or a few firms dominating most industries. That arrangement may be profitable in the short run, although contrary to low prices. The liberal alternative of government ownership or tight regulation tends to mean a government monopoly or stifled private enterprise. That means reduced business profits, although it might mean artificially low prices to satisfy consumers as voters. The mixed economy scores in the middle on both business profits and low prices (see Figure I.2).

Figure I.2
Competition

GOALS / ALTERNATIVES	C Business profits	L Low prices
C Marketplace (monopoly)	+	−
L Government ownership or tight regulation (monopoly)	−	+
N Some of both (mixed economy)	0	0
SOS or Win-Win 1. Stimulate competition through well-placed subsidies 2. Free trade 3. Royalties rather than patents 4. Leasing infrastructure	++	++

Key: C = Conservative; L = Liberal; N = Neutral; + = relatively conducive to the goal (the best of the alternatives on the goal *before* the SOS alternative is considered); 0 = neither conducive nor adverse; − = relatively adverse; ++ = the best of the alternatives on the goal *after* the SOS alternative is considered.

The SOS alternative may draw upon the stimulus to innovation and efficiency of private profit making, and may encourage competition through well-placed seed money and other competition facilitators. Doing so results in lower prices through a competitive marketplace, rather than through a monopolistic one or through artificial price constraints.

The marketplace is associated with capitalism. It may not be associated with competition if the marketplace leads to monopolies or firms working together to decrease competition. Regulation or government ownership is associated with socialism. It is even more likely to lead to monopoly, but monopoly in the hands of the state rather than private enterprise. The marketplace may lead to better business profits rather than regulation. Regulation may lead to better consumer prices than the marketplace.

An SOS alternative is competition, which is likely to lead to even better total business profits than the marketplace, although not necessarily better profits for each firm. Competition is likely to lead to better consumer prices and quality of products than regulation. Competition can be stimulated through laws that (1) require licensing of patents and facilities, (2) lower tariffs to increase international competition, (3) provide seed money to get new businesses established or expanded to make an industry more competitive, and (4) require leasing of networks or electricity, telephone, and cable TV.

Equality in Socialism and Capitalism

Capitalism differs from socialism mainly in terms of government versus private ownership–operation of the major means of production and distribution (see Figure I.3). Capitalism also differs from socialism with regard to the extent to which inequality of income and wealth is allowed. Under pure capitalism, there are no limits to the degree of permissible inequality in income and wealth. Under socialism, there are progressive income taxes and inheritance taxes designed to promote a substantial amount of equality in income and wealth. Capitalism justifies economic inequality as a stimulus to increased productivity. The theory is that people will work harder and be more innovative in order to receive the rewards of greater income and wealth. Socialism justifies having greater income equality as the fair or equitable thing to do, especially in the context of providing a minimum floor regarding food, shelter, and clothing to the poor.

An SOS alternative which does well on both the conservative and liberal goals involves allowing considerable inequality in income

Figure I.3
Equity

GOALS / ALTERNATIVES	C Productivity	L Equity (minimum floor)
C Income inequality (Capitalism)	+	−
L Income equality (Socialism)	−	+
N In between	0	0
SOS or Win-Win 1. Negative income tax or earned income credit 2. Tax breaks for upgrading skills	++	++

Key: C = Conservative; L = Liberal; N = Neutral; + = relatively conducive to the goal (the best of the alternatives on the goal *before* the SOS alternative is considered); 0 = neither conducive nor adverse; − = relatively adverse; ++ = the best of the alternatives on the goal *after* the SOS alternative is considered.

and wealth but providing a minimum floor. That can be done through a negative income tax, whereby people who are below that minimum level receive a payment from the Internal Revenue Service (IRS) instead of paying to the IRS. A better approach is to emphasize the earned income credit, whereby the people below a minimum level who work are rewarded by receiving an IRS payment. Those who do not work receive public aid and assistance in finding a job. The SOS may also provide tax breaks and subsidies for upgrading individual skills in order to increase one's productivity.

Political–Economic Competition and Prosperity

Figure I.4 only includes industrial nations. A separate figure could be made for developing nations. Among industrialized nations, those that provide for competition in politics and economics have more

Figure I.4
Political and Economic Competition as Key Causes of Prosperity

COMPETITION
(Causal Variable)

		NO (In Politics and Economics)	YES (In Politics and Economics)
PROSPERITY OR HIGH STANDARD OF LIVING (Effect Variable)	YES		West Germany (Capitalism) Sweden Socialism
	NO	East Germany (Socialism) Spain Pre-1980 (Capitalism)	

prosperity than those who do not provide for competition in both activities. Industrialized nations that provide for competition in only one of the two activities are likely to have middling prosperity, although competition in politics may be more important to prosperity than competition in economics. Figure I.4 is mainly designed to relate political and economic competition as key causes in prosperity. One could also interpret Figure I.4 as tending to show that countries that have economic competition are more likely to have political competition and vice versa. Figure I.4 also can be seen to show that industrialized nations are more likely to have a higher standard of living than nonindustrialized nations, regardless of political and economic competition. Another conclusion is that whether a country has capitalistic private ownership or socialistic government ownership is virtually irrelevant to prosperity in comparison to political–economic competition and industrialization.

DEMOCRATIZATION

Voting Rights

The conservative alternative to voting rights in South Africa was to deny blacks the right to vote. The extreme left-wing alternative of some of the Pan-Africans was to deny whites the right to vote or even to expel them from the country, denying that they have any right to even live in South Africa. The middling position is one person, one vote, although that could be considered a left-wing position, since the blacks would dominate. The black goal was basically for blacks to be better off. The white goal was not necessarily for whites to be better off than they presently were, but to at least not be much worse off (see Figure I.5).

The conservative position and the more extreme left-wing position would result in a kind of super-optimum position where both

Figure I.5
Voting in South Africa

GOALS / ALTERNATIVES	C Whites well off	L Blacks well off
C Only whites vote	+	−
L 1. Only blacks vote 2. Majority rule without minority safeguards	−	+

N
 	
1. Bill of rights: free
   speech, equal
   treatment, due process
2. U.S. Constitution:
   Senate, electoral
   college, special
   majorities to pass or
   amend
	0	0

SOS or Win-Win Economic rights: economic growth, upgraded skills combined with neutral alternatives	++	++

Key: C = Conservative; L = Liberal; N = Neutral; + = relatively conducive to the goal (the best of the alternatives on the goal *before* the SOS alternative is considered); 0 = neither conducive nor adverse; − = relatively adverse; ++ = the best of the alternatives on the goal *after* the SOS alternative is considered.

blacks and whites would be worse off. The only way the conservatives could succeed in keeping blacks from having the right to vote any longer would be through a system of repression even greater than they had attempted in the past. The country would be in a state of continuous guerrilla warfare with no security from bombing or assassination. There would be no foreign business, or not much, that would want to locate there. Much domestic business would leave. If the extreme blacks had their way and all the whites were driven out, the result would be somewhat similar, in that there would be a lack of foreign investment. Much domestic business would leave voluntarily or involuntarily.

The object was to develop a system in which none of those bad things happen, meaning (1) foreign investment does not shy away from South Africa, but substantially increases; (2) businesses within South Africa stay there and even expand to hire more people and make for more job opportunities; and (3) violence ends, as contrasted to merely being temporarily suspended.

The compromise position is not really one person, one vote. That is the nonextreme left-wing position. The extreme left-wing position is no voting rights to whites at all. At least at the present time, the conservative position is not to deny blacks access to jobs, public accommodations, schools, and so on. The conservative position is to wipe out all apartheid and all segregation except for voting rights. The extreme conservative position is to preserve all apartheid and segregation. A compromise position is one person, one vote combined with some kind of guarantee that whites will not be outvoted in spite of the fact that they have so many fewer people. The proposed devices are as follows:

1. Partition the country into states like the United States. Every state no matter how small gets two senators. There would be basically four states in South Africa, namely, the Cape provinces, Natal, Transvaal, and the Orange Free State. The first two would be black, the last two could be dominated by Afrikaans. There would be eight senators. Maybe each state would have five senators, so there would be twenty senators. But the blacks could not run the Senate any more than the North could run the U.S. Senate. The white states would have the power to prevent even ordinary legislation from being passed, but especially any legislation that requires a two-thirds vote, like the approval of treaties or appointments, and any amendments to the constitution would require a two-thirds vote.

2. Everything that has been proposed is exactly what was adopted in the United States in the constitution. There would be separation of powers, federalism, and judicial review. Everything is designed to enable a minority of states to be able to prevent the majority from exercising

the power that its numbers have. They would have an electoral college in which the president would be chosen on the basis of how many senators each state has, which would have nothing to do with how many people they have since every state would have the same number of senators. They would have a supreme court that would have the power to declare unconstitutional legislation that interferes with property rights or state's rights, all of which would be code words for white people's rights. It is ironic that those who want to preserve white power in South Africa choose as their model the American constitution, including the Bill of Rights. They are all of a sudden very much in favor of minority rights because they are the minority. Here, the word minority means numerical minority, not lacking in power.

A super-optimum solution would have to involve something that would be the equivalent of an internal economic union. It would have to involve a system whereby white business interests would have an environment in which they could prosper, and blacks would have job opportunities accompanied by merit criteria and affirmative action with preferences for people who cannot satisfy a minimum competence level. It basically means going directly to what it is that each side wants to achieve by way of increased voting power and concentrating on how to guarantee that, regardless of the voting rights. It means elevating certain economic rights to a higher status than the status of federalism, separation of powers, and those other constitutional issues.

The key way out is to emphasize both blacks and whites being much better off economically as a result of SOS thinking. That is, political power is directed toward economic well-being for each group. It is also key to get away from stability and look toward continuous economic growth, and to become responsive in regard to upgrading skills, rather than forming a new government. Making rights meaningful includes such rights as the right to sue, but also the establishment of appropriate institutions, like a ministry of international trade and industry.

There are three types of questions that can be asked of revolutionary South African blacks:

1. What is going to happen to the whites? This is an implicitly racist question that shows rather biased sensitivity to what is going to happen to the whites but not what is going to happen to the blacks, who may be in bad shape as a result of white flight, loss of investment, and socioeconomic disruptions.

2. How do you get whites and blacks to make concessions? This is the traditional compromise position, which is better than civil war.

3. The SOS question is how to enable both blacks and whites to be better off than their best expectations.

Voter Turnout

Conservative and Liberal Positions

The United States does not look good relative to the rest of the world when it comes to voter turnout. We have roughly 200 million adults, of which approximately half are registered to vote. But only about half of those who are registered to vote actually do. That is about 50 million. This means if just 26 million out of 50 million vote for a certain candidate for president, that candidate wins. This can be a landslide if each state is hotly contested, even though it is only 26 million out of 200 million possible voters. It is not so good when, in effect, 12 percent of the population can decide who will sit in the Oval Office. We are not undemocratic in the sense of prohibiting people from voting, but less democratic than we should be in the sense of facilitating voter turnout. These figures can be roughly confirmed by the 1990 Census and the 1996 presidential elections.

The true conservative goal might be to promote the election of conservative candidates, but they are not going to say that. What they actually say is that they want to avoid multiple voting (see Figure I.6). They do not want any schemes that will allow cheating at the polls. Liberals, on the other hand, are very concerned about people who do not vote, so they want to decrease nonvoting by adults who could be eligible. The conservative position promotes a decrease in multiple voting in a number of ways. One of the most extreme positions is to purge the voter rolls every ten years and make people register again. This would guard against individuals still being present on the voter rolls who have moved or died. It greatly decreases the number of people who register if you have to do it over and over again. Having advanced registration may make a difference with regard to decreasing multiple voting, but it also decreases the ease in voting procedures. Liberals support ideas like postcard registration or registration at the time you get your driver's license— so-called motor–voter legislation. They also support keeping the polls open a few hours later to make it easier to vote on election day. Unfortunately, the liberal solutions in total would not make much of a difference, as more fundamental change is necessary.

A Win–Win Alternative

What really needs to be adopted is the kind of system presently being used in many countries of the world, including Canada, South Africa, Mexico, and Mozambique, as well as states such as Wisconsin and Minnesota. It involves a few innovations. First of all, there

Figure I.6
Registration and Turnout

GOALS / ALTERNATIVES	C 1. Noneligible registration and voting 2. Increase Republican voters	L 1. Increase registration and voting 2. Increase Democratic voters
C Leave as is	+	−
L Postcard registration	−	+
N 1. Precinct registration 2. Permanent registration	0	0
SOS or Win-Win 1. On-site registration 2. Census registration 3. Vote anywhere 4. Invisible ink check	++	++

Key: C = Conservative; L = Liberal; N = Neutral; + = relatively conducive to the goal (the best of the alternatives on the goal *before* the SOS alternative is considered); 0 = neither conducive nor adverse; − = relatively adverse; ++ = the best of the alternatives on the goal *after* the SOS alternative is considered.

is no requirement of advanced registration. You can register in advance if you want to, but you can also register on-site the day of the election. Many people who do not vote on election day give as a reason the fact that they are not registered. If they could register on election day through on-site registration, that would no longer be a problem. Also, if elections were to be moved to a nonworking day instead of a Tuesday, more people would be able to participate. In Catholic countries, such as Italy, France, and Mexico, election day is on Sunday, when people do not work. Other nations string their elections over a couple of days. Another improvement would allow people to vote in either their home precinct or their work precinct, or to even allow them to vote in any precinct, provided there is some way of checking to make sure they have not voted in another. Multiple-precinct voting can make a large difference in voter turnout.

With all these facilitators, however, the conservative problem of multiple voting rises again. The way that problem is solved in South Africa, Mexico, Mozambique, and other countries is by having voters dip their hand into a bowl of invisible ink. If you show up at a polling place anytime in the day after that, including your original polling place, your hand is viewed under an ultraviolet lamp, and if it shows that you have already voted, you are denied the right to vote again and can possibly be arrested. The invisible-ink method works much better than asking people to sign their names, because names can be forged much more easily than hands. It is a good example of a win–win solution because it would substantially decrease multiple voting and substantially decrease nonvoting. It helps to achieve both kinds of goals simultaneously, like outreach training, or the cleaner, more profitable processes that relate to environmental protection and economic growth. All four aspects of the SOS solution collectively that we have discussed so far are capable of achieving the conservative and the liberal goal more successfully than either the conservative or liberal alternative.

On-site registration, the nonworking election day, multiple precincts, and the invisible-ink method all have a political feasibility problem. This problem is political, in the sense that it is very difficult to get such measures through Congress or through a state legislature. This is because one political party is likely to have enough strength to block them, namely, the party which thinks it will suffer as a result of expanded voter turnout. As long as it has enough power to stop these initiatives, they will never be adopted. If, however, they ever were adopted, they are not likely to be repealed. There is a kind of ratchet effect on new facilitators once they are adopted, because the party in power will look bad if it decreases the ability of people to register and vote. These measures are likely to be adopted when the Democrats have enough influence in the Congress or in the various state legislatures. The traditional thinking is that the Democratic party benefits more from expanded voter registration and turnout than the Republican party, due to the fact that a higher percentage of nonvoters consists of the people who are poorer and less educated than average. Such voters are more likely to vote Democratic. The problem is political, but it may only be a temporary problem as hopefully all the other feasibility problems may be temporary. See, for example, Bernard Grofman and Arend Lijphart, eds., *Electoral Laws and Their Political Consequences* (New York: Agathon Press, 1986), and Frances Piven and Richard Cloward, *Why Americans Don't Vote* (New York: Pantheon Books, 1988).

DECENTRALIZATION

Here we discuss three examples of win–win decentralization. The first involves conflict between the central government and state–local governments. The second involves conflict between governmental and business decision making. The third involves a related conflict between governmental and individual decision making.

Central versus State–Local

Figure I.7 addresses decentralizing. The conservative alternative is to give 100 percent of the jurisdiction to state or local agencies, or all $500 if $500 is being allocated. The liberal alternative is to give 100 percent of the jurisdiction to the central government, or all $500 if $500 is being allocated. Neutral alternatives might include (1) jurisdiction to the central government, with many and strong regional offices; (2) the central government supplies the funding, but state and local agencies make the rules and enforce them; or (3) the central government makes the rules, and the state–local agencies do the enforcing.

The reason conservatives like state–local agencies is because those agencies are often more sensitive to what business firms want because they are seeking to attract business firms to the state or the local communities. Liberals generally like central government, especially the president (holding party constant), because he is more concerned with getting the votes of workers, and a vote from a worker is worth as much as a vote from management, although management might have more money. Likewise, U.S. Senators are sensitive to the needs of the bigger cities in their states because those cities wield the swing vote in determining which senatorial candidate will get elected. See, for example, Thomas Anton, *American Federalism and Public Policy: How the System Works* (Philadelphia: Temple University Press, 1989), and Ellis Katz and Alan Tarr, eds., *Federalism and Rights* (Lanham, Maryland: Rowman & Littlefield, 1996).

Conservatives are generally reluctant to say they like state–local agencies, because those agencies are more sensitive to business profits, landlords, creditors, manufacturers, retailers, and other business interests. Instead, conservatives talk about the need for government that is more responsive to the people, and that state–local agencies are more responsive because they are closer. Liberals are not so reluctant to say they like central government because it is more sensitive to higher wages, better workplaces, and various

Figure I.7
Decentralizing to Lower Agencies or to Provinces

GOALS / ALTERNATIVES	C Responsiveness	L Uniformity or widespread
C 1. State-local 2. Allocate 100 percent or all $500	+	−
L 1. Central 2. Allocate 100 percent or all $500	−	+
N 1. Regional offices 2. Central money, state-local rules 3. Central rules, state-local enforcement	−	0
SOS or Win-Win 1. Both get $500 2. More than $250 apiece	++	++

Key: C = Conservative; L = Liberal; N = Neutral; + = relatively conducive to the goal (the best of the alternatives on the goal *before* the SOS alternative is considered); 0 = neither conducive nor adverse; − = relatively adverse; ++ = the best of the alternatives on the goal *after* the SOS alternative is considered.

consumer interests. In addition, they will emphasize the undesirability of having some states permit low wages and bad workplaces, which will attract business to those places. Thus, liberals tend to talk in terms of the need for national uniformity, meaning uniformly high labor standards, not uniformly low.

If we accept these goals, then we are talking about responsiveness to state–local needs and uniformity of high standards. These are abstract concepts which could be applied to such matters as environmental protection, decreasing unemployment, adequate healthcare, and other substantive matters. In the environmental context, if both sides really want the environment to be healthy in terms of clean air and water, then it makes sense to have both strong central government in the environmental field and strong state–local government. That might mean having an environmental protection agency at all three levels of government, with overlapping jurisdictions. Doing so may not be so efficient in terms of incremental improvement divided by dollars spent, as a measure of efficiency; however, it may be more effective in terms of obtaining clean air and water because three heads are better than one for developing ideas or rules and for enforcing them.

Thus, the win–win solution for greater responsiveness and greater uniformity of high standards and high achievement may be to provide more than $500 for each of the two levels, or at least more than $250 apiece, which would be a split-the-difference compromise. Win–win decentralization tends to mean more authority to all units which have an interest in seeing the goals achieved.

Central versus Business Decisions

Conservatives would like to leave the adoption of new technologies solely to business firms with no government interference (see Figure I.8). Liberals like government agencies, such as the Japanese Ministry of International Trade and Industry (MITI), which makes big technology decisions regarding auto manufacturing, steel, electronics, computers, and so on for Japan. Conservatives abolished the U.S. Office of Technology Assessment, because they viewed it partly as a step toward U.S. MITI. See, for example, Bruce Bimber, *The Politics of Expertise in Congress: The Rise and Fall of the Office of Technology Assessment* (Albany: State University of New York Press, 1996).

In this context, conservatives again talk about responsiveness and business firms knowing best what technologies they need. Likewise, liberals again talk about the need for uniformity on the assumption that most or many business firms will fail to adopt new technologies. The win–win solution might be the one proposed by Secretary of Labor Robert Reich. He once was enamored of the Japanese MITI, but he later thought such an approach involved virtually playing God. Instead, he advocated a 2-percent payroll tax on every business firm in the United States, but with hopes that no firm would pay the tax. The reason they would not pay is because the tax law would provide that they get a 100-percent credit if they used the money to buy new technologies. All they would have to do at payroll-tax time is submit a form indicating how they spent the money on new technologies. They would have a strong interest in not sending the money to Washington. They would also have a strong interest in improving their firm's technology as well as they could.

Figure I.8
Central Government versus Business Firms on New Technologies

GOALS / ALTERNATIVES	C Responsiveness	L Uniformity or widespread
C Business decisions	+	−
L Government decisions	−	+
N Both	0	0
SOS or Win-Win 1. 2-percent payroll tax 2. Not collected if used for new technologies	++	++

Key: C = Conservative; L = Liberal; N = Neutral; + = relatively conducive to the goal (the best of the alternatives on the goal *before* the SOS alternative is considered); 0 = neither conducive nor adverse; − = relatively adverse; ++ = the best of the alternatives on the goal *after* the SOS alternative is considered.

Some people would argue that business firms would spend the money wisely without the payroll tax. Such an argument runs contrary to the fact that when President Reagan gave business firms a 30-percent across-the-board tax break, very little money went into new technologies, in contrast to real estate, luxury goods, and high CEO salaries, and in contrast to the Japanese investment. Thus, the 2-percent payroll tax credit does combine (1) responsiveness to the needs of the business firms, since they know what technologies they need, and (2) the goal of having the United States more uniformly raise its technology.

Central versus Individual Decisions

Conservatives would like to leave the decision to individuals as to whether to get training and what training to get in order to be able to adopt to changing times, especially technologies (see Figure I.9). Liberals would like to have the government set up training pro-

Figure I.9
Central Government versus Individual Decisions on Training

GOALS / ALTERNATIVES	C Responsiveness	L Uniformity or widespread
C Individual decisions	+	−
L Government decisions	−	+
N Both	0	0
SOS or Win-Win 1. Vouchers from government 2. Individual decisions on how to spend the vouchers	++	++

Key: C = Conservative; L = Liberal; N = Neutral; + = relatively conducive to the goal (the best of the alternatives on the goal *before* the SOS alternative is considered); 0 = neither conducive nor adverse; − = relatively adverse; ++ = the best of the alternatives on the goal *after* the SOS alternative is considered.

grams, possibly like the Works Progress Administration of the depression years, or like the public school system but for adults. By leaving it to individuals to make training decisions, conservatives argue that responsiveness to individual abilities and interests is more likely to be met. Leaving it to the individuals is also more likely to be responsive to market forces of supply and demand. Liberals justify a more governmental approach on the grounds that such an approach can bring everybody up to a certain level of computer literacy and knowledge of contemporary science. By raising virtually everybody above such a threshold, a desirable uniformity is obtained.

A win–win solution might involve the federal government giving a $2,000 training voucher to every man, woman, and child, or at least to every adult over age eighteen. Such a voucher could be used to pay for whatever training each individual thought best in

light of their abilities and interests and in light of the present supply and demand for people with the training they pursue. Such a
policy would be highly responsive. It should also result in a high
degree of training, which might not occur if people had to use their
own money. Some people do not have the money available. Those
who do may not be farsighted enough to spend it on training. The
voucher would be worthless unless it is spent for training. It would
be an earmarked voucher, like a housing voucher or food stamps,
that could only be cashed in by accredited training programs or on-
the-job training. The existence of so many vouchers would stimu-
late entrepreneurs to develop worthwhile training programs in order
to attract the voucher holders.

Such a policy would be highly decentralized in terms of the decision making, but yet centralized in terms of the funding. This provides the best of both in a win–win way. The winners are not only
conservatives and liberals, but also (1) individual trainees, whose
training enables them to earn higher and more satisfying incomes;
(2) their trainers, who make money performing a service by upgrading those individuals; (3) the government, which gets more
revenue from the increased gross national product more than the
cost of the vouchers; (4) the children and grandchildren of the trainees, who now have better role models; (5) the customers, clients,
patients, and other beneficiaries of the better trained individuals;
and (6) the taxpayers, from the savings on various forms of public
aid that might be paid to the trainees who might be unemployed
without the training.

RELEVANCE OF THE BOOK

Further details on each of these three issues are given in the
chapters which follow. Under privatization, there are five chapters
giving detailed examples from Africa, Asia, Eastern Europe, and
North America. Under democratization, there are four chapters
giving examples from Africa, Asia, and Latin America. Under decentralization, there are three chapters referring to Latin America,
Asia, and North America.

In each of the chapters, there is a recognition of the dynamics of
synthesizing the best that each side has to offer. That means developing institutions that emphasize the equity and sensitivity of the
public sector to consumers, workers, and the environment, while
simultaneously emphasizing the efficiency or the relative efficiency
of the profit motive and performance measurement of the private
sector. Under democratization, the chapter authors are concerned
with combining majority rule with the rights of the minority to con-

vert the majority. That combination can enable both the majority and the minority to contribute well to democratic institutions. Under decentralization, they try to combine the responsiveness of the local government with the uniformity which central government can facilitate.

Credit should be given to various public-policy organizations that are especially interested in privatization, democracy, and decentralization. They have conducted conferences, conventions, and symposia which have made this book possible. They include the Association for Public Policy Analysis and Management, the American Economic Association, and their counterparts in countries throughout the world and in subfields of political science and economics.

PART I

PRIVATIZATION

1

Government-Owned Companies as Instruments of State Action: Experiences from Botswana

Bonu N. Swami

Botswana is a very large country, with an area of 582,000 square kilometers (about the same as Kenya or France). It is located in Southern Africa, with Namibia, South Africa, Zimbabwe, and Zambia as its neighbors. Though Botswana has a very large area, its population is 1.3 million. Large area and low population pose problems for the efficient working of private markets, because in many areas the population is too small to warrant a person establishing a business, as the costs of providing wares is too high. In addition, it is not justifiable to have many companies established in an area where demand (population) is low. Hence, entrepreneurs are hesitant to establish companies in many parts of the country. In a situation where the free market is unwilling to provide goods or services, and where it is deemed that the services are important to the population of an area, it is the duty of the government to take necessary action to enter the market to provide the goods or services essential to the population, such as transportation, water, electricity supply, and so on.

While delivering his budget speech on March 20, 1971, to the National Assembly of Botswana, his honor Q.K.J. Masire, the Vice President of the Republic of Botswana, made it clear that state action in provision of essential services, such as power, water, housing, and others, was necessary. He stated

At independence [1966] we inherited an economy with a very inadequate institutional structure. Botswana was overshadowed by its economically more developed neighbours. . . . There was no parastatal organisation such as development corporation to promote industrialisation. There was no Housing Corporation to cater for housing needs. There were no public utility corporations concerned with the provision of water and electricity in urban centres. In laying the foundations for development, the Government has striven over the past five years to find ways of creating the basic institutional infrastructure on which to build a dynamic economy. (Masire 1971, para. 4, part II, p. 2)

He further stated

In the past five years, considerable progress has been made. The detailed preparatory work which must inevitably precede the introduction of new institutions occupied by the early period, and in the past year we have seen these efforts bear fruit. In December 1970, this Honourable House passed legislation creating a Botswana Housing Corporation. In April 1970, the Botswana Development Corporation was established as a limited liability Company. In January this year, both Botswana Power Corporation and the Water Utilities Corporation came into existence. Last year also saw a Building Society commence operations. These bodies have yet to prove themselves, but one thing is certain—sustained development would not be possible without them. (para. 5, part II, p. 2)

In this scenario, "Government has created a substantial number of parastatal agencies since Independence, for a variety of purposes and under differing organisational arrangements. Each parastatal has its own statutory mandate, but all are owned by, and responsible to, Government" (National Development Plan 7, 1991–1997: 487). These government concerns are broadly classified into five categories:

1. Financial Institutions
2. Public-Utility Corporations
3. Commercial-Oriented Concerns
4. Sectoral-Policy Implementation Agencies
5. Training/Research Institutions

The government participated directly by contributing to the capital of these organizations, as presented in Table 1.1. In addition the government of Botswana has subscribed to the capital of certain private companies. The share of subscription varies from company to company, as listed in Table 1.2.

Before studying the government-owned companies, it is advisable to have a brief overview of other forms of government concerns

Table 1.1
Government Financing under the Development Budget during National Development Plan 6 (P millions)

Type of Parastatal	NDP 6 (1985/86 prices)	NDP 7 (1991/92 prices)
Development Finance Institutions	102.9	130.0
Public Utilities	375.7	518.0
Commercially Oriented	42.2	27.4
Educational/Research	60.0	213.8
Total	580.8	889.2

Source: National Development Plan 7 1991–1997: 492.

Table 1.2
Government Direct Investment in Industry

	Government equity shares (% of total)	Capital employed (P million)
De Beers Botswana[a]	50	1,497.9
Soda Ash Botswana[b]	48	475.0[c]
BCL Ltd.	15	361.4
Shashe Mines (Pty) Ltd.	15	n.a[d]
Diamond Manufacturing Botswana	15	1.0
Lazare Kaplan Botswana[e]	15	n.a[e]

Source: National Development Plan 7 1991–1997: 490.

Note: Figures are for December 1990 unless otherwise specified.

[a]Diamond Valuing Company (Pty) Ltd. and Teemane Manufacturing Company (Pty) Ltd. are wholly owned subsidiaries of Debswana, in which the government also has 50 percent equity ownership interests.

[b]The government also holds 100 percent of Class C nonvoting preference shares in SAB.

[c]As of March 31, 1991.

[d]In liquidation.

[e]Not yet operational in December 1990.

to trace out the part played by government-owned companies as instrument of state action.

GOVERNMENT PARTICIPATION IN FINANCIAL INSTITUTIONS

The participation of government in financial institutions can be located as follows.

National Development Bank (NDB)

The National Development Bank came into existence on May 1, 1964 (National Development Bank Act 1963) in order to provide financial assistance to newly established undertakings and farmers.

Botswana Cooperative Bank (BCB)

This bank was established in December 1974 under the Cooperative Societies Act of 1964. It is essentially a multipurpose financing institution for the various cooperative societies, such as marketing, credit, consumer, multipurpose, thrift, and loan.

Bank of Botswana (BOB)

Bank of Botswana began July 1, 1975 (Bank of Botswana Act 1975) as a custodian of the money supply and as a bankers' bank.

Botswana Building Society (BBS)

The Botswana Building Society came into existence on January 3, 1977 (Botswana Building Societies Act 1961). The main objective of the Building Society is to receive deposits from the public and lend to Batswana for acquiring houses.

Botswana Savings Bank (BSB)

The BSB was established in 1982, under Botswana Savings Bank (1963), and Amendment Act No. 5 (1982). Its main purpose is to mobilize small savings and use them for national development.

Botswana Development Corporation Limited (BDC)

Botswana Development Corporation Limited was established in 1970 (Companies Act of Botswana 1959) to be Botswana's main agency for commercial and industrial development. All its ordinary shares are owned by the government of Botswana. Initially, the government of Botswana contributed P4 million, and gradually increased its contribution to P123.2 million by 1993–1994. Its main objective is to identify business opportunities in industry, commerce, and agriculture and assist financially and technically for their development. The subsidiary objectives are to conduct feasibility studies of specific projects of interest and to participate in venture capital with private concerns as a partner or by providing required loans. In 1995, BDC held interest in 114 companies in the areas of agriculture, property development and management, industry, finance, commerce, hotels and tourism, and transportation. BDC's contribution of share capital is 100 percent in twenty companies, more than 50 percent and under 100 percent in twelve companies, and less than 50 percent in thirty companies. It participated in fifty-two companies by providing substantial loans as working capital.

PUBLIC UTILITIES

The following are classified under public utilities.

Botswana Power Corporation (BPC)

Established by the Botswana Power Corporation Act (1970), the corporation was made responsible for the generation, transmission, supply, and distribution of electricity in areas approved by the minister of Mineral Resources and Water Affairs.

Water Utilities Corporation (WUC)

Established by the Water Utilities Corporation Act (1970) with the object of supplying a potable water supply.

Botswana Telecommunication Corporation (BTC)

Formed under the Botswana Telecommunications Corporation Act (1980), the main objective of the corporation is to provide, develop, operate, and manage Botswana's national and international telecommunications services on sound commercial lines.

Botswana Railways (BR)

Established under the Botswana Railways Act (1987) as the Botswana Railways Organisation, with the object of provision of services to passengers as well as goods.

OTHER COMMERCIALLY-ORIENTED PARASTATALS

The following are also commercially oriented.

Botswana Meat Commission (BMC)

The Bechunaland (now Botswana) Meat Commission was established by the Botswana Meat Commission Act on December 24, 1965, at Abattoirs at Lobatse.

Botswana Housing Corporation (BHC)

This is a statutory authority operating under the terms and conditions of the Botswana Housing Corporation Act (1970) with an objective of meeting the national housing needs of the country.

Botswana Vaccine Institute (BVI)

The outbreak of foot and mouth disease in the country led the government to build its own unit for the production of foot and mouth disease vaccine in 1978.

Air Botswana (AB)

The country's major domestic and regional carrier, Air Botswana, came into existence as a parastatal corporation under the Ministry of Works, Transport, and Communications on April 1, 1988 by Air Botswana Act (1988).

Postal Services (PS)

Postal Services of Botswana came into existence as a parastatal body in May 1980 with the object of providing both internal and external postal services (Botswana Postal Services Act [1989]).

SECTORAL-POLICY IMPLEMENTATION AGENCIES

Botswana Livestock Development Corporation (Pty.) Ltd. (BLDC)

This is a wholly owned subsidiary of the Botswana Meat Commission, and was incorporated on March 16, 1973.

Botswana Agricultural Marketing Board (BAMB)

The board was established on June 14, 1974 with the object of securing for producers and consumers a market where reasonable prices and products could be made available (Botswana Agricultural Marketing Board Act [1974]).

GOVERNMENT COMPANIES' ORGANIZATIONAL SET-UP

Government companies are classified into four broad types (Thynne 1994):

- Ministry
- Department (nonexecutive/nonministerial), agency, office
- Board, council, commission
- Incorporated company

As stated, an open market is lacking in Botswana. Hence, many concerns are established by government, but at the same time government wants to be away from day-to-day administration of these concerns. The foregoing description reveals that Botswana has a hybrid system of organization. The government, by an act of parliament, establishes the government concerns, the power of administration is handed over to the concerned ministry, and the ministry in turn delegates its powers to the board, council, corporation, or commission established for the purpose. The act empowers the minister to nominate the board, council, corporation, or commission governing body. A few government concerns are established under the incorporated-company organization system, and boards are appointed, nominated, or elected. Even in cases of departmental systems of organization, boards are appointed for governance of the companies. In some companies, the government has assisted by share subscription of less than 50 percent and has the right to nominate the directors.

Government concerns in Botswana are broadly classified into five major categories (as shown in Table 1.3).

Ministry with Independent Board

In this category, the minister has overall command over the body corporate by appointing the board members and issuing instructions on policy matters. NDB, BBS, BPC, BTC, WUC, BHC, BMC, and AB fall within this category. The concerned ministers shall from time to time appoint from among the members of the board a chairman and deputy chairman thereof, and shall publish or cause to publish this in the government Gazette.

Department Agency with Board

In this category, the government concern acts as a government department or an agent to government and discharges duties on behalf of the government. In discharging such duties, specific boards are appointed to look after the governance of the bodies. BOB, BSB, and BLDC may be considered within this category.

Table 1.3
Organizational Set-Up of Botswana Government Concerns

Ministry with Independent Board	Department Agency with Board	Commercial Arm of Government	Incorporated Company	Public and Private Mix
NDB	BOB	BR	BDC	Soda Ash Botswana
BBS	BSB	BPS		BCL Ltd.
BPC	BLDC	BAMB		De Beers Botswana
BTC		BVI		Shashe Mines
WUC				(Pty) Ltd.
BHC				Diamond Manufac-
AB				turing Botswana
				Lazare Kaplan
				Botswana

Source: Compiled from corresponding acts of the Botswana government and public and private concerns.

Commercial Arm of Government

During National Development Plan (NDP) 6 (1985–1991), a new
kind of institution was created, treated here as a parastatal, but
technically a commercial arm of government. Botswana Railways
and Botswana Postal Services fall into this category. They have a
management structure like true parastatals, but remain part of
government, thus rendering them eligible for certain tax advantages within the Southern African Customs Union.

Incorporated Company

BDC comes under this category. It was incorporated as a public
limited company. BDC is a holding company, holding either all or
part of 114 private limited companies' shares. Almost all directors
of the board are nominated by the government on the recommendations of the Ministry of Finance and Development Planning and
participating companies.

The primary task of BDC is to identify investment opportunities in
Botswana for exploitation by both local and foreign investors. To achieve
this the Corporation provides investment advice, loans, guarantees, share
capital, industrial plots and factory premises to investors. As far as possible BDC wishes to limit its involvement in new projects to a minority
interest but will bear the major burden of development where this is of
national interest. (BDC 1995: 4)

Public and Private Mix

In this type of organization, both private-sector and government participation can be seen. The government may substantially subscribe to the share capital of the company. These companies are mostly registered as private limited companies and incorporated under the Company Act of Botswana (1959). In these companies, the government does not hold total control over the registered body.

Debswana which is a unique partnership between the Republic of Botswana and De Beers Centenary AG produces diamonds from three mines in Botswana. Each shareholder in the partnership holds 50 per cent of the equity. This arrangement demands complete unanimity in the decision-making process as well as mutual trust and openness in dealing with each other. . . .

An agreement was signed in 1990 between the Government of Botswana and De Beers Centenary AG to form Teemane Manufacturing Company (Pty) Limited, a diamond polishing operation in Botswana. The company is a wholly owned subsidiary of Debswana. Another wholly owned Debswana company, the Botswana Diamond valuing Company (Pty) Ltd, sorts the entire production of the three mines in Gaborone before the diamonds are sold on the international diamond market through the Central Selling Organisation (CSO) in London. (Botswana, A Review of Commerce and Industry 1993–94: 60).

OWNERSHIP AND INTERNAL CONTROL

The general principle of company ownership is that a shareholder is the owner of that part of the assets of a company which are equivalent to the shareholder's share capital contributed. In government companies, the same rule is applied. Most of the government concerns of Botswana are funded by the government of Botswana, as seen in Table 1.4.

Joint Ventures

In addition to direct participation and having ownership over companies, the government has taken up joint ventures with the private sector, mostly with mining companies (see Table 1.2). The financial obligations and rewards of these enterprises are shared under the respective agreements with the private partners, who exercise managerial responsibility under the supervision of government-appointed board members. The government has also indirectly acquired, through the venture capital investment activities of Botswana Development Corporation, equity in a variety of domestic businesses (National Development Plan 7: 489).

Table 1.4
Government Participation in Share Capital of Parastatals and Commercial
Undertakings (P millions)

Concern	1990	1991	1992	1993	1994
AB	18.5	25.5	41.6	32.7	32.7
BOB	530.1	854.8	1,451.2	1,351.0	2,151.6
BAMB	----	18.5	21.3	21.4	21.4
BCB	2.5	2.5	2.5	2.5	2.5
BDC	61.3	77.0	103.2	103.2	123.2
BHC	0.2	0.2	0.2	0.2	0.2
BLDC	1.4	1.4	1.4	1.4	1.4
BMC	0.2	0.2	0.2	----	----
BPS	----	3.6	9.3	8.6	10.0
BPC	9.2	12.2	49.0	66.6	65.5
BR	----	228.5	237.1	262.4	294.0
BTC	23.3	23.3	23.3	23.3	23.3
BVI	5.0	5.0	5.0	5.0	5.0
NDB	10.6	10.9	12.5	12.4	26.7
WUC	5.6	6.2	6.5	6.7	6.7
BCU	0.1	0.1	0.1	0.1	0.1

Source: Bank of Botswana, Annual Report 1995, p. S68.

GOVERNING BOARD AND TOP MANAGEMENT

Governing Board Constitution

The majority of the government concerns are managed by the board of directors either appointed or nominated by the respective ministry. BMC, BVI, BAMB, and BLDC are under the control of the Ministry of Agriculture. The financial parastatals and Botswana Housing Corporation are linked with the Ministry of Finance and Development Planning. Botswana Railways, Botswana Telecommunications, Botswana Postal Services, and Air Botswana are under the control and direction of the Ministry of Works, Transport and Communications. Botswana Water Utilities and Botswana Power Corporation are under the section of the Ministry of Mineral Resources and Water Affairs. These ministries are generally vested with the power to appoint or nominate the board members of the parastatals. Table 1.5 shows the set-up governance of a few government companies.

Let us examine a few government concerns about the governing boards. Section 9 of the Bank of Botswana Act (1975) regulates the board by stating that "the Board shall consist of the Governor, who shall be Chairman and six other members appointed." In this case,

Table 1.5
Chairmen and Board Members

Concern	Chairman Term (Years)	Appointed by	Board Members (Including Deputy Chairman) Number	Term (Years)	Appointed by
BOB	5[a]	President	6	4	Minister
BDC	[b]	Minister	4–15	[b]	Minister
NDB	3	Minister	4–7	3	Minister
BPS	3	Minister	5–7	4	Minister
BSB	[c]	Minister	5	[c]	Minister
BPC	3	Minister	6–8	4	Minister
BR	3	Minister	5–9	4	Minister
BTC	3	Minister	5–7	4	Minister
WUC	3	Minister	5–8	4	Minister
AB	3	Minister	5–7	4	Minister
BHC	3	Minister	6–9	4	Minister
BMC	3	President	10	3	President
BAMB	3	Minister	8–10	3	Minister

Sources: BOB: Bank of Botswana Act 1975, secs. 9, 10, and 11; BDC: Botswana Development Corporation Limited 1970, article 74; NDB: National Development Bank Act 1964, First Schedule, para. 1, 3; BPS: Botswana Postal Services Act 1989, sec. 4; BSB: Botswana Savings Bank Act 1963, sec. 4; BPC: Botswana Power Corporation Act 1970, sec. 4, 6; BR: Botswana Railways Act 1987, sec. 4, 6; BTC: Botswana Telecommunications Corporation Act 1980, sec. 4, 6; WUC: Water Utilities Corporation Act 1970, sec. 4, 6; AB: Air Botswana Act 1988, sec. 4, 6; BHC: Botswana Housing Corporation Act 1971, sec. 4, 5; BMC: Botswana Meat Commission Act 1965, Schedule: Part I, para. 2, 3; BAMB: Botswana Agricultural Marketing Board Act 1974, sec. 4, 5.

[a]Chairman is Governor of Bank of Botswana

[b]There is no time limit of length of appointment (years) for chairman and other members of the board. They can resign at their own will, or the minister can terminate their services at any time.

[c]The minister decides the term of office of each member of the board at the time of appointment.

the experts from finance and banking are selected and appointed as governor and deputy governor and other board members are nominated by the concerned ministry. Similarly, the board of BDC is appointed by the Ministry of Finance and Development Planning. In this case, the chairman will be the Permanent Secretary of the Ministry of Finance and Development Planning, the vice chairman will be the Permanent Secretary of the Ministry of Commerce and Industry. Directors are nominated from the constituent companies, and there are nine board members selected from a wide spectrum of industries. One can see a public–private mix in this organization.

In almost all cases, the chairman and board members are selected and appointed by the concerned ministry. In other words, government, indirectly, has a major role to play in the management of all government concerns, including Botswana Development Corporation Limited.

Top Management

Each concern has a top management team but "the degree of managerial autonomy accorded to the parastatals differs depending on their activities and their ability to generate net revenues rather than relying on Government financing" (National Development Plan 7: 487).

In the case of Bank of Botswana, the top management team consists of a general manager and managers of the departments, such as administrative services, banking, finance, financial institutions, international, and research.

The top executives of BDC are a managing director, deputy to managing director, financial controller, and projects manager.

The principal officers who are responsible for the management of Botswana Power Corporation are a chief executive, financial manager, divisional managers, operations manager, and projects manager.

The general manager of Botswana Railways is responsible to the minister for the administration of railways on commercial lines.

The top management team of Botswana Telecommunication consists of a chief executive; deputy chief executive; group manager commercial; group manager corporate services; financial controller; group managers of planning and development, systems and operations, information systems, and telephone south and north; and chief internal auditor. The chief executive is appointed by the concerned minister and other senior officers are appointed by the board on the recommendations of the chief executive.

The corporate management team of Water Utilities consists of a chief executive, deputy chief executive/manager development, manager finance, and manager operations.

Section 10 of Air Botswana Act No. 4 (1988) empowers the concerned minister to appoint the general manager. The board considers the appointment of other members with the recommendations of the minister.

The general manager of Botswana Housing Corporation will be appointed by the Minister of Finance and Development Planning, and must be "a person with a proved record of success in having administration, preferably within a large organization and with experience in all aspects of the subject, namely, housing designs, construction, administration, finance and management" (Botswana Housing Corporation Act 1970: sec. 12).

"Subject to the approval of the Minister, the Board of Botswana Agricultural Marketing Board will appoint a General Manager. The General Manager is the Chief Executive Officer of the Board and shall, subject to the directions of the Board, manage the undertakings, operations and property of the Board and exercise such of the powers of the Board as the Board may from time to time delegate to him" (Botswana Agricultural Marketing Board Act 1974: sec. 3).

Disqualifications and Termination of Board Members

More or less in all government concerns, the following persons are disqualified to be appointed as chairman or member of the board:

• a member of the National Assembly
• a person of unsound mind
• a declared insolvent
• a convicted person
• a professionally disqualified person
• a person of legal disability
• a person absenting without leave consecutively for three meetings

Any member other than a managing director can resign from a board membership by sending his or her written application to the concerned minister. The President of Botswana or the concerned minister may appoint a tribunal or a commission to investigate the chairman of a board and, on the recommendation of such a tribunal or commission, the chairman may be removed from the position at any time if found guilty.

In most cases, board meetings are called by the chairman at least once every three months. Two board members can request a special board meeting, and then the chairman must call such a meeting within a month's time. Decisions are taken by majority votes. In case of a tie, the chairman has the deciding vote. A member who has an interest in a matter does not take part in the voting.

FINANCING ARRANGEMENTS

All parastatals will be expected to manage their financial affairs in a manner which permits timely payment of all debt servicing obligations. Commercially oriented enterprises will be expected to demonstrate financial viability, including the payment of regular dividends to Government. Government will encourage those parastatals that have developed commercially viable subsidiaries to consider divestment to private sector investors—either by issuing equity shares or outright sale. The resources generated from such liquidations will be used to retire parastatal debt or to finance new investment. Furthermore, consideration will be given to possibilities for privatisation of some discreet functions or entire agencies. (National Development Plan 7, 1997: 493)

Many of the commercially oriented government companies, such as Water Utilities, Botswana Telecommunications, Botswana Housing Corporation, Botswana Railways, and Air Botswana, have to follow the same principle in fixing their user charges. The boards of the corporations have to recommend these charges to the concerned ministry and the final authority of approval or disapproval lies with the minister. The tariffs may be uniform or different, depending on the amount of consumption and the type of user. As far as possible, tariffs are uniform, but the element of cross-subsidization is found, especially in water charges, where up to a certain consumption the charges per unit are low and gradually the charges are increased. In other words, the high-income-bracket people subscribe for the low-income group by cross-subsidization.

In some cases, users associations have a say in the tariff fixation, like International Air Transport Association (IATA) in the fixing of Air Botswana tariffs. In the majority of cases, the concerned ministry acts as a pace setter in tariff fixing and works as a mediator between the government companies and consumers.

Bank of Botswana, Botswana Power Corporation, Botswana Telecommunications, Water Utilities, Housing Corporation, Meat Commission, and Postal Services are monopolistic concerns, and hence the government takes proper action in fixing of fair prices, providing the consumer with a reasonable price and the concern with a reasonable return on investment. Through active government participation, there is not much uproar from consumers in Botswana, as in many other developing nations. Subsidization is also seen in Botswana Housing Corporation, where the government controls the rent to be collected from the tenants. The rents are much lower than market rents and the government is gradually increasing the rents to see that they are finally equal to market rents.

EXTERNAL CONTROL

Almost all government concerns are monopolistic by nature and business. Because of the lack of a wide market due to a small population and the spreading of population over a wide area, private entrepreneurs are not forthcoming. Hence, the government has to enter into utilities and commercial enterprises. At the same time, the government has given freedom to the boards. Monopoly and freedom may lead to many economic and social ills, and so the government has instituted many controls, such as insisting on external audits by certified public accountants or by an auditor general. In some cases, audits may be taken up by the auditors approved by the minister and, at the same time, the auditor general may be requested to examine the accounts and report the matter to the concerned minister.

CONCLUSION AND SUGGESTIONS

The limited population and wide physical area of the country posed a problem of lack of entrepreneurship in Botswana, as entrepreneurs feared to go where no sufficient demand existed. Prior to independence in 1966, there was no infrastructure development, and so the government had to take an active part in the establishment of various financial institutions, public-utilities corporations, commercial-oriented concerns, and sectoral agencies. The parastatal concerns such as utility services were given freedom to work on commercial lines, and to generate their own income. In certain cases, the government joined in partnerships with private organizations in the establishment of companies, such as De Beers Botswana and BCL Ltd.

Government concerns are organized under five categories, namely, companies directly under the control of ministries but with independent boards; department agencies with boards; commercial arms of government; incorporated companies; and public and private mixed companies. With respect to ownership and internal control of government concerns, in most cases the government is the sole owner, but the internal control is vested in nominated board members who are responsible to act on commercial lines. In most cases, the governing boards consist of a board of directors with a chairman nominated by the government and other board members, also nominated by the government. In most cases, a chairman is appointed for a period of three years, a board member is appointed for a period of four years, and the board consists of a wide spectrum of specialists.

The top general management of government concerns is vested in the hands of the chief executive or general manager and his or her team of functionary heads, who take day-to-day actions. Policy matters are decided by the board with the concurrence of the government. Government companies have become the source and means for government actions on policy decisions. The entire economy is tuned through these concerns. In the area of financial management, concerns are expected to manage their financial affairs in a manner which permits timely payment of all debt-servicing obligations and, in most cases, they are expected to manage their affairs on sound commercial lines.

On the whole, the government of Botswana, through its government concerns, manages the economy of the country on a laudable basis, compared to many countries in the African continent.

REFERENCES AND BIBLIOGRAPHY

Air Botswana Act. 1988 (Act No. 4 of 1988).
Annual Report. Bank of Botswana. 1995.
Annual Report. Botswana Livestock Development Corporation (Pty.) Ltd. 1974.
Bank of Botswana Act. 1975 (Cap. 55:01).
Botswana, A Review of Commerce and Industry, 1993–94, 13th ed. Ed. Brad Lambertus. Gaborone: B & T Directories (Pty.) Ltd.
Botswana Agricultural Marketing Board Act. 1974 (Cap. 74:06).
Botswana Agricultural Marketing Board. 1974.
Botswana Building Societies Act. 1961 (Cap. 42:03).
Botswana Development Corporation Limited, 25th Anniversary. 1995.
Botswana Housing Corporation Act. 1970 (Cap. 74:04).
Botswana Live Stock Development Corporation (Pty.) Ltd. 1973.
Botswana Meat Commission Act. 1965 (Cap. 74:04).
Botswana Postal Services Act. 1989 (Act. No. 22, 1989).
Botswana Power Corporation Act. 1970 (Cap. 74:01).
Botswana Railways Act. 1987 (Cap. 70:01).
Botswana Savings Bank Act. 1963 (Cap. 56:03) and Amendment Act No. 5. 1982.
Botswana Telecommunications Corporation Act. 1980 (Cap. 72:02).
Companies Act of Botswana. 1959 (Cap. 42:01).
Cooperative Societies Act. 1963 (Cap. 42:04).
Masire, Q.K.J. 1971. Address to the National Assembly of Botswana.
National Development Bank Act. 1963 (Cap. 74:05).
National Development Plan 7. 1991–1997. Ministry of Finance and Development Planning.
National Development Plan 6. 1985–1991. Ministry of Finance and Development Planning.
Post Office Act. 1980 (Cap. 72:01), repealed by Botswana Postal Services Act 1989.
Post Office Savings Bank and Savings Certificate Act. 1982 (Act No. 5 of 1982).
Thynne, Ian. 1994. "The Incorporated Company as an Instrument of Government: A Quest for a Comparative Understanding." *Governance* 7 (1): 63.
Water Utilities Corporation Act. 1970 (Cap. 74:02).

2

Government-Owned Companies as Instruments of State Action: The India Case

Pradeep K. Saxena

The economic sciences have a very peculiar problem of defining development and determining the role and limits of the state, its apparatus and enterprises, and their operation in making the strategies of development, particularly in developing countries. The problem arises due to the limitations and failures of socialist and capitalist economies. The welfare economics which underlie the failures of both kinds of economy have called in to question the long-term sustainability of socialist and capitalist systems. The emergence of the market economy has provided a new alternative, a choice, and a strategy of development in which the role and limitations of the state and private capital are redesigned in order to abolish the check, licensing, bureaucratic obstacles, and unlimited discretion of the government. The market economy will provide a base for sustainable growth and development to the participants in the economy. It will provide economic choices, private capital, and an interest-articulation system in the modern political economies of developing countries like India as the experience of these economies show that socialism has not been successful at providing choices and private capital to the state and, hence, the state became imperfect, noninformative, inefficient, and highly politicized and corrupt in distributing the fruits of growth, if there were any.[1] These socialist economies also failed to take risks, realize potential, and create institutions and norms of development. On the other side, the capitalist economies have generated unproductive capital, labor problems, social disintegration, and political problems like terrorism, violence, and so on. Both types of economies ignored the real path of development of the poor, nonmarket sectors and the basic values and institutional mechanism of society. Capitalist economies created more complex problems than their solutions.

The market economy is, therefore, viewed as an innovative response to the failures of the traditional economies and provides a new alternative with varied choices to evolve a more efficient, effective, responsive, and competitive system to integrate state and private capital. The basic idea behind the GATT/WTO was to evolve a market system in which the role of the state would be to set the rules of the game (economy) and to provide an environment for efficient and flexible operation of the institutions, because environment is more important than ownership. In creating such an environment, the state was to focus its attention not only in the policy fields, but also on the institutional setting, as institutions are the expression of a state's intentions, motives, and alliances with the market forces.[2]

In the market economy, the question of incentive-cum-information constraint is to some extent resolved, as the state is to act as information-cum-incentive desk in order to create market socialism on the one hand and to generate competition on the other. However, it is the administrative competence of the state which manages the "desk." In the developed economies, the weaknesses of administrative competence are compensated by insurance, technology, capital, cultural heterogeneity, and social diversities, while in developing countries, administrative competence is reviewed in terms of its influence and interference in the politicoeconomic system due to lack of prerequisites such as technology, capital, and openmindedness. Since developing countries are forced to the idea of welfare state, the state is forced to ignore profits, competition, and quality and a rent-seeking system is protected.[3] Moreover, the responsibility of future generations is avoided. The experiences of Southeast Asian economies have also generated problems about the market-economy approach. Due to the lack of a public-policy approach, institutional and infrastructural mechanisms and the process of modernization have generated ethical and moral questions in society which have become obstacles to the free expression of the state.[4]

The responsibility of the state to emerge as a dynamic leader of the market economy in these developing economies is a big challenge before their governments. India's former finance secretary, Mr. Montek Singh Ahluwalia, has suggested the theory of "redistribution with growth" through new institutional mechanisms.[5] The World Bank Report of 1996 pointed out that the developing countries are focusing their attention on "redistribution" rather than "growth," and therefore losing the benefits of growth, as the cost of redistribution is very high and the benefits of growth are being either monopolized or manipulated. Further, the government, in the redistribution, avoids renegotiations with growth-prone forces and tries to regulate economic forces on dictatorial terms rather than on administered contracts.[6] In the redistribution process, imperfect and asymmetric information between government and economic forces generally leads to prolonged bargaining and fewer options for renegotiations. Opportunism persists on both sides, which reduces renegotiation options and calls for costly arrangements for renegotiation. Lack of well-defined ownership rights also make it difficult to determine when the government will act in an expropriatory manner. As such, both the opportunism and imperfection of information increase the transaction costs of the redistribution sometimes caused by institutional reforms. A reform entails both benefits and costs. Benefits stem from the efficiency gains that accrue from the public enterprises and costs arise from the new institutional mechanisms created to reduce risks.

Reforms of public-sector enterprises (PSEs) are undertaken by the government, particularly in developing economies, on the basis of potential gains which compensate the losers and provide incentives for new partners.[7] PSE reforms reveal government intentions, gains, transfers, and distributive processes of growth. In developing economies like India, any public-sector enterprise reform package is viewed as a government's signed contract with various socioeconomic groups. Several empirical studies show that PSEs are government vehicles of "tenure-maximising regime" for as long as possible, because PSEs offer a support-sustaining system through various contracts.[8] Redistribution through PSEs does not mean transfer of wealth from rich to poor, but transfer from the less influential to the more influential because they are better in organization and providing support to the government. Governments pay attention to the demands of influential groups (for example, a meeting of the Indian prime minister Mr. Devegowda with top industrialists on December 31, 1996), and these demands include some form of transfer. Therefore, PSEs are politically motivated redistributive arrangements. However, if the PSEs fail in providing support to politically designed motives or politics, leaders in government try to search out new alternative forms of PSEs which can provide gains to them both from the market economy and the mass support. For this, the company form of PSE is the most suitable form of PSEs, and can provide opportunities and incentives to the regime and also to the economic forces to oblige each other. Government-owned companies (GOCs) increase the credibility of the government and minimize the cost of redistribution, as they speed up the volume of redistribution because the information imperfections and asymmetries are cleared through the close connections with influential economic forces, thereby decreasing the cost of policy renegotiations.[9] GOCs are to ensure protection of rent on the basis of political bargaining and guarantees of continued rent flow. Such companies are the best institutional mechanisms of promises, incentives, and rewards, as these adjust with new information and unfolding events. As such, GOCs are input suppliers and transactional institutions to provide gains of rents to influential groups, consumers, the political regime, and interest blocs. GOCs enjoy credibility in the market in the sense that they are able to sustain themselves in the market economy by augmenting capital and resources from the open market. Last, GOCs are able to capitalize on the political environment and put major claims to gain influence in the political system.

The literature on macroeconomics and business in government shows that PSEs are converted into GOCs to meet the challenges of economic crises and policy change. Economic crises may be in the total economy of the country or at some sector or industry level. At the national level, as in India during 1990–1991, when a balance of payment (BOP) problem emerged due to a shortage of foreign reserves, GOCs are a support–sustenence system to the political regime by offering capital, reserves, and resources in order to get more investments and relaxations from the domestic and foreign markets and to bring political–economic equilibrium at the national and international levels. During such crises, GOCs move fast to use government resources to help growth resume. GOCs also force the government to bring major policy change, mainly when the companies foresee the economic crises in the country. If the government delays policy reform, the GOCs redesign their operations to get economic gains during uncertain situations, as these are flexible in comparison to PSEs.

The degree of inefficiency in GOCs generally remains low or at marginal level, as the types of production are maintained at a standard level due to competition with private-sector enterprises (PRISES), and information imperfections tend to be smaller. GOCs calculate the size of gains on the basis of information and interact with PRISES for distribution or utilization of gains. However, GOCs operate under government directives and policy packages, so inefficiency persists and imposes informational costs upon the GOCs and policy-reform packages, but the informational cost remains low in comparison to PSEs. In company form, the complexity of information is resolved through the simple organization of the company. Further, GOCs set up their linkages in the different sectors on the basis of the capacity to extract information, and the complexity of information is automatically resolved. The structural characteristics of the GOCs also help in resolving the complexities of information. GOCs increase the potential gains from the market economy, make reversals more costly, and increase the probability of adherence to the market orientation and information.[10] The market-friendly orientation of the GOCs creates efficient systems of financial disclosures, environment protection, enforcement of contracts, protection of intellectual property rights (IPR), labor, antitrust regulations, and simple taxation, which not only increases the perfection of information but also produces quality, efficiency, and effectiveness. To ensure the system, GOCs enjoy autonomy and the government is thereby able to maintain a distance in their market operations and avoid any managerial interventions, as the management is to consist of specialized personnel with business orientation and competence to deal with market forces. However, government intervention cannot be totally ignored, because market regulations are designed by the government in view of the country's economy. In this situation, GOCs are required to persuade the government to intervene less than in the past. However, the political reality is inevitably injected into interventions in order to achieve political objectives.[11] GOCs are, as such, subject to political directives but are now being insulated in such a way that political interventions should generate inefficiency in the companies.

Further, GOCs are being reoriented to maximize profit as the alternative choice of governance, competition, cost conditions, or public interest, but political interventions are not as supportive as for private enterprises. On the question of maximizing profitability, the issues of regime sustenance and power enhancement contradict the democratic and political situations as the profit of enterprises are utilized for political purposes. However, the dynamic commitment of government for profit in the liberal economy and global competitiveness may protect the enterprises. With dynamic commitment, GOC's investments, capital, cost, property, and information can be protected and make the GOCs feasible and desirable. Sometimes, international donor agencies like the World Bank or the International Monetary Fund (IMF) act as insulators by imposing conditions on the government, and save the profits of GOCs from misutilization for political purposes. Organizational strength and power also act as insulators in the GOCs.

In GOCs, technological gaps exist, but not as deep as in PSEs. Private enterprises exchange technology to increase quality of products, efficiency, and cost effectiveness. GOCs make contracts under the severe control of government. Most of the GOCs tend to be heavily dependent on explicit and implicit capital transfers from the government. Since GOCs are not a nexus of treaties, the government's discretion to transfer capital depends upon political interests.

Capital generation in GOCs is not a crucial problem in comparison to PSEs because GOCs are designed to collaborate with the private sector on certain terms and conditions like ownership or management by the government and capital investment by the private sector. Joint ventures in GOCs are easily carried out when there is a clear-cut agreement on inputs and control/regulation over the outputs. Capital generation in GOCs is based on profit motives. Social services are not provided, but public interest is preserved.[12] The quality of products is also maintained to ensure capital generation. The question of national interests or safety provides ample opportunity for political interventions, but in such situations the companies lose either capital or quality. The situation is more visible in developing countries.

Similarly, transfer of technology or knowledge is not provided at scale to the GOCs in comparison to PRISES. Medium-level technology is transferred to the GOCs. It is true that the latest technology and knowledge is not transferred to the GOCs due to government political interventions, lack of autonomy to use the technology, bureaucratic procedures, and lack of trained staff and dynamism in the management of GOCs.[13] It is also true that GOCs do not participate in agreements on the latest technology because the government prefers to organize competition in the market economy rather than participating in the competition. Market forces and private-sector companies compete to obtain the latest technology and knowledge at higher prices from the open market. When the latest technology and knowledge are sold at affordable prices, the GOCs try to monopolize them. However, GOCs try to buy the latest technology in some sectors where the questions of national security and interests are at stake, as in space and atomic sciences. However, in such cases, technology and knowlege are transferred with great reservation by multinationals or foreign powers.[14]

The issue of capital generation and transfer of technology is interlinked with the mode of operation of GOCs and sentiments of the market. GOCs take a liberal view on capital generation, as it dilutes the financial burden of the government. GOCs provide services on a cost-payment basis, and invite private capital for investment on the one hand and make efforts to ensure technological advancement on the other. The limitation of GOCs in the economy of any country is the government's reservations, political programs, and international agreements. GOCs express the economic intentions and agendas of government. The issue of transfer of technology and knowledge is also linked with market failures, particularly in those sectors where market failures occur occasionally. In economies like India, GOCs intervene in market failures and help to improve market sentiments and sustainability. In such situations, GOCs sacrifice cost–benefit capital generation and transfer of technology.[15] To avoid this situation, GOCs intervene indirectly in market failures in the form of incentives, restrictions, and preferential regulation. Government interventions through GOCs use the power of the market or market forces for the strength of the market mechanism, political support, and interest articulation. More particularly, when the trade liberalization process takes place to establish the economy, GOCs become the vehicles of the export–import system. GOCs are empowered to transfer imported items to the private sector, and thus these companies become an international partner of trade. During the structural-adjustment process, GOCs get international aid to repay the cost of reforms and trade liberalization. Although conditions are imposed by donor agencies, the cost of conditions are transferred to market forces, the private sector, and consumers directly. For example, the Indian government, in the opening of the telecom sector, has imposed the cost of IMF conditions upon private telecom companies and users. As such, GOCs are beneficial in transferring cost conditions.

On the whole, we find that the economic crisis will drive public-sector enterprises to reform and government-owned companies will emerge as a more flexible, liberal, autonomous, and competitive form of government action, voice, and will. Such companies will provide a dynamic and liberal set of operations to the government in the business sector, both as facilitators and regulators of the market economy and the new international economic order created by the GATT/WTO. GOCs will operate as links for information, cost–benefit, service, quality, and consumer satisfaction, efficiency, and operational effectiveness. Since the complexities of economies are increasing at the global level, GOCs are the most suitable organizations to extract the benefits and gains of economies' complexities.

In India, economic reforms were driven by the politico–economic crisis in the country (political instability and the problem of balance of payments) and the pressures of international organizations like the World Bank and the IMF after 1991. The main focus of the reforms was upon the liberalization and opening of the economy for multinational corporations in order to lessen the role of the state in the economic development of the country by withdrawing, selling, and redesigning public-sector enterprises. The main reason of limiting the role of the state was to slash the burden of sick and heavy PSEs upon the government and to convert the most essential of the PSEs' unprofitable enterprises by redesigning them. An amendment was made in 1993 to the Indian Companies Act of 1956 to enable the government to declare public-sector boards/enterprises as state companies so that these PSEs could be empowered to play a key role (by raising capital through shares, debentures, bonds, etc.) in the market economy and to do important business in the essential sectors. For example, roadways, electricity, and water boards were empowered to change from loss-making to profit-making government units. The main burden of these reforms was to release PSEs from the network of politics and the rigid bureaucratic administrative system and to lessen the influence of politics in the business activities of the government. Besides this, the government also tried to locate the capital to fill up the budget deficit by selling the shares of public-sector enterprises in the open market, as well as slashing the burden of PSEs through foreign direct investment (FDI). Further, to promote capital and investment, the tax structure was redesigned in order to promote corporate sector enterprises like Steel Authority of India (SAIL), Oil & Natural Gas Commission (ONGC), and so on, and also to restructure the management boards of public-sector companies like AIR-Indian Airlines Corporation. The PSEs were also provided different facilitations and relaxations in price determination, wage determination, labor relations, marketing, and so on. Last, the PSEs were permitted to start new ventures with private and foreign investors. On the whole, the economic reforms in India were aimed at shifting the focus of the state to more vital and important matters of international politics, rather than economic matters in order to find a proper place in the world governance mechanism. Developing economies have been dominated by the traditional theories imposed by colonial rule and the legacies of socialist thought.[16] New economic reforms have supported the idea of depoliticizing the economy, improving the quality and efficiency of services, and increasing exports and imports in the world economy. In order to achieve these policy options, the Indian government has modified its export–import (EXIM) policy, eased the convertibility of the Indian rupee in the current account, and improved FDIs, Foreign Exchange Regulation Act (FERA), labor laws, trade-related practices and rights, and primary and secondary market-related rules and regulations.

Further, the government has taken initiative in selling the shares of PSEs to the private sector and MNCs, but the capital gained was not reinvested in the PSEs for upgrading the enterprises, and was instead utilized for the budget deficit and the oil-deficit pool. Therefore, the basic purpose of PSE privatization was defeated. Moreover, GOCs were directed to adopt policies that either protected Indian industry or subsidized the social and agroindustrial sectors, which increased their deficit. Those GOCs in profit have become loss-making units. However, the government's strategy to acquire capital by selling the shares of major PSEs like ONGC has paved the way for converting PSEs into GOCs which are controlled and regulated by the central government through the policy framework or by independent regulatory commissions/authorities. The strategy of the central government has made it easy for PSEs to act as shareholding companies rather than as enterprises. Another significant change in the PSEs is that organizational autonomy was provided to the GOCs and the government will refrain from intervening in the management boards or in the appointments of chairmen or managing directors so that political and bureaucratic interference is restricted. However, the government may intervene if the GOCs are becoming sick, loss-making units, or burdens upon the budget of the government. GOCs have also been permitted to make direct contact with foreign investors or sell shares to private/foreign companies or partners.[17] GOCs have also been liberated from the clutches of the licensing system by a single-window permission system subject to the laws and regulations of the central government, as with protection of the environment, historical monuments, defense locations, and so on. As such, the PSEs have been converted to GOCs in order to get a competitive place in the global economy and the market-oriented economy of the country.

In India, the process of making PSEs into government-owned companies started in 1994–1995, when several committees recommended the change. The government initiatives to reform the PSEs have not been drastic and revolutionary, and their pace has been slow, as has been indicated in a survey of the World Bank and IMF.[18] In India, the Industrial Credit and Investment Corporation of India (ICICI) conducted a survey on the public limited companies of the central government and the state governments in 1996 on the economic reform period (1991–1996), which pointed to several interesting results. The survey showed that the public limited companies have not been able to sustain their profits. In 1995–1996, the profits of these companies were very low in comparison to previous years. During 1994–1995, the total profit was 17.5 percent, and in 1995–1996 it came down to 16.8 percent. Similarly, the operational profit came down from 12.5 percent (1994–1995) to 11.5 percent (1995–1996), but the profit level remained the same on invested capital in 1994–1995 (15.5%) and in 1995–1996 (15%). These companies have been able to attract foreign investments in comparison to domestic investments. The foreign investments went from 45.1 percent in 1994–1995 to 53.2 percent in 1995–1996.

The ICICI Survey was conducted on 675 companies. It pointed out that the business of these companies increased tremendously after the new economic policy of 1991, but the profit did not increase as the cost of production increased. The reasons for increasing production costs were modernization of technology, the increasing cost of raw materials, higher salaries, loss of value, higher interest rates (30.3%), and a higher tax rate (14.1% in 1994–1995 to 17.7% in 1995–1996). Therefore, the operational profit was 17.4 percent and net profit was 12.5 percent. The permanent property rate has been significant, and touched the highest score of 28.2 percent in 1995–1996. The survey brings out the fact that companies have not been able to earn maximum profit, even after the economic reforms (1991–1996). Although these companies earned a good profit in comparison to the prior reform period, the profit did not increase significantly during the reform period. The reasons outlined for the decline in profit are increasing operational costs for raw materials, higher wages, technological upgrades, increasing interest rates on loans and cost of production, tough competition in pricing in the market, and conditions imposed by the World Bank and the WTO as well as by some developed countries on exported goods. Another significant fact emerging from the survey is that the companies concentrated their attention on foreign rather than domestic investments, and therefore fluctuations in the foreign currency market and the ratio of difference between Indian currency and the U.S. dollar increased the cost of foreign collaboration or joint ventures. Besides this, competition on market prices and tax structures also severely affected the performance, profit, and quality of goods. In India, the capital markets, both primary and secondary, were promising until 1994, and companies were able to attract investments from the domestic market. After 1994, regular interventions of government and the SEBI (a regulatory body of the central government to control capital markets in India) have demolished the primary capital market and the share bazaar collapsed. Big and reputed companies were not able to generate money from the primary market. Several companies were in trouble and forced to mortgage their permanent properties in the secondary capital market. Consequently, there were more interventions from the SEBI and the government, more closing of the capital market was seen in 1995–1996, and the sensitive index (SENSEX) of the Bombay Stock Exchange touched the lowest point in three years (2,500) in December 1996. Besides this, the survey also pointed out that the companies have been able to enlarge their capital property, production, and capacity during the reform period (1991–1996), which will significantly gear up the market economy in India. The survey expects that the companies' profits will increase in the coming years as they are able to stabilize themselves in the market economy; however, there are possibilities of a volatile market system and political instability, which will affect the growth of the GOCs in many ways.

CONCLUSION

The reversal of economic theories in the field of economic sciences and the emergence of new policy options and alternatives have created dilemmas and contradictions in transitional socialist economies like the Indian economy. These economies are under pressures and constraints from both politics and economics, and the governments are not able to take hard and quick decisions in the market economy. Hence, the pace of economic reforms is slow and based on a "wait and watch" policy which is creating uncertain situations and suspicions in the market economy. For example, delays in announcing the reform package had a negative effect on the market economy in India in December–January 1997. Since the market economies in these societies have not been able to get the support of the masses and the social systems, the pressure to go slow and fear of losing power in the political system have not yielded better or expected results from the reforms in the economic sectors. Besides this, the legal system is rigid and traditional, which provides little flexibility to the government to convert public enterprises into GOCs. For example, the central government has to promulgate a Presidential Ordinance if it wants to convert any PSE into a GOC (recently, the president of India promulgated an ordinance to convert the Industrial Reconstruction Bank of India [IRBI] as a GOC). Another major problem is that the coalition government (a mixture of thirteen major political parties including Communist/Marxists) was not able to take the major economic decisions to liberalize the economy by making or converting PSEs into GOCs in India, in spite of its commitment to a market economy. Further, the bureaucracy is a big hurdle in setting more GOCs, as it loses power and dominance in the administrative system and, more particularly in the present situation, it is capitalizing on the political situation for its own purposes. The rigid administrative system is holding the PSEs by capturing the key positions (chairman and management director) which prohibit the government from converting the PSEs into GOCs. Moreover, the concept of the welfare state is preventing the government from liberalizing and opening the service sectors for private and foreign investors. The government declining to per-

mit the entry of foreign media into India has had a negative effect
upon the GOCs in taking major economic decisions. Last but not
least, the vote bank of rural India is prohibiting the government
from establishing GOCs, as subsidies will not be available to the
rural people in the GOCs system. The continued emphasis on subsidy to rural people has generated a psyche of dependence upon the
government, which creates a big problem for the PSEs.

The crisis of 1991 in India, both politically and economically,
forced the government to reengineer the economic system and to
prepare it for future economic challenges. The government's will to
redesign the economic system has yielded better results in the
peformance of PSEs, as the survey of the ICICI showed that profit
has increased in the public limited companies, and the initial reforms were significant in bringing change in the economic scenario
of the country. After 1994, the situation changed and the profit
level in the companies could not be maintained due to the slow
pace of economic reforms, unstable political conditions, and the tax
structure of the country. The government's will to continue the economic reforms was appreciated, but the coalition government has
not been able to speed up the economic reforms. However, companies have shown remarkable performance during the last five years.

Although companies have been successful in the Indian economy
during the initial period, several apprehensions were expressed
about their role and future performance. In the Indian economy,
the PSEs are the expression of the government's policies and the
constitutional commitments like a socialist pattern of society, equality, and justice, which will not allow the government to enforce the
basic principles of the market economy. There are some examples
of when the Supreme Court of India has intervened and directed
the government to restore the earlier situation in the public interest, as in the Narbada Valley project or the Enrone Power project
in Maharastra. Such judicial interventions will significantly affect
the market-economy approach of the government. Another point of
interest is that the bureaucratic set-up of the country does not permit the government to allow the increasing role of the private sector,
as it will diminish their importance. Further, government-owned
companies have been insulated by the political interventions which
will be a big problem in the future of companies. For example, the
investments made by companies in the market, joint collaborations
of these companies in the industrial sector, and business deals are
not easily approved by the political managers in these GOCs. Moreover, political involvement creates informational constraints and
generates incapacities in these GOCs. Besides this, politics intervene in the routine management of the companies. Last, the infor-

mational incapacities of GOCs have been crucial in the market economy, because the GOCs will not be able to compete and maintain quality with profit, pricing, and marketability in the near future, as the MNCs are more competitive, quality oriented, service minded, and reasonable in pricing.

To conclude, in developing countries like India, PSEs are the vehicle of maximizing the tenure of the political regime. The theory of redistribution with growth is to support the vote bank of rural people, political masters, and the rent seekers of the developing economy. The market economy cannot serve the interests of politico-bureaucracy, as it avoids distributing the profit among them (political and administrative masters) which they extract from the socialist economy in different ways. GOCs are the compulsions or the result of the conditions imposed by the World Bank and the IMF. However, these are emerging in the country. The future of these GOCs will depend upon the autonomy, financial and administrative flexibility, and professionalism with a pure business outlook. The commitment of the government to continue subsidies through the GOCs will not be possible in the near future. If it continues, the GOC experiment will fail as in Mexico and Brazil. GOCs will have to take nonpolitical decisions and compete in the market economy on the terms and conditions of the global economy. Modern economic theories are not now country political-regime centered. Economic sciences have now reached the point where politics or country/culture can prohibit it in its endeavor to become global. This has to be realized by the political masters in India, who should make necessary arrangements (not only regulatory systems but also policy options). India is the largest democracy in South Asia and is crucial in leading the region for the global market economy. We can only expect that the Indian government will understand the situation and capitalize through GOCs. Otherwise the country will be exploited by the MNCs. India is a model economy for the South Asian region. The South Asian Association for Regional Cooperation (SAARC) will become a platform for regional bargaining or an interregional trade center. Now it is up to the Indian government to decide the future of government-owned companies, either for its own purposes or for global purposes.

NOTES

1. Sebatian Edwards, "The Political Economy of Inflation and Stabilisation in Developing Countries," working paper 4319, NBER, Cambridge, 1993.

2. Jose Edgardo Campos and H. S. Esfahani, *Credible Commitment and Success with Public Enterprise Reform* (Washington, D.C.: World Bank, 1995).

3. Anne O. Krueger, "The Political Economy of the Rent-Seeking Society," *American Economic Review* 64 (1974): 291–303.

4. Pradeep Saxena, *Public Policy, Administration and Development* (Jaipur: Rupa Books, 1988).

5. Montek Singh Ahluwalia, "Redistribution with Growth," World Bank Development Conference, 1995, pp. 40–45.

6. Victoral Goldburg, "Regulation and Administered Contracts," *Bell Journal of Economics* 7: 426–448.

7. Dani Rodrik, "The Rush to Free Trade: Why So Late? Why Now? Will It Last?" in *Voting for Reforms: Democracy, Political Liberalisation and Economic Adjustment*, ed. Stephen Haggard and Steven B. Webb (New York: Oxford University Press, 1994).

8. John Waterbury, *Exposed to Innumerable Delusions: Public Enterprises and State Power in Egypt, India, Mexico and Turkey* (Cambridge: Cambridge University Press, 1993).

9. Robert Bates and Anne O. Krueger, *Political and Economic Interaction in Economic Policy Reform* (Oxford: Basil Blackwell, 1993).

10. Christopher Clague, "Relative Efficiency, Self Containment and Comparative Cost of Developed Countries," *Economic Development and Cultural Change* 39 (1991): 507–530.

11. Roger Nell, "The Politics of Regulation," in *Handbook of Industrial Organisation*, vol. 12, ed. Richard Schmalensee and Robert Willig (Amsterdam: Elsevier, 1989).

12. Pradeep Saxena, "The Strategies of Development: The Indian Case," in *Strategic Planning and Development: Developing Economies in Perspective*, ed. Sony Nwankwo (Sheffield, 1996).

13. Pradeep Saxena, "Science, Ethics and Transfer of Technology: A Case of India" (paper presented at the International Symposium on FMTs, Paris, France, 16–18 September 1996).

14. Ibid.

15. Joseph E. Stiglitz, "Technological Change, Sunk Costs and Competitions," *Brookings Paper on Economic Activity* 3 (1987): 883–947.

16. Pradeep Saxena, "Decline of Development State," in *Research in Social Sciences*, ed. J. P. Mishra (New Delhi: Agam Kala Prakashan, 1993).

17. Planning Commission, Government of India, "Approach Paper of VIII Five Year Plan," in *Eighth Five-Year Plan* (New Delhi, 1992).

18. "World Bank Survey," *Hindustan Times*, 27 September 1996.

3

Economic Transition and Public Service in Slovenia

Stanka Setnikar-Cankar

Modern times are times of change. This does not apply only to Slovenia, which together with other Eastern European countries is trying to extricate itself from the old system which has proven to be less efficient, above all economically (even though its citizens like to emphasize upon certain occasions that geographically, cultur- ally, and even economically and politically, Slovenia is in fact more part of Central Europe). Such changes are taking place all over the world and differ only in type and intensity.

Changes in the field of public administration in developed coun- tries take place under the umbrella of the general trend of develop- ment of industrial society toward postindustrial society. Taking into account the power and significance of public administration, it could play a positive role in this process and even be a motivation factor. Mechanization, new forms of organization resulting from the divi- sion of work, increasing production of public services, a high de- gree of specialization, and technical professionalization are trends which also characterize work in public administration. The criti- cism of negative phenomena in industrial society is therefore also addressed to the state and its administration, and requires appro- priate redirection. Postindustrial society is a "society of services." Developments in the field of education and research have led to a flourishing of the quaternary sector. The terms "information soci- ety," "leisure society," and "risk society" obviously indicate new fea- tures and changes that public administration must face. It is interesting that the finding that the characteristics of postindustrial development exert an influence of expanding this field has been accepted almost unanimously in most developed countries. Public administration is on the increase, not only because it is one of the characteristics of the society of services, but also due to the shortcomings of the market-economy mechanism in the field of public services. In developed countries, the best and most acceptable characteristics of market-economy mechanisms are combined with necessary intervention by the state, and the extent of both mechanisms varies.

The standard administrative system has survived all political instabilities and changes: from monarchies to republics, from dictatorship to democracy. One could say, with a slight ironic twist, that bureaucracy is older than democracy. It will therefore continue to exist in the future, preferably to support the modern positive developments in society, taking into account the historical, political, cultural, sociological, and economic features of the environment. It is a fact that historical differences exist between the more "managerial bureaucracy," as in the United States, Great Britain, Canada, Australia, and lately New Zealand, and the more "legally oriented bureaucracy," as in France, Germany, and Slovenia.

Naturally, Slovenia, as a less-developed country in the company of the most-developed ones, also lags behind in the public sector. However, it need not make all the mistakes developed countries have made on their way to industrial society and toward postindustrial society. Taking into account the positive and negative experiences of other countries, we must aim our vision of the development of public administration toward creating an administration for the needs of a postindustrial and postmodern society.

PUBLIC EXPENDITURE IN SLOVENIA

At the beginning of the 1990s, Slovenia inherited a large inflation rate and a negative growth of GDP. After 1991, the inflation rate was considerably reduced, since the monthly price index growth was only one-third of what it had been, but the annual inflation rate in 1992 was still 200 percent, while per capita GDP fell to US$6,320. Essential structural changes occurred in the Slovenian economy: The contribution of value added from industry fell from 50 percent before 1989 to 40.6 percent in 1992, while the contribution from services increased from 45 percent to 54 percent. All these changes were accompanied by a high rate of unemployment, which officially amounted to 13 percent; the actual level was about 9 percent. The greater openness of the Slovenian market caused additional pressure toward unfavorable movements, since economic policy could not neutralize the increased vulnerability of the Slovenian economy, even to small changes of the external conditions of the economy.

Recently, the economy has been additionally burdened by higher taxes and contributions for social services. Small countries are as a rule "expensive" in terms of their budget. At present, the revival of commercial activities and restructuring of the economy are priority tasks. In the short term, this orientation is not compatible with the growth of investments in the public sector and the noncommercial infrastructure, an increase in the country's material expenditure, increased social rights, and increased national debt. On the contrary, the view that a reduction in the amount of public expenditure is economically desirable in order to unburden the economy is quite widespread.

The entrepreneurial-managerial culture is being introduced, both in developed European countries and in countries in transition, also in the public sector. A large share of those who seek the services of the public sector will still depend on the operation of that part of the public sector which will not be privatized. The issues of financing, organization, and economic efficiency (i.e., productivity in the public sector) are therefore extremely important.

The basic characteristic of the economies of the majority of countries in transition is large changes which result from real economic questions. First, the issue of the lack of efficiency of the economy appears. In Slovenia, this is certainly in part a result of secession, the loss of traditional markets, the process of privatization, and introduction of the laws of the market into all segments of commercial and even noncommercial activities. To be honest, it must be admitted that the attitude toward public expenditure in Slovenia is still very much under the influence of the old opinion of its consuming nature. Employees in the public sector cannot expect a large amount of support and sympathy from the public when they fight to improve their material position. In 1996, this was demonstrated most obviously in two cases.

In mid-1996, doctors went on strike for the first time after many decades. Dissatisfied with their "wage slave" relationship with the state, which treats them as state employees who should be happy to have permanent employment without the risk of losing it, they demanded salaries which would be equal to other employees in public administration, above all to those of judges, who have managed to gain a better material position. Since 1996 was an election year, the doctor's strike was also politically charged, which many parties naturally took advantage of. In defending the doctors' demands, they did not forget to draw the attention of voters to the incompetence of the government. According to public-opinion polls, the Slovenian public responded traditionally: A relatively high percentage of people interviewed did not support the doctors' strike, because the published salaries for doctors were higher in absolute terms than others (e.g., the salaries of employees in companies with economic problems). In conditions of unemployment, bankruptcies, ownership transformation, loss of markets, and other economic difficulties, the high level of education, specific work conditions, stress, and high responsibility of doctors became irrelevant.

Employees with low salaries and unemployed people with social support on which they cannot live normally are not interested in differences in the level of education, difficulty of work, and responsibility, but only in the absolute amounts of salaries. It is understandable that a part of the Slovenian public which has found itself in an unenviable position has not shown any sympathy for the employees in the public sector whose existence is not endangered. However, a similar response was seen from the part of the population which supported the thesis that by striking the doctors violated the principles of medical ethics, since during their strike they only treated the most severe cases, while other, less urgent cases had to wait for the end of the fortnight's strike. Their dissatisfaction helped form the public opinion that above all the patients were the victims of the doctors' strike, because the doctors "set their material interests above the ethical ones" (Gorjup 1996).

The second, worrying response was shown in opinions that this is a sector which does not create new value, but only spends it, since it is financed from taxes and contributions of the impoverished economy. This completes the circle: The economy which can hardly keep its head above the water due to the objectively straightened circumstances after Slovenia's secession pays increasingly higher contributions to the spendthrift state and the public sector. According to their opinion, employees in the noncommercial sector obviously still cannot understand that the funds for their salaries and other costs of activities are created by employees in the commercial sector, which must deal with liquidity problems and bankruptcies. The employees in the public sector are therefore expected to share the fate of employees in economic activities and agree that their work is valued lower. A series of comments on the organization and work of the public sector was given. On the occasion of the doctors' strike, critics emphasized the insufficient number of doctors and poor organization of work, which causes long waiting periods, above all for specialists. The dissatisfaction of patients is higher, since these same doctors are willing to see the same patients immediately in their private surgeries for payment.

Such strikes are certainly a challenge for sociological research and an alarm signal for changes in government policy in this field. When the strike by doctors, who partially succeeded with their demands, was followed by a strike by teachers demanding the same evaluation criteria as those which apply to doctors and judges, the dissatisfaction of employees in the commercial sector increased further. The threat of teachers to strike immediately before the end of the school year, when pupils in secondary schools were preparing for their final examinations, which are decisive with regard to their ability to enter university, and pupils in primary schools were facing external exams, which are decisive for their continued education in secondary schools, annoyed parents. Under these conditions, the degree of solidarity with teachers was even lower than it had been for doctors.

If one neglects the political and sociological aspects of this problem, these strikes sounded a clear warning about the open issues of financing, organization, and the extent and quality of services of the public sector in Slovenia. Even though some criticism of health care and education was politicized and intended to collect preelection points, there were also justifiable comments as to the quality of the operation of the public sector, which should be taken seriously and reacted to. In addition to the government, competent ministries, and employees in the public sector, this is also the task of professionals.

IN SEARCH OF A ROLE FOR THE PUBLIC SECTOR

The responses to the doctors' strike, threats of a teacher strike, and dissatisfaction of employees in the police and the judicial system have clearly drawn our attention to the difficult material situation of these activities. With regard to the objective economic circumstances in Slovenia as one of the central European countries in transition, their situation could be presented as a reflection of the general situation. But major changes are in fact taking place in these activities. The public sector is facing the process of privatization in the environment with which it cooperates, and this affects its operation. At the same time, its own system is changing. Not only is the privatization of certain noncommercial activities spreading extremely rapidly, the rules for activity within the framework of the former "state" sector are also being demolished.

The terms "privatization" and "introduction of market economy criteria" are probably most often used to briefly describe the changes in the field of the economy in Slovenia. Both should enable the economy to increase the growth of created national product. Ideas about the significance of development and stimulation of entrepreneurship in the economy through market order are therefore generally accepted, even though they have not been fully implemented in practice. Due to the large amount of interweaving, interconnection, and mutual dependence of the private and public sectors, it is almost impossible for the latter to remain unchanged with systemic changes occurring in one segment of the society. The demands for the privatization and introduction of market elements in the public sector have therefore appeared almost simultaneously.

The first extreme demands were followed by more tolerant ones, the objective of which was to assess and take into account arguments for and against privatization in the public sector. Privatization is closely connected with politics and fiscal problems, since it includes the issues of equality, economic efficiency and commercially based operation, and the relationships between the public and the private sectors. One argument for a certain degree of privatization of the public sector is above all economizing, which is made possible by managerial and entrepreneurial methods. The entrepreneurial instinct seems to be universal. The economic theory is very clear: Due to ownership and incentives, state ownership cannot be as efficient as private ownership in the production of the same product or service. The negative efficiency of the state sector is covered by redistributing income or printing an excessive amount of money, which leads to inflation, unemployment, and economic regression.

Naturally, there is a series of content and technical issues in the transition of state ownership to more competitive forms which demand gradual implementation. Noncommercial activities provide the population with services of an existential nature and their unthinking transformation and privatization would bring more damage than benefit. One possible solution is the sale of state companies in entirety or partially through the sale of a controlling packet of shares. Difficulties in this form arise in Slovenia, above all from the lack of interest in buying such shares as a result of the very poor economic situation of state companies which are offered for sale. Another reason for this is a lack of capital among potential buyers and attempts to sell such companies below their market value, which means that previous objective analysis of the company's situation and capabilities is necessary.

Ownership transformation of infrastructure is an essential part of the overall ownership transformation process of socially owned companies in Slovenia as a prerequisite for the establishment of market economy. In line with the Law on Business Public Services, passed in 1993, partial nationalization of public utilities has been implemented as the first stage of ownership transformation. The second stage of ownership transformation, which will facilitate genuine privatization, will start as soon as the Law on Privatisation of State Ownership, which has been discussed in Parliament since October 1994, most recently at this writing in summer 1999, is passed. The Slovenian approach in ownership transformation of public utilities could be considered unique. In the first stage of ownership transformation of public utilities, the infrastructure has initially been nationalized. Second, the remaining social capital of public utilities has been split between the state and/or local authorities. The company becomes a public enterprise if the socially accumulated sources exceed 51 percent. The remaining social capital—49 percent or less—has been transformed according to the law (Hrovatin 1997). The rationale for separating the infrastructure from companies and transferring it to state or local community ownership could lie on economic grounds. In spite of economic justification for competitive restructuring of sectors in conformity with the role of infrastructure there are at least three key shortcomings:

1. Infrastructure has been split up into national and local solely according to the scope of the accumulated sources by the state and local communities over the past years.

2. The legal status of public utilities (i.e., whether they are public or private) is determined solely on the basis of the system of their financing in the past.

3. Infrastructure has been withdrawn from the companies. Through such a solution, management of infrastructure and investment decisions have been transferred from companies to governmental and local authorities, which are less experienced and devoted to efficient management than companies themselves.

The separation of infrastructure in Slovenia would be justified if the state or local authorities organized a bid to contract out the operation of public utilities. The more efficient solution would be to nationalize the infrastructure companies as whole entities—without separation of network—in the first stage, and to schedule them for privatization—where appropriate—in the second stage, applying experiences in other EU countries. Another possible form would be granting concessions to the private sector to perform public services. Even though ownership would remain unchanged, initiative would be on the side of the concessionaires. Some concrete problems related to concessions in Slovenia appeared due to a lack of interest of concessionaires and a lack of experience in determining the elements of concession relations. In some cases, only an exchange of the state monopoly with the private monopoly occurred. Concessions therefore do not automatically mean better quality services, nor lower prices. The third form is an introduction of a partial private payment for public services, which should reduce the budgetary expenditure for such activities. Experience to date has shown that the amounts of additional payments are not high and are therefore mostly acceptable to users of such services. However, this is also the reason why they do not have a significant influence on a reduction of budgetary expenditures for these activities. The fourth form is public financing of services performed by the private sector. An example of this could be services in which the social criteria are more important than the economic ones (health care services, social security services, etc.). As a rule, professionals do not object to the introduction of various forms of privatization in the public sector, but the illusion that privatization can solve all problems is quite unacceptable, since it brings a series of new social, political, and economic problems. Practice to date has shown that Slovenia is facing a large lack of domestic capital, a poorly developed capital market, and a low interest in the investment of foreign capital in joint ventures. This is also reflected in investments of the private sector in the field of noncommercial activities. The majority of investments still come from the budget. Public companies which are being organized according to entrepreneurial principles face a work overload. Different forms of privatization therefore cause a reduction in the number of employees and an increase in the already high unemployment rate. The prices of services have increased for certain activities. As a rule this has happened in fields in which a high degree of competitiveness is not possible and profitability rates are low.

The public utilities are usually the activities where a natural monopoly arises. The fact is that the firms in the public-utilities sectors in Slovenia are, due to historical and developmental reasons, monopolies. This was the first cause for society to explicitly control prices. In order to prevent this monopolistic situation, the society—before the transition—strictly controlled prices and often fixed them under the level of production costs. At the end of the 1980s and the beginning of the 1990s, the prices of the public utilities were caught unchanged and have been submitted to changes only on specific demand. The present system of limitations for the pricing systems of the local public utilities was determined first of all by the wish for the macroeconomic regulation of inflation and not the microeconomic criterion of efficiency. On the other hand, the level of living had to be protected. The data show that not even one of the expenses of households paid to the public-utilities sector represents any significant expense and proportion of the households' budgets, including the expenses for drinking water (Fabjančič 1997).

The current improvement in the performance of public utilities and the simultaneous adoption of the latest innovative methods for lower costs cannot be expected without the stimulation of better business.

NEW FORMS OF PERFORMANCE IN THE PUBLIC SECTOR

Privatization forms have created the possibilities of choice, the implementation of which largely depends on the purchasing power of customers. Slovenian society is becoming increasingly more stratified, inequalities are increasingly greater, and the benefits of economic growth are nonuniformly distributed between those who receive income.

In the period from 1991 to 1994, 62 percent of employees received income lower or equal to the average gross salary in Slovenia. The concentration of gross income in 1994 was the following: 20 percent of employees with the lowest gross income received only 7 percent of total gross income, 60 percent of employees with medium gross income received 52 percent of total gross income, while the remaining 20 percent of employees with the highest gross income received as much as 41 percent of total gross income (Borak and Pfajfar 1995). Since these differences will probably increase, a large number of customers will depend on the services of that part of the public sector which will not be privatized. The issues of its extent, quality, organization, and accessibility are therefore even more important.

On the other hand, the radical and political changes during the 1990s raised discussion concerning the state of ethics in Slovenia (Glas 1997). Ethical issues occupy a prominent place today due to the following:

- The destruction of the former moral and value system, which created uncertainties concerning appropriate behavior.
- The new ownership structure, which exposed social property to the challenges of new business strata and holders of political power.
- Slow legal changes and contradicting regulations, which opened "gray zones."
- The economic recession, which offered an easy "alibi" for some ethically unacceptable acts.
- A liberal, highly permissive environment.

One can find a series of articles on illegal transactions involving budgetary funds between new institutions (funds) and the private sector which brought unjustified income to individuals. After many years of constant attacks on public services and employees in the public sector as being old fashioned and rigidly bureaucratic, it now seems that the old-fashioned ideas of the responsibility, integrity, and honesty of state employees are not all that bad.

The systemic changes no longer allow the unchanged performance of services in the public sector. The principles of financing, organization, and operation must be adapted to the economic, legal, and political social circumstances. In an environment in which the principles of market behavior and competitiveness are affecting every facet of social life, the public sector cannot operate according to established principles. Patients, citizens, and pupils are no longer adjuncts to the process of creating services, who must be satisfied merely by having access to services. They are becoming active, critical individuals who want to participate actively, express their opinions, and influence the course and quality of services rendered, and also to judge the attitude and method of rendering them.

In setting new rules for the functioning of the public sector in Slovenia, it is primarily necessary to do the following:

· Establish standards for organizations in the public sector.
· Establish mechanisms for the influence of users of services.
· Establish clear relationships of responsibility.
· Improve financial management.
· Improve information management.

The following principles should above all be observed:

· Detailed standards must be determined for different levels of services.
· Consultation with users of these services is essential in establishing these standards.
· Availability of clear information on services, objectives, and results.
· Openness about achieved goals and people who provide services.
· Complaints procedures must be user friendly and efficient.
· Harmonization between created value and funds: value for money.

Findings from one survey (Setnikar-Cankar 1996) have shown the following principles and rules:

· Development toward clearly determined and budgeted management is beneficial and positive.
· It is quite clear to the majority of people in public administration that employees in the highest positions in public administration have knowledge and capabilities, above all in the field of public policy, but there are

relatively few people with direct experience in managing and direct providing of services.

- Employees in public administration inevitably take into account the priorities of their ministries and the parliament.
- A large variety and complexity of work and the information requirements of the parliament and the mass media cause an excessive workload in state administration.
- In comparison with private and public organizations, public administration is too extensive and varied to be managed as a whole.

On the other hand, user involvement is limited and is more reactive than proactive. This suggests that the user voice is still weak and that the crucial issue is to identify the users.

MEASURING OUTCOME IN THE PUBLIC SECTOR

There are pressures because of budgetary spending and demands to reduce it. Activities in the public sector are controlled, but insufficient attention is paid to results achieved with spent funds. On the other hand, there is still relatively little pressure from the outside to improve the operation.

Organizations in the field of public services are also expected to function in a more entrepreneurial manner. But managing a company in the field of noncommercial activities is not the same as managing a company in the field of commercial activities. Differences arise from the fact that organizations in the public sector have a different purpose of business operation and specific relationships with users of their services. Traditional relationships in the public sector can be illustrated with the frequently heard statements of school principals that they wish to lead the pedagogic process and not be managers and accountants. In addition, the ability of individual managers to efficiently manage and bear responsibility are limited in the public sector. Not only are the use of funds and the subject and content of activities controlled, but so are their managerial methods, employment and dismissal of personnel, salaries, promotions, working time, evaluation, organization, accommodation, use of information technology, and so on. The rules are determined centrally and their changes do not depend on individual managers.

The reason for control is supposedly the ensuring of a better quality of services within the framework of available funds for the benefit of taxpayers and employees. Independent or government agencies are established to provide services, due to the size of the state administration which prevents efficient management. But the practice of establishing agencies did not bring only positive results. In some countries, they even speak of "agencymania," expressed in an unreasonably large number of agencies, which is a typical example of exaggeration in introducing a new type of institution even where this is not necessary. There is no need to establish separate executive agencies to improve the operation of an organization. There are a number of instruments for improving operation: decentralization of responsibility for the selection of the majority of inputs, better specification of operation, clear responsibility relationships, or improvement of financial and information management.

We are in favor of alternative forms of organizational pluralism in the public sector, due to the large variety of tasks. It is therefore understandable that some organizations need more supervision by ministers, while others must be protected from unnecessary interference by ministries in the interest of independence of the executive function.

In designing organizational forms, one must take into account the functions and their environment: the possibility of competing in the market, the nature and extent of the social function of the organization, whether it primarily deals with counselling, whether it accepts the regulatory function or the function of a policy designer, whether it provides services for the public, and the possible degree of the commercialization of its services. The result must be the founding of numerous different types of organizations (agencies, departments, institutes, public companies, and institutions), all with tasks, financial structures, and regimes of responsibility which are suitable to the nature of their tasks. Under these conditions, it is possible to use different managerial styles with different degrees of autonomy.

Better organization, lower costs of operation per unit of service, and higher quality of services are hopefully also achieved by encouraging competition. Simulation of circumstances similar to those in the commercial activities sector in market conditions with a sufficient degree of competitiveness is expected to be achieved through contracting out or market testing. "Competing with quality" means introducing competitiveness in activities which have so far been performed only in the public sector. A clear relationship is being created between users and providers of services. This encourages innovation among internal and external competitors. Attention is moved from the results, procedures, and objectives to improving efficiency and successfulness. It is hoped that the threat of competition itself will improve quality and efficiency. The experiences of countries which have had such practices for a longer period of time have shown that the positive aspects of market testing are above all the following: savings in costs, higher efficiency, greater flexibility, and innovation due to the threat of job loss. Its negative sides are the consequences of the absence of competition, which are shown in poor quality and inappropriate services (dirty streets; poorly maintained schools, hospitals, and parks; etc.).

Naturally, the issue arises of proving that services will be better as a result of this and that the benefits to taxpayers, users, and employees will be higher. It is possible that new organizational units are rigid and that so-called "freedom" does not ensure higher efficiency.

Programs for improving the quality of the public sector and managerial reform have opened the question of evaluation of the operation of the public sector. Even though there are a certain number of indicators, organizations use them more for cosmetic purposes. The objective of programs for improving the quality of the public sector is to develop procedures for the monitoring, controlling, and evaluation of its operation in order to integrate these procedures and their results into strategic and operative management. Agreements on salaries have been decentralized, employment contracts for a determined period of time and salary incentives have been introduced, both for the highest and middle positions in public administration, and so on. A new relationship between ministries and managers of administrative units who conclude annual contracts on operation has been established. A managerial committee which consisted of experienced managers from the private sector of the economy participated in auditing. Changes in the public sector were part of general systemic, economic, and social changes: monetary policy reforms, introduction of microeconomic liberalization, changes in the structure and functioning of local self-management, and changes in the educational and health care systems, and in residential and social policies.

The increasing role of economic indicators has an influence on the relationships between corresponding ministries (Ministry of Finance, agencies, administrative units) and contractors. Data based on indicators make it possible for the Ministry of Finance to control the use of funds with regard to different activities. These indicators have a double meaning: On one hand there are fewer opportunities to cover up inefficiency, on the other they enable transparency in any limitations of services.

Economic indicators are especially important when they serve as a basis for financing. A large part of the public sector in Slovenia (e.g., regular education from primary school to university, a part of health care, social security) is financed on the basis of norms which take into account planned programs and their implementation. The example of norms in higher education shows that the basis for financing is the extent of services with regard to allowed (normative) items (input—number of hours of lectures, exercises, and seminars with regard to the number of students), while the extent of the product is considered to a lesser degree (output—number of students who graduate) and the quality of that product is almost not considered at all (outcome—acquired professional knowledge, creativity, innovation, ability to work in teams, etc.).

To a large extent, this is a consequence of budgetary financing of the public sector in the past. The budget or appropriate ministries used to be the only source and address for requests and demands for funds. The fact that it is quite normal in market economies that organizations in this field obtain only a part of their funds from the budget and create the rest themselves is quite unpopular in Slovenia, even though it is essential.

Wherever possible, commercial functions should be separated from noncommercial functions and organized in state–public for-profit organizations (international airports, ports, radio, TV). Research and development organizations can be established on completely commercial bases. A systematic and wide program of commercialization, which means a full or partial coverage of costs or payment by users, can comprise services which have to date been financed exclusively from the budget: agricultural counselling service, statistical data service, meteorological service, water analysis service, and so on. In the field of education, this objective is expected to be achieved through the system of financing basic programs. Educational institutions can acquire additional funds by organizing supplementary and counselling activities and through research projects with which they can compete for additional funds equally with others. They will be successful if they offer better programs.

It is of interest that in Slovenia such practices were very widespread from 1986 through 1996 at the level of university education. Even more, certain faculties obtain up to 80 percent of all funds through research and counselling activities. On the other hand, there are some faculty members at the university level who still strictly adhere to the principle that faculties are primarily academic institutions which should not pursue profit. An example from the field of language education: Interest in foreign languages has always been great in Slovenia, but the educational system has been poor, above all in the 1950s and 1960s. However, the teaching of the English, German, Italian, and French languages experienced a true boom in the middle of the 1980s and since 1991. Since the middle generation speaks foreign languages less well, they wished to obtain such knowledge at additional courses and seminars. This great demand has encouraged the establishment of new, mainly private, language schools, which faced a lack of professional teachers. This was an opportunity for the language faculty to provide for the additional education of teachers, pass on foreign experience, and assist in organizing high-quality education.

But the faculty administration did not think in an enterpreneurial manner and did not see a market niche in this situation. It is paradoxical that this faculty is at the University of Ljubljana, which battles extreme problems of space, inappropriate work conditions, and low salaries. Constantly dissatisfied professors, tired by their constant complaints over their poor material position, which have mostly been ignored, evidently did not find enough energy to have a direct influence on their own material position. An argument they expressed during a discussion with their colleagues at a facility which has ten educational centers and organizes supplementary education for employees on weekends was that university teachers are not travelling salesmen. This reply would be appropriate for an ideal situation at the university level, which should above all enable professors to perform scientific and research work. But even in this case the faculty which wishes to be flexible would respond to practical needs. Perhaps institutions just need more time to be organized appropriately. Unfortunately, market opportunities work in such a way that lost opportunities do not recur and the competition is stronger every day.

Naturally, we are not in favor of economic criteria becoming dominant in the field of public services. The example given does not mean that language education should be accessible only to those who can pay for it. Counselling and educational activities that are organized for certain groups of users against payment of attendance fees perform the function of improving the quality of all services. If additionally collected funds enable the purchase of equipment or literature, education of teachers abroad, cofinancing of textbooks, participation in nonprofit projects, and better salaries, regular students also benefit from that. Among other things, in the long term and in conditions of strong competition it is impossible to sell mist and old stories to those who pay for services themselves.

OPEN QUESTIONS

Statements related to the changes in the operation of the public sector seem to be of an economic–financial and managerial nature, but it is a question whether they are not also political and constitutional. The most pressing issues related to the changes in the operation of the public sector are the following:

- How will the systemic-managerial changes affect the rights of citizens?
- What power over the rights of citizens can the private sector acquire?
- How can equal opportunities for citizens using the services of the public sector be preserved when public services are provided by different organizations?
- What extent of control over the "production" of services should ministries retain and how will this affect parliamentary responsibility?

These issues are of fundamental importance. Unfortunately, it is not possible to find appropriate and carefully weighed answers to them. The answers are general: Competition is positive, private practice is clearly better, the rigorousness of the market will undoubtedly bring benefits, and efficiency will increase.

What is more efficient? Is the competition discussed by the government the same competition under which private companies operate? Is it better for services to be performed by organizations which could go bankrupt and are no longer controlled by the parliament? Is it an incentive for employees in the public sector to be constantly exposed to somebody proving to them that their work is of lesser value than that performed by people employed in the private sector?

It has been established in New Zealand (Boston et al. 1996) that there is no accurate data on the effect of fixed contracts (which enable the competition of the private sector) on the mobility of employees and ethics in the public sector. However, data show that employees in high positions in public administration have accepted the system of employment for a definite period of time and payment based on performance. The data that only 6 percent of candidates for positions have come from other fields, not from the public sector, is not surprising, since the nature of work in the public sector is essentially different and the labor market is different (there may be some overlapping in financial management and human resources management). However, there are always political and budgetary limitations to salaries in the public sector which would be interesting for "high-flyers" in the private sector.

The reason that this issue is insufficiently discussed is that the issue of public administration in Slovenia is not politically highly valued. In addition, there is usually no professional opposition to government reforms among employees in public administration in Slovenia. Even more, the public always receives the opinions of employees in the public sector (i.e., "insiders") with some reservation and skepticism with regard to their objectivity, saying that they are above all trying to preserve or even improve their position.

Last but not least, the demands for and execution of reforms in the public sector mean a considerable frustration for employees.

Responsible behavior therefore demands a large amount of critical capacity: It needs to be shown that the work of the people who provide public services (i.e., civil servants, policemen, postmen, doctors, teachers) is appreciated. The constant threat of a "cultural revolution" with which the value of public services is lowered, employees are demoralized, and traditional structures destabilized is unacceptable. Reform must be based on the identification of shortcomings and a coherent and consistent plan for the removal of these shortcomings, taking into account the positive and negative effects of changes prior to their implementation.

Without consensus regarding the terms "efficiency," "equivalent value," and "quality," and an accurate definition of exactly what they mean in practice and what political and constitutional changes will be caused by the changes, it is not possible to count on their success. Even then, the reforms may have undesired effects. Without previous consideration, the pursuit of higher economic efficiency may only change the method of performing services, but not ensure its fulfillment and possibility of use.

CONCLUSION

In Slovenia, the process of transition from a socialist economy into a market economy was conducted differently than in most other Eastern European countries. Radical political and economic changes during the 1990s raised discussion concerning the state of the public sector in Slovenia. The situation produces growing problems and the need to define the organization and rules of the public sector.

The views on the changes in the functioning of the public sector are changing. The inefficiency and quality of services of the public sector in comparison to the private sector are significant. The objective of change is primarily to increase efficiency through different degrees of privatization and market-oriented measures. The principles of functioning, organization, and operation must be adapted to the economic, legal, and political–social circumstances. In an environment in which the principles of market behavior and competitiveness are affecting every facet of social life, the public sector can no longer function according to established principles. Naturally, we are not in favor of economic criteria becoming dominant in the field of public services.

Programs for improving the quality of the public sector and managerial reform have opened the question of evaluation of the operation of the public sector. Even though there are a certain number of indicators, organizations use them mostly for cosmetic purposes. The objective of programs for improving the quality of the public sector is to develop procedures for the monitoring, controlling, and evaluation of its operation in order to integrate these procedures and their results into strategic and operative management.

Better organization, lower costs of operation per unit of service, and higher quality of services are hoped for also by encouraging competition. Simulation of circumstances similar to those in the commercial-activities sector in market conditions with a sufficient degree of competitiveness is expected to be achieved through contracting out or market testing.

We are in favor of alternative forms of organizational pluralism in the public sector due to the large variety of tasks. The current improvement in the performance of public utilities and the simultaneous adoption of the latest innovative methods for lower costs cannot be expected without the stimulation for better business.

Patients, citizens, and pupils are no longer adjuncts in the process of creating services who must be satisfied merely by having access to services; they are becoming active, critical individuals who want to participate actively, express their opinions, and influence the course and quality of services rendered, and also to judge the attitude and method of rendering them.

REFERENCES AND BIBLIOGRAPHY

Bailey, S., and C. Davidson. 1997. "Did Quality Really Increase Under Local Government CCT?" In *Public and Private Sector Partnerships: Learning for Growth*, ed. L. Montanheiro, B. Haigh, D. Morris, and Z. Fabjančič. Sheffield: Hallam University Press.

Borak, N., and L. Pfajfar. 1995. "Analiza neenakosti v delitvi dohodkov v Sloveniji" (Analysis of Inequalities in the Division of Income in Slovenia). *Slovenska ekonomska revija* 47: 87–99.

Boston, J. 1995. *Lessons from the Antipodes: New Zealand*. Dartmouth: Aldershot.

Boston, J., J. Martin, J. Pallot, and P. Walsh. 1996. *Public Management: The New Zealand Model*. Auckland: Oxford University Press.

Fabjančič, Z. 1997. "A Water Pricing Model for Slovenia." In *Public and Private Sector Partnerships: Learning for Growth*, ed. L. Montanheiro, B. Haigh, D. Morris, and Z. Fabjančič. Sheffield: Hallam University Press.

Falconer, P. K. 1997. "The New Public Management: Principles and Practice in the UK." *Javnauprava* 1: 98–108.

Glas, M. 1997. "The Ethics of Business in Slovenia: Is It Really Bad?" In *Public and Private Sector Partnerships: Learning for Growth*, ed. L. Montanheiro, B. Haigh, D. Morris, and Z. Fabjančič. Sheffield: Hallam University Press.

Gorjup, Viktorija. 1996. *Privatisation in the Fields of Education, Health Care and Culture*. Ljubljana.

Greer, P., and N. Carter. 1995. *Next Steps and Performance Measurement.* Dartmouth: Aldershot.

Hrovatin, N. 1997. "Ownership and Competitive Restructuring of Infrastructure in Slovenia." In *Public and Private Sector Partnerships: Learning for Growth*, ed. L. Montanheiro, B. Haigh, D. Morris, and Z. Fabjančič. Sheffield: Hallam University Press.

König, K. 1996. *Public Administration: Post-Industrial, Post-Modern, Post-Bureaucratic.* Budapest: EGPA.

Ministrstvo za finance (Ministry of Finance). 1996. *Bilten javnofinanĒnih prihodkov in izdatkov* (Bulletin of Public Income and Expenses). Ljubljana.

O'Toole, Barry J., and A. G. Jordan. 1995. *Next Steps, Improving Management in Government.* Dartmouth: Aldershot.

Saner, Raymond, and L. Yui. 1997. *Pilot Projects for Improving Working Procedures in Slovene Public Administration and Training Modules.* Ljubljana: Inštitut za javno upravo; Geneva: Centre for Socio-Economic Development.

Setnikar-Cankar, S. 1996. *System of Measuring Outcome and Control in the Public Sector.* Budapest: EGPA.

4

Maintaining the Mission of Nonprofit Organizations under Government Contracting

Sherry J. Fontaine

Fundraising and philanthropy are what commonly come to mind when the general public considers sources of funding for nonprofit organizations. What is not widely understood is that government funding has become a significant source of revenue for nonprofit organizations. This is not a recent phenomenon. The Filer Commission (1975) found that the nonprofit sector had increasingly become a "mixed-realm" which was supported by private philanthropic and government sources of funding. Greater government funding was and continues to be welcomed by nonprofit organizations as sources of private funding have declined. However, what was disturbing to the commission was that increasing dependence on government monies threatened the independence of private, nonprofit organizations.

What the Filer Commission reported in 1975 accurately predicted a continuing trend of increasing government funding of nonprofit organizations. Government funds, including government contracts and reimbursement, accounted for 31 percent of nonprofit-service-organization income in 1989 (Salamon 1992). Since this figure includes the delivery of health services and education, it does not reflect the percentage given to human-service agencies. While the budgets of the latter agencies are comparatively smaller and would attract less overall government funding, there is a marked trend for contracting out social services to smaller nonprofit agencies as well. The various types of nonprofit social services that are often candidates for government contracting include child care, homeless shelters, services for the elderly, employment training, and counseling (Nathan 1996).

The trend of government funding of nonprofit social-service agencies had its most dramatic rise in the 1970s and 1980s (Smith and Lipsky 1993). This is underscored by Lipsky and Smith (1989), who reported that federal social-service expenditures to nonprofit organizations were nonexistent in the 1960s but rose over 50 percent over the last twenty years. This growth trend experienced setbacks beginning in the Reagan era and continuing into the 1990s, when governments began a period of retrenchment. During this period, funding for social services was cut back (Salamon and Abramson 1996). A consequence of these cutbacks was less funding for and, consequently, a greater uncertainty regarding the continuation and level of funding provided through government contracts.

What is of interest in this examination of the government–nonprofit social-service contractual relationship is whether or not nonprofit organizations abandon or stray from their mission as a result of their contractual obligations. Second, is it prudent from a strategic-planning or management perspective for nonprofit agencies to alter their missions in order to successfully compete for government contracts? The objective of this chapter is to begin to answer these questions through a review of theories on the role of government and third-sector relationships, as well as the concepts and applications of strategic planning. The relationship between government and the nonprofit sector as analyzed from a political-science perspective and the practice of strategic planning as understood from a management perspective offer other means of exploring the conflicts and compromises in maintaining the stated missions of nonprofit organizations.

THEORIES ON THE WELFARE STATE AND THE NONPROFIT SECTOR

Theories on the relationship between the public and the nonprofit sector, particularly in terms of human and social services, view nonprofit organizations as (1) providing services not offered by the public or private sectors, (2) an alternative or substitute for government as a provider of services, or (3) a middleground which provides a complimentary, mutually beneficial relationship between government and the nonprofit sector.

The first perspective contends that the role of the voluntary sector is to provide services the government and the private sector cannot or do not provide. This theory has also been termed the "market failure" theory (Weisbrod 1987). Nonprofit organizations have also been viewed as an alternative or substitute for the public sector in providing public goods. Conservative political arguments suggest that relying on nonprofit organizations to provide social services rather than government is actually a desirable goal. From this perspective, the community orientation, missions, and independence of private nonprofit organizations make them more preferable than government for the delivery of human services (Filer Commission 1975). In his book, *The Tragedy of American Compassion*, Orlasky (1992) provides a moral argument for relying on nonprofit agencies rather than government to provide social services. Historically, voluntary associations provided human services. As our country grew and as the welfare state expanded, government replaced nonprofit organizations as social-service provider. Government is impersonal and has removed both the giver and the recipient from the personal contact and feelings of compassion that Orlasky believes have traditionally characterized the voluntary sector. Nostalgia aside, the sheer numbers of needy individuals cannot be met by the resources of the nonprofit sector alone.

A collaborative or partnership relationship between the nonprofit sector and government best explains the present relationship between both sectors (Mohr and Guerra-Pearson 1996). The growth in federal spending has not resulted in a decline in the nonprofit sector. In fact, the opposite has occurred. Expansion in the provision of public welfare services, particularly at the federal level, has resulted in an increasing amount of government contracting with nonprofit agencies to provide these services (Mohr and Guerra-Pearson 1996; Lipsky and Smith 1989). This partnership, in which government supports nonprofit organizations, is part of a pattern which Salamon (1987) has termed "third-party government," whereby government uses nonprofit organizations to carry out government programs. Salamon acknowledges that nonprofit organizations have unique institutional characteristics that give them an advantage in delivering human services, but he rejects the "market failure" theory, which views the role of nonprofit organizations as compensating for the gaps in the public- and private-sector markets. Salamon's unique perspective is that the government–nonprofit partnership is actually an outcome of voluntary-sector failure. The nonprofit sector was not able to fulfill its role in providing for those in need. Nonprofit agencies may be more flexible than government bureaucracies in how they provide services and to whom they provide services; however, because they can use their own criteria in selecting who will have access to their services, the principle of equity is comprised. As a result, there are many needy individuals who have no service providers in the voluntary sector. Government expansion into the provision of social services was necessary to cover the gaps in coverage which existed in the voluntary sector.

The Pros and Cons of Government–Nonprofit Partnerships

The resulting government–nonprofit partnership for delivering human services is in many ways a mutually beneficial one. By contracting with nonprofit agencies for the delivery of social services, governments are able to expand the welfare state without expanding the bureaucracy. On a more practical level, through contracting, governments are able to expand access to services without a corresponding expansion in government institutions or staff. There are a number of additional advantages found in the government–nonprofit partnership for the delivery of social services:

1. Nonprofit agencies are considered more innovative and flexible than large government bureaucracies. Private nonprofit agencies can be innovative and flexible because they are independent organizations that theoretically are not bound by the restrictions and "red tape" often found in government agencies (Filer Commission 1975; Gates and Hill 1995).

2. Because nonprofit organizations are often community based and community focused, they can offer services best suited to local needs (Saidel 1989; Lipsky and Smith 1989).

3. Nonprofits are considered a more cost-efficient provider of social services. State and local governments have lowered the costs of delivering social services by contracting with nonprofit organizations. There are various reasons why nonprofits are more cost efficient. These reasons include greater use of volunteer staff, lower-paid staff, scale economies which favor smaller organizations for the production of social services, and, at least theoretically, competition among nonprofits, which allows governments greater bargaining power (Ferris 1993).

4. Governments depend on the trustworthiness and experience of nonprofit organizations in the delivery of social services (Ferris 1993).

5. Governments can shift political responsibility for the delivery of social services to nonprofit organizations.

This partnership is of course beneficial to nonprofit organizations as well. The most obvious benefit to nonprofit organizations is that government contracting provides a more reliable source of funding. It relieves the burden of launching large fundraising campaigns and dealing with the problems of donor preferences for funding of specific programs, and provides nonprofit organizations with the ability to develop new programs and expand their existing client base. (Salamon 1987; Smith and Lipsky 1993). By virtue of their participation in the contracting arrangement, nonprofits have also increased their influence and involvement in the policy-making process (Saidel 1989). Although, as Smith and Lipsky (1993) point out, the policy process affecting nonprofit activities is dominated by government officials, not by the nonprofit agencies, which are placed in a financially vulnerable position as a result of the contracting relationship.

Counterbalancing the advantages to the government–nonprofit contractual relationship is a number of concerns which indicate problems inherent in this partnership. Foremost is the loss of independence of nonprofit agencies engaged in government contracting (Filer Commission 1975; Salamon 1987; Lipsky and Smith 1989). Independence and autonomy, characteristics which enable nonprofit organizations to be innovative and flexible in the development and delivery of programs, are jeopardized when organizations depend on government contracts for a significant portion of their funding. Government organizations have their own set of criteria for program recipients. As Lipsky and Smith point out, these organizations operate under differing organizational norms. Government is concerned with the equitable distribution of services and relies on mechanisms such as predetermined eligibility criteria to ensure an objective means for service delivery, but, as we are aware, criteria tend to be rigid and do not account for individual differences and circumstances. Nonprofits, while they have been criticized for selecting clients according to organizational preferences embodied in their missions, are more concerned with responsiveness to clients. For these clients, services are more personalized and applicable to their individual needs. Under government contracting, it is assumed that compliance with government regulations and criteria for eligibility will take precedence over the responsive, individualized nature of service delivery offered by private nonprofit organizations.

A loss of independence can result in diminishing other attributes that make nonprofit organizations desirable partners. For nonprofit staff, dedication can outweigh relatively lower salaries. Will this dedication continue if staff feels restricted by following government regulations? Will contracting require the use of more professionals and less reliance on volunteers? If so, nonprofit organizations would not be as cost efficient in delivering social services. Another issue that has been raised is that rather than being equal partners, nonprofit organizations have become another arm of the government, one which is dependent upon and vulnerable to the uncertainties of government funding (Smith and Lipsky 1993; Smith 1994).

An additional concern is that of accountability (Gates and Hill 1995). Nonprofit agencies are not accountable to legislatures or the voting public. While nonprofit agencies are subject to compliance with government regulations imposed within a contractual agreement, nonprofit organizations, like any other essentially independent organization, can find ways to circumvent the application of regulations and eligibility criteria, or staff simply will be lax in conforming to them. The end result is that nonprofit organizations can maintain some degree of independence in terms of how and to whom they choose to deliver services. This problem may be lessened as governments, as well as funding intermediaries such the United Way, place greater emphasis on the development and use of performance measures for determining the success of programs they are funding.

IMPACT ON ORGANIZATIONAL MISSION

If the contractual relationship between nonprofit organizations and government threatens a nonprofit organization's independence, it can be assumed that it threatens its mission as well. The literature on the government–nonprofit contracting relationship supports this assumption (Salamon 1994; Smith 1994; Smith and Lipsky 1993; Montes 1997). This chapter is concerned with the impact of the government–nonprofit contracting relationship on the nonprofit mission because the mission embodies the purpose of an organization. This is particularly the case in nonprofit organizations. As Lester Salamon has stated, "Where for-profit organizations acquire their organizational raison d'être fundamentally from the pursuit of profit, nonprofit organizations get theirs from pursuit of mission, a purpose that binds the agency's personnel, supporters and beneficiaries together in a common purpose" (p. 95).

Government funding and the regulatory requirements that follow may not necessarily be incompatible with a nonprofit organization's mission. They can, however, have an impact on its purpose, as it will change the way and/or type of clients the organization serves. The impact of government will depend upon the type of nonprofit agency involved in the contractual relationship. Agencies which were formed on the basis of government funding are already dependent on the government and are more likely to reflect the same mission or purpose as their funding partners. Agencies with multiple sources of funding (e.g., Red Cross) can maintain their original mission and have a higher degree of independence. Agencies which are most vulnerable in terms of maintaining their mission and independence are community-based agencies, which generally do not have a strong financial base or numerous funding options (Lipsky and Smith 1989; Ferris 1993).

Role of Organizational Missions:
The Strategic-Planning Perspective

Strategic-planning literature, which focuses on the operational aspects of planning, presents a somewhat different perspective on the importance of maintaining a nonprofit organization's mission. The mission of a nonprofit organization in the strategic-planning process is defined through the organization's mission statement. Much of the strategic-planning literature for nonprofit organizations offers a market-oriented or business-strategy approach when analyzing the role of mission statements in nonprofit organizations. The mission statement defines a nonprofit organization's core values and purpose. An equally important function of the mission statement is that it reflects a shared vision of an organization's employees and stakeholders (Drucker 1992; Bryson 1994). In operational terms, mission statements guide the goals, strategies, and actions of an organization.

In *Managing the Non-Profit Organization*, Peter Drucker (1992, 7–8) lists three "musts" of a mission statement: opportunities, competence, and commitment. Commitment is reflected in the shared vision of the mission statement. Competence refers to a self-assessment by the agency's staff and stakeholders to determine, in essence, what they do best. Opportunities are the more questionable "must" of the mission statement. They are questionable because they can potentially conflict with the value-expressive content of the mission statement. When Drucker lists opportunities as an essential component of the mission statement, he is referring to the opportunities that exist external to the organization. Opportunities should be commensurate with the needs of the nonprofit organization's publics and reflect the organization's mission. The opportunities considered should also match the organization's competencies and available resources.

Pursuing government contracts would be an example of human-service nonprofit organizations pursuing external opportunities. The government–nonprofit contractual relationship is based on the belief by both parties that nonprofit organizations have a demonstrated competency in delivering human services and can assist government in effectively meeting their obligations to provide these services. Yet government contracting, as already noted, can conflict with a nonprofit organization's ability to maintain its mission.

How is the conflict reconciled in the strategic-planning literature? To begin with, this particular relationship has not been explored in depth in the management literature. From a business standpoint, government contracting is simply another opportunity that a clever executive or governing board should exploit. However, there is always the caveat that opportunities such as this should only be explored if they are consistent with the organization's mission (Drucker 1992; Bryson 1994, 1995). What differs is how public and nonprofit policy analysts view the role of a nonprofit organization's mission versus how strategic planners or business strategists define it. There is a common view that an organization's mission should reflect its core values. Similarly, there is an acceptance that the mission of a nonprofit organization is inseparable from its reason for being and, therefore, plays a distinctive and critical role for voluntary agencies.

When considering the definition of the mission statement from the strategic-planning and business-strategy perspectives, there are additional characteristics of the mission statement which allow it to be more flexible or vulnerable, depending on your point of view. The first is that the mission statement itself is constructed in such a way that it is not only simply stated, but also very broad and open to interpretation. Thus, an organization can have a great deal of latitude in choosing the opportunities it wants to pursue and still claim to be acting in accordance with their mission.

Consider the following exemplification of a mission statement from a regional nonprofit organization:

Northeast Regional Job Training Center—To advance the economic well being of the Northeastern Region. The Center is designed to foster family development, enable individuals self-sufficient through employment, and to provide employment and training services to employers.

While this mission statement exemplifies the appropriate concepts and values of the organization as the strategic-planning process recommends, it does not represent the true range of services that this type of organization provides. This is, in fact, not an uncommon problem in nonprofit mission statements (Espy 1986). It is also important to note that this organization is involved in government contracting. The result has been that the original client base that this organization was founded upon has significantly expanded.

For example, in the case of the job training center, deteriorating economic conditions in the region called for an increase in services for displaced workers. In addition, these workers were transitioning from a disappearing manufacturing sector and needed training to develop new technical skills. Since the organization is increasingly dependent upon state government contracts for its funding, the agency staff is always concerned with meeting state government performance criteria, measured in terms of job placements for clients. This measurement is based on a percentage of job placements for those that complete training. The higher the number enrolled, the higher the number that needs to be placed. Although this performance measure is subject to criticism, what is of concern in this analysis is how adherence to these criteria has posed critical questions regarding the organization's mission. For the past several years, the organization has exceeded the targeted number of enrollments. Demand for job training has been high in the region, and the mission of the organization is to provide employment training for any individual in need, which would include all dislocated workers. Yet to meet the quantitative performance measure for the state contract it would be more prudent for the organization to limit enrollments and give priority to clients that are more likely to find employment. This would allow the organization not only to maintain but also to increase their placement rates. It would not strictly speaking be a population outside of the organization's mission, but it would be a selective population that is more educated and probably less economically disadvantaged. There is an immediate concern to keep with an unstated but inherent part of the organization's mission, which is to serve the economically disadvantaged.

A second aspect of the strategic-planning perspective is that, while the mission statement or the values it represents is considered almost immutable, the strategies or goals can and should be changing in response to the external environment (Drucker 1992; Nutt and Backhoff 1992; Bryson 1995). If the mission statement guides the goals and strategies of a nonprofit organization, it is likely that changes in goals and strategies will eventually conflict with the organization's mission statement. If strategy has primacy over a nonprofit organization's mission, the net effect will be to diminish the importance of the organization's mission relative to the individual strategies.

Going back to the case of the job training center, if the organization chose to prioritize the selection of clients, it would follow an appropriate strategy from a market-oriented perspective; however, the original mission would be jeopardized. The organization could also choose to look for additional sources of funding in order to maintain their enrollments and, consequently, their mission. Unfortunately, this is not always the outcome when the government provides significant funding for a nonprofit organization (Wolch and Rocha 1993). The desire for government funding, the pursuit of an opportunity, or a market-driven strategy often becomes the overriding objective. The consequence is that fewer services are provided to the population defined in the organization's mission.

Challenges of a Changing Client Base

When we consider the mission of a nonprofit organization, we are also aware of the types of clients that the mission statement reflects. Yet demographic changes, new treatments and technologies, and changes in funding sources all have an impact on the original service base. Girl Scouts of the United States of America is a good example. Their original members were young women from seven to seventeen years of age who could not be characterized as culturally diverse. If we looked at the young women that are Girl Scouts today, we would find a very diverse population of young women. The organization responded to changing demographics and changing needs.

But what occurs when shifts in the client base bring enhanced reimbursement or more lucrative funding opportunities for nonprofit organizations? Nonprofit organizations that are lured by the financial benefits derived from serving a particular client group will drift from the charitable functions of their mission. As nonprofit organizations become more market driven, the individuals that fall through the public sector "safety net" have fewer agencies to turn to for assistance. Compounding this problem are cutbacks in government social-service programs which translate into funding cuts for nonprofit organizations who were contracted to provide these services. Interestingly, rather than turning back to their philanthropic roots, nonprofit agencies have become increasingly more market driven (Salamon 1994). Just as these agencies pursued new funding streams generated through government contracts, many nonprofit human-service agencies are now pursuing fee-for-service alternatives. It appears that when nonprofit agencies become more market driven than mission driven they weaken their charitable purpose and thus the characteristics that make the third sector unique.

ALTERNATIVES

The question posed at the outset of this chapter was how nonprofit agencies can maintain their mission under government contracting. The obvious answer is that nonprofit managers and boards should seek a middle ground that will balance the financial needs of organizations and adhere, as much as possible, to the organizations' missions. This is a simplistic answer, since striking this balance is an ideal goal but not necessarily an achievable one. Another, perhaps obvious, conclusion is that for nonprofit organizations to maintain their independence as well as their mission they should seek diverse funding sources. This could, for example, be a mix of government contracts, donations, foundation grants, fee-for-service alternatives, and so on. Once again, this is an ideal alternative that will minimize an organization's dependence on any one funding source. Unfortunately, not all agencies will be able to secure sufficient funds from alternative sources to maintain their financial solvency (Smith and Lipsky 1993). This would be particularly true of smaller, less well-established human-service nonprofit organizations.

What needs to be noted, however, is that when we consider the vulnerability of an organization's mission when facing financial incentives and disincentives that are incompatible with the mission we are generally considering the founding mission and purpose of the organization. Business strategists are simply realistic in assuming that externalities such as demographic changes, treatment advances, and differing solutions to social problems could compromise the original mission of an organization. March of Dimes is often cited as an example of an organization that revised its mission and strategies in response to changing needs. Adherence to its original mission and the primary service population would have made this organization obsolete.

In some instances it would be preferable for an organization to close its doors or merge with another nonprofit organization rather than completely compromise its mission as a nonprofit service provider. In instances where a nonprofit organization maintains its charitable intent and does fulfill a need, the immutable nature of the mission has to be questioned. This is particularly the case if changes in the service population are not reflected in the mission. This does not mean that the primary purpose of the organization changes; instead, its mission should be broadened to reflect the differing service needs of the population it currently serves and the potential population it could be serving.

In order to maintain the mission of human-service nonprofit organizations, if not in its original form at least its original intent, the mission statement should maintain (1) the core values of the organization and (2) the same or similar population that the nonprofit organization intended to serve and upon which the mission was developed. However, for human-service agencies, branching out to a broader population has to be approached with caution. The danger in government contracting is that the population that is currently being served will be "crowded out" by a service population that promises increased revenue. A nonprofit organization cannot be true to its mission if it does not continue to provide services to the population originally defined in its mission.

Adherence to an organizational mission also demands a recognition of the political context of the government–nonprofit partnership. Operating under government contracts requires that nonprofit leaders be able to manage stakeholders and be adept corporate political strategists (i.e., influence policy and social issues impacting the organization) (Bigelow, Middleton, and Arndt 1996; Billis 1993). Maintaining a sense of mission and a significant measure of independence in a highly politicized environment requires that nonprofit managers become skilled in influencing public-policy decisions. This includes not only influencing legislatures, but also educating and mobilizing all organizational stakeholders regarding the political and social issues affecting the organization. Funders are certainly critical stakeholders, but nonprofit organizations must also consider soliciting support from and mobilizing community groups, advocacy groups (which are often comprised on beneficiaries of their relatives), and other nonprofit agencies with related concerns (Bigelow, Middleton, and Arndt 1996). Last, nonprofit organizations must consider the role of the governing board. Saidel's (1993) research on the role of governing board members in relation to government indicates that board members have played an important political-advocacy role. In so doing, they have served a buffering function which protects the autonomy of an organization as well as protecting its mission.

Future Research

The analysis presented in this chapter was derived from the literature and from experiential knowledge of nonprofit organizations. The analysis raises other questions which merit further investigation. It would be beneficial, for example, to determine the mix of differing populations a nonprofit agency can serve without adversely impacting the population defined in its mission. A case study of agencies that have successfully maintained a financially diverse mix of clients without sacrificing services to any client group would be one means of understanding how this difficult balance between adherence to the mission and the necessity of achieving financial stability can actually be reached. Conversely, in instances where the balance is tipped in favor of clients who offer more lucrative funding sources, investigators have to consider the thorny issue of whether or not a nonprofit organization should continue to maintain its tax-exempt status. Yet another area that merits further empirical investigation is diversifying funding sources. Since the availability of a diverse funding base is a critical factor in maintaining the independence of an organization, what alternative approaches can a nonprofit organization pursue (i.e., interorganizational networks, collaborative efforts, stronger advocacy role) to acquire a greater mix of funding sources? Hopefully, through continued research we will be able to further our understanding on how nonprofit organizations can accomplish the difficult tasks of maintaining their missions and successfully managing their organizations.

REFERENCES AND BIBLIOGRAPHY

Bigelow, B., M. Middleton, and M. Arndt. 1996. "Corporate Political Strategy: A Framework for Understanding Nonprofit Strategy." *Nonprofit Management and Leadership* 7 (1): 29–43.

Billis, D. 1993. "What Can Nonprofits and Businesses Learn from Each Other?" In *Nonprofit Organizations in a Market Economy: Understanding New Roles, Issues and Trends*, ed. David Hammack and Dennis Young. San Francisco: Jossey-Bass.

Bryson, John M. 1994. "Strategic Planning and Action Planning for Nonprofit Organizations." in *The Jossey-Bass Handbook of Nonprofit Leadership and Management*, ed. Robert D. Herman. San Francisco: Jossey-Bass.

Bryson, John M. 1995. *Strategic Planning for Nonprofit Organizations: A Guide to Strengthening and Sustaining Organizational Achievement.* San Francisco: Jossey-Bass.

Drucker, Peter F. 1992. *Managing the Non-Profit Organization: Principles and Practices.* New York: HarperCollins.

Espy, Siri. 1986. "Corporate Identity and Directions." In *Handbook on Planning for Nonprofit Organizations.* New York: Praeger.

Ferris, James M. 1993. "The Double-Edged Sword of Social Service Contracting: Public Accountability versus Nonprofit Autonomy." *Nonprofit Management and Leadership* 4: 363–375.

Filer Commission on Private Philanthropy and Public Needs. 1975. *Giving in America: Toward a Stronger Voluntary Sector: Report of the Commission on Private Philanthropy and Public Needs.* Washington, D.C.: The Commission.

Gates, Scott, and Jeffrey Hill. 1995. "Democratic Accountability and Governmental Innovation in the Use of Nonprofit Organizations." *Policy Studies Review* 14: 137–148.

Lipsky, Michael, and Steven R. Smith. 1989. "Nonprofit Organizations, Government and the Welfare State." *Political Science Quarterly* 104: 625–648.

Mohr, John W., and Francesca Guerra-Pearson. 1996. "The Effect of State Intervention on the Nonprofit Sector: The Case of the New Deal." *Nonprofit and Voluntary Sector Quarterly* 25: 525–539.

Montes, Guillermo. 1997. "Public Funding and Institutional Reorganization: Evidence from the Early Kindergarten Movement." *Nonprofit Management and Leadership* 7: 405–420.

Nathan, Richard P. 1996. "The Nonprofitization Movement as a Form of Devolution." In *Capacity for Change: The Nonprofit World in the Age of Devolution*, ed. Dwight Burlingame. Indianapolis: Indiana University Center on Philanthropy.

Nutt, Paul C., and Robert W. Backhoff. 1992. *Strategic Management of Public and Third-Sector Organizations: A Handbook for Leaders*. San Francisco: Jossey-Bass.

Orlasky, Marvin N. 1992. *The Tragedy of American Compassion*. Washington, D.C.: Regency Press.

Saidel, Judith R. 1989. "Dimensions of Interdependence: The State and Voluntary-Sector Relationship." *Nonprofit and Voluntary Sector Quarterly* 18: 335–347.

Saidel, Judith R. 1993. "The Board Role in Relation to Government: Alternative Models." In *Governing, Leading and Managing Nonprofit Organizations*, ed. Dennis Young, Robert M. Hollister, and Virginia Ann Hodgkinson. San Francisco: Jossey-Bass.

Salamon, Lester M. 1987. "Of Market Failure, Voluntary Failure, and Third-Party Government: Toward a Theory of Government–Nonprofit Relations in the Modern Welfare State." *Journal of Voluntary Action Research* 16: 29–49.

Salamon, Lester M. 1992. *America's Nonprofit Sector: A Primer*. New York: Foundation Center.

Salamon, Lester M. 1994. "The Nonprofit Sector and the Evolution of the American Welfare State." In *The Jossey-Bass Handbook of Nonprofit Leadership and Management*, ed. Robert D. Herman. San Francisco: Jossey-Bass.

Salamon, Lester M., and A. J. Abramson. 1996. "The Federal Budget and the Nonprofit Sector." In *Capacity for Change: The Nonprofit World in the Age of Devolution*, ed. Dwight Burlingame. Indianapolis: Indiana University Center on Philanthropy.

Smith, Steven R. 1994. "Managing the Challenges of Government Contracts." In *The Jossey-Bass Handbook of Nonprofit Leadership and Management*, ed. Robert D. Herman. San Francisco: Jossey-Bass.

Smith, Steven R., and Michael Lipsky. 1993. *Nonprofits for Hire: The Welfare State in the Age of Contracting*. Cambridge: Harvard University Press.

Weisbrod, B. A. 1987. *The Nonprofit Economy*. Cambridge: Harvard University Press.

Wolch, J. R., and E. M. Rocha. 1993. "Planning Responses to Voluntary Sector Crises." *Nonprofit Management and Leadership* 3: 376–395.

5

Privatization of State-Owned Utility Enterprises: The United States Has Done It Too

Douglas N. Jones and Bradford H. Tuck

There is a great deal of current interest in the phenomenon of privatization of public utilities that is taking place around the world.[1] At least nine countries in Latin America, a dozen countries in Europe, and a half-dozen countries in Asia are in one degree or another transforming state-owned and -operated businesses. Government-owned telephone facilities are commonly candidates for sale, and privatization of this sector has taken place (or is well underway) in countries like Argentina, Bolivia, Brazil, Chile, Mexico, Malaysia, New Zealand, Hungary, Poland, Belgium, and elsewhere.[2] What is less readily recalled is that the United States had its own notable case of privatization of a nationally owned telephone enterprise in 1968, when Congress authorized the sale of the U.S. Air Force's Alaska Communication System (ACS) into the private sector. Bought by RCA in 1968 for $29 million, the current owner is AT&T, with several others in-between. This chapter looks backward to the motivations for privatization of ACS and the hoped-for results and weighs these against what actually has eventuated. Too seldom is such a retrospective done on a significant public-policy initiative. It also sketches the similarities and contrasts between the Alaska case of telephone-utility privatization and recent global privatization initiatives. Many more similarities than differences are found, despite the obvious differences in cultural and economic circumstances.

MOTIVATIONS FOR THE SALE OF ACS

At least a half-dozen reasons may be cited for the privatization of ACS in 1966–1967. Before doing so, however, a brief chronology of events leading to the actual sale of the Alaska Communications System is helpful to understanding.

Beginning in the early 1960s, the U.S. Army, the Air Force, and the Bureau of the Budget showed an interest in preparing for the sale of ACS. A year after the Air Force inherited the system from the Army, it commissioned a study of the financial circumstances of the Alaskan long-lines communications activities and their salability.[3] In 1965, a definitive study was done by the Air Force for the secretary of defense presenting "the Air Force position" favoring sale of ACS, setting out guidelines for a public-interest disposal of the system, and posing near-term alternative solutions should a sale not be authorized or made.[4] About the same time, the Air Force contracted for a management study on the feasibility of financing ACS under an industrial fund concept, used elsewhere by the military to apply more of a "business approach" to some of its commercial-type activities.[5]

In the meantime, an ad hoc presidential committee created by President Lyndon Johnson (the Federal Field Committee for Development Planning in Alaska), which was operating in Alaska to help do the analytical work in rebuilding the state after the 1964 Alaska earthquake, worked closely with the secretary of the Air Force's office in framing the Department of Defense (DOD) proposal for sale. It saw a sale as conducive to longer-term economic development in the state. Accordingly, the Federal Field Committee recommended to the parent Cabinet Committee on Alaska that the sale be authorized.[6] By the turn of the year, legislation was introduced in the 89th Congress in both houses for disposal of the government-owned, long-line communication facilities in Alaska, and letters were sent by the Air Force to seven prospective private bidders.[7] These letters enumerated the plant and equipment that was up for sale or lease, the fair value thereof, and inquired about the bidders' interest.[8] A day of hearings was held in the U.S. Senate in May 1966 and legislation was passed there in October, but time ran out for consideration in the House of Representatives. Legislation was reintroduced in January 1967 and became law on November 14, 1967.[9]

An important motivation for sale of the Alaska Communication System was the realization by the Air Force and the Department of Defense that ACS was always going to be a budget problem for them. Faced with increasing growth of private demand for communications services in Alaska, the resulting need to increase investment in the system was not likely to be met in annual budget battles with competing weapons and personnel requirements within the Department of Defense—or, for that matter, within the Air Force itself or Congress. This consideration is the close counterpoint to the motivation of foreign countries now privatizing their utilities (including telephone), because of the difficulty in servicing existing public debt for these enterprises, borrowing additional money for expansion, or deploying scarce resources away from competing needs.

A second motivation for the sale of ACS was worry over the need for modernization and efficiency improvements in serving the communication needs of Alaskans. By 1967, the system had gone seven years without capital improvements.[10] There was no direct distance dialing (DDD); no channel capacity for live TV, Telex, or news facsimile transmission; and no private lease lines, electronic data processing (EDP), or data transmission facilities. As with many state-owned enterprises (SOEs), employment levels to run ACS were relatively high, and cost consciousness was probably not a watchword. It was felt that a private entity would have the incentive and wherewithal for efficiency improvements through modernization of equipment and operations. (Partly for this reason, the Air Force favored outright sale of ACS rather than a leasing of facilities or contracting out the operation of ACS, as it would still be responsible for providing the network assets.) A belief in the superior efficiency and readiness to modernize on the part of private companies also characterizes current reasons for utility privatization in other countries.

A third reason was the aversion on the part of the Air Force to "meeting the public" in a continual business relationship. The military was always more or less uncomfortable in retailing communications and all that is involved (e.g., billing, collections, customer service, marketing). Moreover, it was a chance to redeploy into other more central military operations some portion of the 900 employees that worked at ACS. This motivation is not really found in the privatization movement in other countries. For one thing, state-owned enterprises are typically not run by the military and, for another, SOEs are often viewed as sources of public employment for the citizenry which are only reluctantly relinquished. Major labor protests in Brazil (described in a CNN report July 30, 1998, by K. Barrett and K. Pilgrim) upon the government's authorization to sell Telebras provide a recent example of this last point.

A fourth element in the sale of ACS is U.S. society's widespread ideological preference for private ownership of anything that is commercially feasible. This is to say that as long as telephone and telegraph activity in Alaska remained below the financially viable level in revenue/cost terms, there was little call for privatization. With growth in usage, indications of additional significant pent-up demand, and collections that annually exceeded likely attributable costs of providing service, the idea of sale into private ownership became increasingly salient. This motivation is also one that does not have a clear counterpart in privatization overseas, though it could be argued that the increasingly widespread preference for capitalist solutions and reliance on markets is a similar phenomenon.

A related fifth reason behind the sale of ACS was the qualitative one of "normalizing" Alaska as a state. While recognizing individual differences, public policy at the broadest level has an interest in all of the nation's states having fundamental similarities. Thus, Alaska, having achieved statehood politically just eight years before, needed to amalgamate itself into the union fiscally, structurally, and perhaps otherwise. One of these aspects of fundamental similarity was a privately owned rather than a state-owned infrastructure where possible. This federalist aspect is probably not currently found elsewhere, with the possible exception of Canada.

A sixth factor, and one that is sharply mirrored in utility-privatization rationales in other countries, was hoped-for economic development. Always a powerful force, virtually all the parties to the sale cited the encumbrance that an outdated communications system posed for economic growth in Alaska and, conversely, the likely benefits to the development of the state's economy that a modernized, efficient, and affordable system would provide.[11] This belief in the linkage between infrastructure (a relatively little-used term at the time) and economic activity is now a driving force in privatization efforts everywhere. Almost all countries that are embracing liberalization invoke participation in worldwide economic growth and global competitiveness as reasons for doing so.

Finally, there was the motivation of expanding the tax base in Alaska. Being a big state with a very small tax base resulting from constrained growth, a huge amount of public lands, and a large public sector (federal, state, and local), the opportunity to place an additional $30 million in valuation on the property tax rolls in Alaska from the privatization of ACS was particularly attractive. Moreover, the prospect of additional tax receipts to the state based on expanded sales volumes by the winning private bidder further enhanced the transaction. Foreign governments typically feature this motivation when securing legislation and citizen support for the sale of SOEs into private hands.

The commonalities between the motivations for privatization of commercial telecommunications service in the U.S. case of Alaska in 1966–1967 and the current cases of utility privatization around the world now, a third of a century later, have been identified. Some qualifications should be acknowledged, however. It is, of course, a much larger leap to go from a history of national public enterprises to private ones than to merely "adjust" the ownership pattern in one state against the backdrop of traditional private ownership.

Also, it really cannot be said that the United States is in any way starved for new capital or has serious difficulty with servicing debt.[12] Not only are the magnitudes of the changes quite different, the institutional differences as to the readiness with which the population accepts changes in ownership are substantial. Still, similarities abound, and it is noteworthy that both the Alaska case and recent overseas cases have involved getting legislative approval to one degree or another to authorize privatization of state-owned utility assets. Finally, since ACS was part of a defensive early warning system in the midst of the Cold War era, there were national security concerns that might not be quite as salient in today's context— except, perhaps, for Russia, as the former Soviet Union privatizes telephone systems. Even here, it is common for the military in liberalizing countries (e.g., Egypt and Jordan) to be particularly wary of private ownership of their telecommunications systems.

CONDUCT OF THE SALE OF ACS

The crafting of the features that characterized the sale of ACS into the private sector was thorough and imaginative. Also, the basic approach to privatization that was chosen is very different from what countries have recently done in selling off their state-owned utilities. In the latter case, the simple idea was to auction the assets to the highest bidder with the goal of returning as much money to the treasury as possible. In the Alaska case, the innovative idea was to make the auction focus on facilities improvements and reduced rate schedules while requiring every bidder to pay the same "upset price," equal to the fair value of the existing property.[13] The genius of this approach was that the transaction would fit well within the public utility regulatory setting, would not result in Alaskan ratepayers being burdened forever with "too high" rates for recovery of the premium paid by a winning bidder (a problem arguably faced in the wake of other country disposals), would achieve the two public interest goals of the sale (better service with lower rates), and would assure that the U.S. government got a reasonable (though not "top dollar") price for the assets.

Getting agreement for such an innovative approach among the parties in the legislation was no small feat. Neither the U.S. Treasury, Congress, the Department of Defense, or the Federal Communications Commission (FCC) on the federal side, nor the state of Alaska, the local governments, the business interests, or the Alaska Public Utilities Commission (APUC), on the state side had identical interests. And the telecommunications companies that were expected to be the bidders would have much preferred to simply bid on the basis of price and not be faced with devising binding bids regarding investment upgrades and lowered tariffs. Successful orchestration of this fundamental framework and other important provisions of the transaction can largely be attributed to the close collaboration of the U.S. Air Force Office of Installations and Logistics and the Presidential Committee for Development Planning in Alaska.[14]

The concerns of the participants were proper and well focused. They can be grouped into those primarily dealing with the U.S. government interest and those dealing with Alaska's special interest. The Senate wanted assurances from Air Force witnesses that the sale price of ACS would fairly recover the government's investment, that military preparedness would not be endangered, that the Air Force would not be faced with higher prices when it bought back communications services from the purchaser of ACS, and that civilian and military employees at ACS would be reasonably accommodated in the transition.[15] The Air Force was also asked what the costs of conducting the disposal might be, and the answer was "not more than $500,000."[16] From the Federal Communications Commission witness, Senator Stennis extracted somewhat reluctant promises that the FCC would review the interstate rates proposed by the winning bidder (rates which would be frozen for the first year under the Air Force sale provisions), would recommend a downward adjustment if the rates were found to be too high, and would work closely with the APUC as to the issuance of regulatory documents like a Certificate of Public Convenience and Necessity.[17]

Senior Air Force witnesses responded to the committee's concerns affirmatively. They pointed out that they would in effect control the prices that the military as well as civilian users of the system would pay by the requirements in the bidding procedure itself. Fair-cost recovery would result from the Air Force determining the upset price based on a consultant's evaluation of the value of the ACS facilities involved in the sale (and preparatory to it). Importantly, they also testified that national security could well be enhanced by privatization of ACS, since system improvements would be an integral part of the outcome. As to providing for ACS employees, the Air Force said it would try to get the purchaser to signal in advance the potential for continued employment of ACS personnel. Employees in the civil service system would also have an opportunity to accept another position with the federal government, and uniformed ACS employees would be reassigned.

With respect to Alaska, the senators wanted to make sure that the outcome of privatization was really going to be beneficial to the state generally and that the rural population would be served and served better. They also wanted to know that the governor of Alaska was explicitly for it.[18] The question of "service to the bush," as it is often described, is a perennial issue in Alaska, with its great distances, sparsely populated rural areas, and often high-cost operations. As such, it still today commands a good deal of the regulatory agenda on communications at the Alaska PUC and sometimes at the FCC.[19] The testimony of the chairman of the President's Committee for Development Planning in Alaska outlined the problem and a solution in saying, "The volume of service required by [these remote] communities is inadequate to permit the establishment of a separate commercial network. The Department of Defense believes that it can, on some reasonable economic basis, continue to provide (village service into the toll centers over the military lines) without prejudicing its military system."[20]

The "reasonable economic basis" that designers of the sale had in mind involved allocating costs in remote areas on a usage basis between national defense, defense standby, and commercial carriage. The idea would be that charges to bush subscribers would be predicated only on the costs allocated residually to the commercial traffic, an approach that might have some merit in the pricing policies for rural customers in some reforming countries.

Historically, it has not been common for national legislatures, in the United States or elsewhere, to focus in any detail on the arcane field of public-utility regulation. The legislative history of the privatization of the Alaska Communication System was, therefore, somewhat unusual. The hearing record read a bit like a public-utility textbook, with frequent references to concepts of used and useful, universal service, the revenue requirement, fair and reasonable rates, cost allocation, common carriage, demand elasticities, rate base valuation, and Certificates of Public Convenience and Necessity. But it was just this thoroughness in understanding by the committee that made the disposal action possible, and the bill became law on November 14, 1967.

ASPIRATIONS AND OUTCOMES

In this section, we note the expectations that were associated with the sale of the Alaska Communications System, and attempt to measure some of the outcomes. Our interest is in the outcome of the sale of ACS, the degree to which expectations were met, and the broader results revealed by the post-sale history of communications in Alaska. Some outcomes can be directly linked to the sale, while others cannot be so directly attributed, for various reasons.[21]

Sale and Certification

The innovative sale of the ACS system was to be based on a fixed price plus guarantees of rate reductions and commitments to specified types of future investments, including consideration of satellite service.[22] Seven bidders responded, and the sale was finally awarded to RCA Global Communications (Globcom). Key terms of the sale included the following:

1. A purchase price of $28,431,132 (with adjustments to be made at the time of transfer).
2. A commitment to rate reductions over the first three years of operation estimated to be in excess of $40 million.
3. Capital expenditures of about $27.7 million within three years from the date of the transfer, including expansion of landline intercity facilities, direct distance dialing, acquisition of part ownership in the COMSAT earth station in Alaska, and expansion of service to 142 remote communities.

Shortly after the sale, RCA Alaska Communications (a subsidiary of RCA Globcom and referred to hereafter as RCA Alascom) was incorporated in the state of Alaska as the corporation applying for the Certificates of Convenience and Necessity to both the FCC and the APUC.

The certification process at the state level was not without its difficulties, and was indicative of the problems that a newcomer to Alaska telecommunications could expect to encounter. The experience also supports the point made earlier that the success of privatization is not only dependent on the form of the privatized firm, but is also tightly linked to the form and expertise of the regulatory bodies under which the firm operates. This observation cannot be overstated when it comes to privatization overseas. After a few countries "learned the hard way," legislation authorizing the privatization of state-owned utility enterprises now commonly includes the establishment of a regulatory regime as a key provision of the bill, often replete with indications of the commission structure, size, authority, and responsibility. International financial agencies like the World Bank, the Agency for International Development (AID), and the International Development Bank (IDB) now nearly insist on it.

In the Alaska instance, the APUC was itself a young body, with limited experience in the regulation of long-line communications, but with a fair amount of experience in the regulation of local exchanges. It should be noted that RCA Alascom was entering a market in which a number of sizable local exchanges were well established with their own interests and agendas. Turf battles over who would be allowed to offer which services erupted before RCA Alascom got to carry its first long distance call. What was at issue was the future shape of the Alaska telecommunications market.

The commission recognized the complexity of the issues raised, and also realized that resolution of these issues could take years. The commission's imaginative solution was to exclude from consideration what it identified as "peripheral" issues, with which it would deal in future proceedings, and focus only on the provision of "public long-lines and toll telephone services and telegraphic services."[23] RCA Alascom received its certificate in August 1970. By January 1971, RCA Alaska Communications was operating Alaska's long distance system, a little over three years after Congress authorized the sale.

The next several years would prove to be difficult but generally financially rewarding years for the carrier. Dealing with the regulatory environment and local exchange competitors was a part of daily life, and not something that RCA Alascom was especially prepared for or comfortable with. By 1979, RCA Alascom was ready to pass the reins to a new owner, Pacific Power and Light (and its subsequent subsidiary, Pacific Telecom, Inc.), perhaps foreshadowing the convergence of telecommunications and electric utilities currently being discussed. Pacific Power and Light was a well diversified public-utilities firm, and, upon assuming ownership, what had been RCA Alascom became, simply, Alascom, Inc.[24]

Results and Evidence

There are no absolute standards by which to judge the performance of the first private carrier in the aftermath of the sale. However, a good starting point is to focus on the terms of the sale: major modernization investments, reduction in the price of service, and expanded service to rural Alaska. In general, we look mostly at the early years, up to the time that RCA Alascom was sold to Pacific Power and Light (June 1979), with the AT&T ownership performance too recent to evaluate with any perspective.

Investment

The amount of investment envisioned as being warranted by market conditions at the time of the sale was estimated by RCA Alascom to be about $28 million over the first three years of operation. Events quickly rendered these estimates grossly inadequate. Demands related to construction of the TransAlaska Pipeline System, development of the oil find at Prudhoe Bay, rapid expansion of the overall economy, needs of the "bush," and rapid technological change all contributed to the need for greatly accelerated investment. Recall that the whole system at the time of sale by the Air Force was valued at about $28 million. Table 5.1 summarizes net plant and gross and net revenues for RCA Alascom and its successor owners from 1971 through 1992. First, it is clear that the levels of investment stipulated in the sale were rapidly met and exceeded. Further, gross revenues, which had been growing at about 10 per-

cent a year in the 1960s (Air Force–owned ACS revenues) grew at
an annual rate of about 13.6 percent through the 1970s under
privatization. Net revenues grew at an even more dramatic rate of
38.3 percent per year. It is worth noting that these growth rates
are in constant dollars. Growth during the 1980s continued to be
substantial, but less dramatic.[25]

The average change in net plant for the 1971 through 1979 period was about $28.1 million per year. Investments were wide rang-

Table 5.1
RCA Alascom Net Plan and Equipment, Gross Revenues, and
Net Revenues (1971–1995)

Year	Net Plant	Change in Net Plant	Gross Revenue	Net Revenue
	Millions of Constant Dollars (1982 - 1984 = 100)			
1971	92.78		66.50	1.23
1972	106.99	14.21	79.57	2.64
1973	151.53	44.54	90.51	4.82
1974	212.31	60.79	117.45	13.93
1975	326.01	113.70	150.70	24.29
1976	290.36	-35.65	177.68	22.45
1977	390.79	100.43	183.64	28.21
1978	386.85	-3.94	190.14	25.60
1979	376.78	-10.07	194.33	25.51
1980	355.96	-20.82	193.99	28.10
1981	360.97	5.01	216.81	39.57
(shift to calendar year)				
1983	458.20	97.23	279.09	58.68
1984	409.82	-48.37	264.16	43.36
1985	354.31	-55.51	274.97	38.65
1986	323.65	-30.66	264.91	39.34
1987	304.09	-19.56	259.73	39.24
1988	270.26	-33.83	261.32	40.88
1989	261.29	-8.97	253.47	53.70
1990	316.12	54.83	226.02	40.72
1991	313.92	-2.19	277.59	4.06
1992	222.45	-91.48	261.77	30.80
1993	202.88	7.59	243.93	29.12
1994*	130.87	-67.79	246.38	38.24
1995	234.63	107.43	239.69	29.16

*Associated with sale to AT&T.

ing and included major reorganization to the switching networks, stored programming technology for DDD (for Anchorage in 1972 and elsewhere by 1975), heavy investment in emerging satellite technology, and much more. By the end of the first decade of operation, over $400 million had been invested.[26]

Table 5.1 (continued)

		Millions of Current Dollars**		
Year	Net Plant	Change in Net Plant	Gross Revenue	Net Revenue
1971	39.25		28.13	0.52
1972	46.43	7.19	34.53	1.15
1973	68.64	22.21	41.00	2.18
1974	106.58	37.94	58.96	6.99
1975	186.15	79.57	86.05	13.87
1976	178.57	-7.58	109.27	13.80
1977	256.36	77.79	120.47	18.51
1978	271.57	15.21	133.48	17.97
1979	292.38	20.81	150.80	19.80
1980	304.35	11.96	165.86	24.03
1981	333.53	29.19	200.33	36.56
(shift to calendar year)				
1983	454.53	121.00	276.86	58.21
1984	423.35	-31.18	272.87	44.80
1985	374.86	-48.48	290.91	40.90
1986	348.90	-25.97	285.57	42.41
1987	329.03	-19.87	281.03	42.46
1988	293.50	-35.53	283.79	44.39
1989	291.86	-1.64	283.13	59.98
1990	374.91	83.05	268.06	48.29
1991	389.27	14.35	344.21	5.03
1992	285.17	-104.09	335.59	39.48
1993	268.20	10.03	322.47	38.49
1994	176.68	-91.52	332.61	51.63
1995	325.90	149.22	332.93	40.51

**Current dollar data are taken from the annual reports of the APUC. There is no 1982 report due to the transition from reporting year to calendar year reporting. Data have been deflated using the Anchorage Consumer Price Index. In 1979, RCA Alascom, Inc. was purchased by Pacific Power and Light, Inc. The name changed to Alascom, Inc.

Table 5.2
Employment and Wages in Alaska Telephone and Telegraph (SIC 481)

Year	Average Monthly Employment	Annual Wage and Salary ($ millions)	Average Monthly Wage (in $)	State Total Average Monthly Employment	SIC 481 as Percent of State Total
1970	150	1.673	930	92,465	0.162
1972	793	10.687	1,123	104,243	0.760
1975	1,644	33.592	1,702	161,315	1.019
1980	2,027	66.371	2,729	170,018	1.192
1985	1,895	81.420	3,580	228,076	0.831
1990	1,832	81.750	3,719	236,227	0.776
1991	1,961	93.039	3,954	241,024	0.814
1992	2,059	94.912	3,841	245,845	0.838
1993	2,104	100.881	3,996	251,216	0.838
1994	2,148	106.417	4,129	256,829	0.836
1995	2,183	109.299	4,176	259,771	0.840
1996	2,240	111.664	4,155	261,613	0.856

Source: Alaska Department of Labor, Statistical Quarterly, selected issues.

Employment

Another consequence of the sale of the ACS system was an expected increase in private-sector employment in the communications field. Table 5.2 shows the growth of Alaska employment and wage and salary income of workers in the telephone and telegraph industry (primarily standard industrial classification [SIC] 481). From a base of 150 workers in 1970 just before RCA entered Alaska, employment grew to almost 2,200 by 1995, with an annual payroll of nearly $112 million. Some perspective on these figures is given by looking at SIC 481 employment as a percentage of total employment. The figure has grown from 0.16 percent to about 0.85 percent by 1996, and seems to have become a relatively stable share of total employment.[27]

Tax Base

In addition to expansion of the private-sector employment base, expansion of the tax base was also envisioned as one of the positive outcomes of the sale, particularly in a new state with a narrow tax base. Data for the early years were not obtainable, but in 1977 RCA Alascom incurred the following tax liabilities: Federal Corporate Tax, $10.21 million; Alaska Corporate Tax, $2.32 million; Alaska Gross Receipts Tax, $0.5 million; and property taxes within Alaska, $0.86 million. Thus, after several years of operation, RCA Alascom was contributing over $3 million of tax revenue annually to Alaska state and local governments (and over three times that to the federal government). By 1995, however, the successor company paid $21.38 million in federal taxes, $6.02 million in state and local income taxes, and $2.40 million in property taxes, a grand total of $29.8 million in taxes.[28]

Rural Service

According to the sale package, approximately 142 bush communities were to receive either new or upgraded service. In most cases, this was to consist of a single phone available for public use at some central location. Connection was to be by VHF links to existing exchanges or toll centers.[29] By 1974, the APUC decided to open a docket (APUC, U-74-87) to inquire into the progress of the bush program. The findings were mixed, but it was clear that the program was well behind schedule, both in terms of scope and quality of service.

With the bush program lagging, RCA Alascom actively explored the feasibility of using satellites to increase bush service. Coincidentally, the state of Alaska, increasingly dissatisfied with the rate of bush progress, began to aggressively pursue independent development of bush service through the use of satellites and earth-station links. The state appropriated several million dollars for the acquisition of earth stations and at one point was actually seeking certification to provide service. A compromise of sorts was finally reached in 1975, in which the state purchased the equipment and Alascom installed and operated about 100 small earth stations.[30] It is interesting to note that this model of government ownership and private operation of the facilities is currently being repeated in several countries around the world as an alternative to either full public or full private ownership of utilities. Build, operate, and transfer or various lease-back arrangements are examples of this.

Despite problems, the connection of local areas via satellite, and subsequent expansion of the system concurrent with the development of more sophisticated technologies, were positive factors in the rapid expansion of local exchanges in rural Alaska.[31] Prior to 1980, about 45 rural (defined roughly as not connected to the highway system) villages were connected to RCA Alascom. Between 1980 and 1989, in excess of 135 communities were added.[32]

Prices

Perhaps the most important element of the sale package was the price for service.[33] A general interstate rate reduction was to go into effect at the time that RCA Alascom assumed operation. The initial rate reduction averaged 25 percent, and was expected to "save" consumers about $40 million over the first three years of operation. Even with these cuts, Alaska rates were well above national rates, but a look at the Alascom interstate rate history shows an unbroken downward trend in tariff prices.

It was asserted in congressional testimony by those supporting the sale of the ACS system that demand for Alaska telecommunications services was both price and income elastic. We attempted some preliminary investigation of this hypothesis using RCA Alascom revenues as a measure of quantity, with prices and per capita disposable income as the independent variables. Linear and log linear regressions suggest that the volume of calls is price elastic (i.e., greater than one) and that the income elasticity is positive and greater than one.[34]

Concern was also expressed in presale testimony that reductions in the price of long distance service would occur at the expense of local exchange rates. A cursory review suggests that in the larger systems (e.g., Anchorage, Fairbanks) rates, measured in real terms, actually did fall. Rates in some of the smaller systems appear to have increased in some cases and declined in others. The massive expansion of bush service makes generalizations over time very difficult. However, total costs to consumers overall have decreased in real terms (see Table 5.3). For those who make significant use of long distance calls, the decrease has been substantial.[35]

Perhaps the most dramatic changes observed are in the rapid decline of the price of interstate long distance calls. Table 5.3 compares the cost of a 1969 $10 Alascom call to subsequent rates. The rates for the first minute and for additional minutes for selected city pairs are shown in Table 5.4. Based on these rates (direct distance dialed calls, daytime rate) a three-minute call from Anchorage to Washington, D.C., would cost $0.87. In 1966, a comparable call (station to station) would have cost $7.50.[36] Juneau to Seattle was $3.50 and Nome to Seattle was $5.50. These same calls cost $0.78 in 1995. If the 1966 call were measured in 1996 dollars, the price of the Anchorage–Washington, D.C. call would be $29.30.

Service Quality and Performance

In 1971, the completion rate for toll calls through the primary Alaska toll centers averaged 38 percent. By 1976, the completion

Table 5.3
Alascom Rate-Reduction History

Date	Rate (Compared to $10 Call in 1969)
January 10, 1971	$ 7.50
March 26, 1976	$ 5.59
July 1, 1977	$ 3.91
January 1, 1979	$ 3.52
May 25, 1984	$ 3.31
June 1, 1985	$ 3.12
June 1, 1986	$ 2.67
January 1, 1987	$ 2.11
July 1, 1987	$ 2.02
January 1, 1988	$ 1.89
December 1, 1988	$ 1.82
April 1, 1989	$ 1.70
July 1, 1989	$ 1.69
January 1, 1990	$ 1.59
July 1, 1991	$ 1.56

Source: Pacific Telecom, Inc., San Francisco, submission to APUC, July 1991, in commission files, Anchorage.

rates were as follows: Anchorage, 47 percent; Fairbanks, 42 percent; Juneau, 69 percent; and Ketchikan, 66 percent.[37] By way of comparison, a standard of 95 to 99 percent would be used by most U.S. telecommunications systems. Current data on this measure of service quality are difficult to come by, but indications are that they are converging on the national standard.

Toll separations were another matter of concern. In the mid-1960s, toll revenues to local exchanges nationally, as a percentage of total revenues, averaged about 35 percent, and local exchange revenues were 65 percent. The city of Anchorage was receiving just under 8 percent of its total revenue from long distance toll revenues. By 1976, the balance had shifted somewhat. Nationally, the toll revenue fraction had increased to about 52.5 percent. Anchorage was at 35.4 percent, while Fairbanks and Ketchikan were at about 44 percent.

Table 5.4
Current Direct Distance Dialing Rates between Selected Cities (First Minute and Each Additional Minute)

City		Barrow	Juneau	Nome	Seattle	Wash. D.C.	Miami
Anchorage	1st	0.588	0.588	0.588	0.26	0.29	0.29
	Add.	0.38	0.38	0.38	0.26	0.29	0.29
Barrow	1st						0.29
	Add.						0.29
Juneau	1st	0.588		0.588	0.26	0.29	
	Add.	0.38		0.38	0.26	0.29	
Nome	1st				0.26	0.29	
	Add.				0.26	0.29	

Source: GCI, Inc., 1995, *Phone Quote of Rates*, February 16, Anchorage.

Table 5.5
Percentage of Alaska Households with Phones

Year	Alaska	Urban	Rural	Pop. 1-2.5K
1960	60.0	74.2	47.8	NA
1970	73.4	84.8	61.1	NA
1980	83.3	82.0	65.3	83.0
1990	91.7	95.2	83.4	92.3

Source: Alaska Census of Housing, 1960–1990, U.S. Department of Commerce, Bureau of Census, Washington, D.C.

Note: In 1960 and 1970, the percentage measures "phone available," whereas 1980 and 1990 measures are for phone in unit.

Juneau was at 52 percent. Thus, while Alaska was converging toward national averages, it still tended to lag substantially.

Comparisons of U.S. and Alaska phones per capita prior to the sale indicated that Alaska was grossly underserved, with telephones per 100 persons at about one-half the national average. Table 5.5 shows the percentage of Alaska households with phones. As indicated in the table, expansion of bush service was slow to respond following the sale. While modest gains are made between the 1970 and 1980 census, the real surge occurred after 1980. It is also worth noting that even communities of 1,000 to 2,500 in population are on a par with the state average. Only in the smaller villages and communities does it appear that significant potential for expansion remains.[38]

The Telephone Company and the Institutional Setting

It is clear that significant growth in the communications industry occurred during the 1970s, and that the winning bidder in the sale was a significant contributor to that growth. RCA Alascom did meet the initial stipulations of the sale, though there was strong sentiment that there was much room for improvement. Here we review some of the perceptions and relations of the telephone company in the institutional setting in Alaska, particularly with the Alaska Public Utility Commission. The APUC–RCA Alascom relationship was often strained, and by 1978 the commission had contracted for a major external performance audit of RCA Alascom. Undertaking of the audit was indicative of substantial dissatisfaction with the performance of the carrier.[39] The main findings can be summarized in three main groups.

The first addressed the relationship between RCA Alascom and its parent corporation, RCA, Inc. The parent corporation had little experience in the operation of a regulated public utility and did not provide RCA Alascom with any clear sense of direction, goals, or objectives relative to relationships between the parent and subsidiary. Moreover, the subsidiary appeared to suffer from a lack of autonomy, particularly with respect to investment decisions. A second area of difficulty was the relationship between RCA Alascom and other major players in the development of Alaska telecommunications policy, including the Alaska legislature, the office of the governor, consumer interest groups, and the APUC. These groups were often at odds with each other, and there was no meaningful comprehensive state policy to provide direction for the development of telecommunications. The third problem area was tied directly to the management of RCA Alascom. The study recognized that substantial progress had been made in solving many of the problems identified, but highlighted some remaining difficulties: (1) a failure to recognize the concept of "public servant" implicit in the award of the Certificate of Public Convenience and Necessity, (2) the absence of long-run strategic planning and budgeting focused on meeting acceptable levels and quality of service, (3) an inability to provide regulatory bodies with data normally expected of regulated public utilities, (4) many instances of staffing with inexperienced or less than fully qualified personnel, and (5) high employee turnover rates.

These and other problems resulted in an unfavorable public perception of the company and may have underlaid the decision to sell. However, the sale of RCA Alascom to Pacific Power and Light was not a "magic wand" and, not surprisingly, subsequent owners have had their own difficulties in living up to government and public expectations.

SUMMARY AND CONCLUSIONS

Thirty-two years ago the disposal of the Alaska Communications System was initiated, and it can be viewed as one of the early experiments in privatization in the utility sector. Our review and analysis has explored both the successes and problems associated with this experiment, the extent to which public-policy objectives were met, and the similarities and dissimilarities of the Alaska case with the worldwide interest in privatization in the utility sectors.

The fact is that most, if not all, of the basic goals of the framers of the sale were met. In many cases, the goals were substantially exceeded. In addition to meeting the basic stipulations of the sale, the privatization resulted in a significant increase in private-sector employment, development of needed infrastructure, a modest expansion of the tax base, and a substantial contribution to the quality of life in Alaska. Consumers benefitted from an expansion of telecommunications services, both in terms of scope and kind, and from significant reductions in the overall cost of communications. From this perspective, the sale must be viewed as an unqualified public-policy success. When viewed from the more focused perspective of how well a regulated public-utility firm performed in the aftermath of privatization, the record is a bit more mixed. A number of problems relating to the adequacy, quality, and reliability of service were experienced. The primary source of these difficulties was the ownership structure and management of RCA Alascom, but the rapid growth of demand, an uncertain regulatory environment, and state intervention in the industry were contributing factors as well. Of course, utility performances in other states (and countries) are not without some similar blemishes.

Finally, what implications can be drawn with respect to current privatization efforts around the world? First, there may be an advantage from the public-policy point of view to not auction off state-owned utility assets to the highest bidder. The privatization of ACS was imaginatively done on the basis of bidding based on reduced rates and improved service rather than garnering the highest price for the government's assets. While the latter approach helps the treasury of a country, it may saddle future ratepayers with inordinately high prices to compensate the winning bidder for its high bid. This can be a real drag on growth and development and facilities modernization. Privatization in foreign countries has typically not followed the Alaska model in this regard, as governments have striven to get top dollar for the assets, but the approach is worthy of consideration if a longer-term view is taken.

Second, privatization that simply is the transfer of monopoly power from public ownership to private ownership requires the existence of strong regulatory oversight to ensure production efficiency, service quality, and pricing fairness. The Alaska experience suggests that this can be a challenging task for a regulatory body, especially a new one. However, over time the emergence of competition tends to lessen the detailed regulatory burden, while at the same time the regulatory commission gains experience and stature. This maturing experience is being played out in other countries that have privatized state-owned enterprises (e.g., the United Kingdom, Chile, and Argentina), but not without false starts, turmoil, and considerable friction.

Third, privatization will likely result in a firm (or firms) that are more responsive to public demand. RCA Alascom was much more responsive to the growth in aggregate demand and the demand for new services than one could have expected from the government-owned system. (Recall that one of the justifications for the sale was lack of responsiveness on the part of the U.S. Air Force through its ownership of ACS to changing public needs.)

Fourth, privatization does not guarantee economic efficiency in production. RCA Alascom was a more efficient supplier of public communications services than its government predecessor, but there remained a great deal of room for improvement. Perhaps AT&T will be more efficient, and competition may make it more so.

Finally, the overall public-policy sphere within which both production and regulation occur can have a significant impact on performance of the privatized industry for good or ill. In the case of Alaska, the lack of a coherent, comprehensive telecommunications policy in the immediate post-privatization period was repeatedly found to be one of the major problems in the orderly development of the industry. Improvement in the policy environment has been accompanied by improvement in industry performance. It may well be that planning and privatization are not really the opposites they have long been held to be. For the latter to work, the former would seem to be required.

NOTES

This chapter is a revised version of a 1997 report for the National Regulatory Research Institute, Ohio State University.

1. Privatization is one of several forms of industry restructuring that is going on. "Commercialization" is perhaps the broader phenomenon that encompasses—in addition to privatization—intermediate approaches like

"corporatization" (making the utility service behave more like a firm and less like an agency), contracting and leasing for privately provided services, and joint ventures of the "capitalization" or "crown corporation" public/private type. Sometimes the term "liberalization" is used to describe the broad movement.

2. Of course, the privatization of British Telcom in the United Kingdom was accomplished a good bit earlier (1984) and in some sense "started it all."

3. Middle West Service Co., *Middle West Study*, report prepared at the request of the Air Force, September 1, 1963.

4. Deputy of Transportation and Communications, *Perry Report*, submitted as an attachment to a document sent by the Assistant Secretary of the Air Force to the Assistant Secretary of Defense (Installations and Logistics), March 9, 1965.

5. *Stone Study*, report prepared at the request of the Air Force by the consulting firm of Stone and Webster, 1965. Under an industrial fund arrangement, a military supply activity, for example, is designed to be managed in such a way that users "pay" into it an amount that covers all operating costs and perhaps some contribution to capital costs.

6. Federal Field Committee for Development Planning in Alaska, *Economic Development in Alaska*, a report to the president, August 1966, p. 36.

7. Senate, Preparedness Investigating Subcommittee, Committee on Armed Services, *Hearings on S. 2444, "Government-Owned Long Lines Communication Facilities in the State of Alaska,"* 89th Cong., 2d sess., 31 May 1966, 11.

8. Somewhat surprisingly—and surely ironic in light of its 1995 acquisition of the Alaska telephone system for a reported $365 million—AT&T voiced disinterest in the sale and declined to join the bidding for the $29-million asset-disposal price.

9. Public Law 90-135, 90th Cong., 1st sess. (14 November 1967).

10. Senate Committee, *Hearings on S. 2444*, 49.

11. Ibid. The most thorough case for this was laid out in the testimony of Mr. Joseph H. FitzGerald, Chairman, Federal Field Committee for Development Planning in Alaska, *Hearings on S. 2444*, pp. 47–51.

12. However, in the course of the Air Force's testimony explaining its desire to sell the Alaska telephone system the Deputy Assistant Secretary said, "Proposals to appropriate funds for the purpose of modernizing and expanding facilities for commercial communications in Alaska have, of course, had to compete in the establishment of the Department of Defense budget with proposals to expend funds for military purposes." *Hearings on S. 2444*, ibid., 29.

13. An independent financial audit of ACS was conducted using traditional utility accounting methods to determine the value of the assets used and useful in the provision of the communications services.

14. It was fortunate and somewhat unusual that S. 2444, "a bill to authorize the disposal of the government-owned long-lines communication facilities in the State of Alaska," went to the Preparedness Investigating Subcommittee of the Senate Committee on Armed Services for consideration. The prime sponsor of the bill, Senator Bob Bartlett of Alaska, had

only recently left that subcommittee. Other senators comprising the sub-committee, several of whom participated in the May 1966 hearing, were John Stennis, Henry Jackson, Robert Byrd, Stuart Symington, Margaret Chase Smith, Strom Thurmond, Leverett Saltonstall, and Howard Cannon. This was a powerful group indeed, and favorable consideration by this subcommittee would bode well for S. 2444 in full committee in the Senate, and in the Congress itself.

15. Ibid., 10, 34, 36, 47, 103.

16. Ibid., 35.

17. Ibid., 39–42.

18. Ibid., 58–59, 62.

19. We have in mind here, for example, various Alaska Joint Board FCC discussions held intermittently from 1989 to 1993.

20. Senate Committee, *Hearings on S. 2444*, 50.

21. First, the observed outcomes reflect the interaction of the new RCA Alascom, the young and (at the time) inexperienced APUC, and a proactive state of Alaska. Second, the period following the sale was marked by rapid technological change in telecommunications nationally and worldwide. Third, the state was to enter an unprecedented boom related to the construction of the TransAlaska Pipeline, development of the Prudhoe Bay oil fields, and government spending of large and initially unanticipated revenues. Finally, the industry, both at the national and state level, was headed for major restructuring, reflecting both the introduction of significant competition within markets and a concomitant relaxing of regulation.

22. This discussion is drawn primarily from material in T. H. Bivens, "The Question of Earth Station Ownership in the Alaska Bush: An Analysis of Regulatory Policymaking," Ph.D. diss., Graduate School, University of Oregon, 1982; William H. Melody et al., "Telecommunications in Alaska: Economics and Public Policy: A Report to the State of Alaska," April 1978, Simon Fraser University, British Columbia; and APUC Order No. 3, U-69-24, Juneau, Alaska.

23. APUC Order No. 3, U-69-24, 11.

24. Shortly thereafter, competition within many markets in the telecommunications industry was a fact at the national level, and in 1982 General Communications, Inc. (GCI) began interstate commercial operations in direct competition with Alascom. Then, in 1991, GCI entered the intrastate market (General Communications, Inc., Form 10-K, December 1993). As noted, in 1995, AT&T acquired the stock of Alascom, and Alascom is currently operating as AT&T–Alascom.

25. In nominal dollars, the growth rate per year of gross revenue was over 23 percent, and net revenue grew at about 45 percent. From this it can be seen that the testimony of the chairman of the presidential committee for developing Alaska as well as the Air Force itself with respect to the likely commercial feasibility of the privatized system was amply borne out.

26. George Shaginaw, 1982. "Alaska and Alascom: A Decade of Telecommunication Development," paper in support of the Alaska Case Study Presentation to the 1982 Pacific Telecommunications Conference, Honolulu, Hawaii, January 17–20, p. 29.

27. It should be noted that not all of this employment is private-sector employment, in that several of the local exchange utilities (including the Anchorage Telephone Utility) are municipally owned.

28. Alascom, *Annual Report to the Alaska Public Utilities Commission*, various years.

29. During the 1971–1975 period, Alascom installed Improved Marine Telephone System (IMTS) units to about fifty communities but, reportedly, the system was less than adequate. In some instances, as many as five or six villages would share a single channel. Call-completion rates as low as 10–15 percent were common (Vinod K. Batra, "Local Exchange Growth in Bush Alaska," paper in support of the Alaska Case Study Presentation to the 1982 Pacific Telecommunications Conference, Honolulu, Hawaii, January 17–20, 1982, p. 36).

30. Shaginaw, "Alaska and Alascom," p. 29.

31. Other equally or more important factors include restructuring of local, intrastate, and interstate rate systems.

32. Proceedings of the Chugach Conference: Discussing the Future of Communications in Alaska, Chugach, Alaska, August 18–19, 1989.

33. It is recognized, of course, that the problem of correct pricing signals is often a matter of raising telephone rates, not lowering them in other countries.

34. These results are based on only eleven observations, so care must be taken with the quantitative conclusions.

35. The fact that during the period observed (roughly 1971–1990) significant changes in the structure of local rates were taking place makes for some caution in imputing causality. These included changes in the distribution of local and long distance charges, and ownership of the customer's telephone equipment, for example.

36. In closing the hearings on the sale of the Alaska communication system that afternoon in May 1966, Senator John Stennis quipped, "We hope this matter will all be wrapped up. I want to put a telephone call through before too long to Alaska, and I don't want to have to pay $12.50 or $15.00." Senate Committee, *Hearings on S. 2444*, 105.

37. William H. Melody, Telecommunications in Alaska: Economics and Publix Polixy, Final Report to the State of Alaska, Juneau, April 1978, pp. 55–56. Performance problems also abounded in other standard measures of service quality (e.g., operator response time, equipment blockage and failure, and trunking and switching operations), though the overall trend was toward improvement.

38. For the 1960 and 1970 censuses, the measure of phone service is availability (roughly, "a phone nearby"), versus a phone in the dwelling unit for later census years. Thus, the figures tend to understate the growth of service availability, and certainly understate the growth in the quality of service.

39. Before the audit was completed, however, RCA Alascom was sold to Pacific Power and Light (1979), and the audit findings were rendered moot for purposes of the Commission (APUC Order No. 43, U-78-4).

PART **II**

DEMOCRATIZATION

6

Democratization and Conflict Resolution in Africa

John W. Harbeson

No theme for an International Political Science Association triennial meeting could be more pertinent to contemporary sub-Saharan Africa than "conflict and order." The magnitude and complexity of conflict throughout Africa in its postindependence era, its destructive and debilitating effects, and its seeming resistance to durable amelioration require no rehearsing. What is new and important in sub-Saharan Africa is the wide array of democratic transitions carrying the promise not only of citizen rights and political empowerment but of structures that will transform potentially violent conflicts into constructive public debates producing negotiated, broadly acceptable public-policy outcomes. These prospects may be enhanced by the foundations of economic liberalization that African states have begun to establish at the behest of both international agencies and African entrepreneurs. The question is whether, how, and in what ways democratization will diminish and ameliorate conflict and establish the durable roots of political order required for democracy itself, as well as for a long-sought, heretofore elusive African socioeconomic renaissance.

But why should consolidated democracy in Africa, or anywhere else for that matter, yield such an extraordinary payoff, alone or in concert with other factors? The literature of empirical democratic theory has tended to emphasize causation in the reverse direction: democracy as the culmination of successful resolution of conflict between authoritarian rulers and insurgent movements for democracy.[1] Democracy's role in facilitating conflict mediation and humane political order has been more generally assumed and than it has been explained.

At least one strain of democratic scholarship, however, has explored the contribution of democratic institutions to conflict mediation and peaceful order, one that hypothesizes that democratic regimes interact with each other to maintain peace through negotiation and mediation of differences in international relations. The theory of the "democratic peace" has arisen from long hibernation during the Cold War to flower once again with the emergence of democracy's "third wave" and the dawning of the post–Cold War era, wherein economic and political liberalization has enjoyed a degree of normative hegemony with few modern historical precedents. Building philosophically upon the teachings of Immanuel Kant and the global vision of U.S. President Woodrow Wilson, the democratic peace literature has examined the proposition that there are logical, empirically grounded connections between stable democracy and the avoidance of violent conflict. Roughly during the lifespan of democracy's third wave, this theory has emerged to challenge realist and neorealist theories of international relations which generally discount the influence of domestic state structures and political cultures.[2]

The theoretical, policy, and human importance of the democratic peace thesis for the post–Cold War world in general, and for Africa in particular, can scarcely be overstated. To the extent that the theory itself withstands rigorous empirical testing, democracy's claims to be in the best interests of all states are greatly strengthened and become correspondingly less dependent on the hegemony of democratic states in the post–Cold War era. To the extent that democratically governed states are significantly more likely than authoritarian regimes to resolve their differences through negotiations rather than through resorting to violence, democracy's third wave holds great promise for international relations. For Africa, the spread of democracy could potentially mean an era of peace that would permit nations and peoples to turn swords into plowshares and to rebuild economies and societies that in turn will enhance democratic consolidation. It offers African peoples relief from the ravages of violent conflict and new hope for healthy, productive lives. Not least important, African membership in a global family of democratic nations could mean a diminution of the pervasive marginalization the continent has suffered since the independence of its nations. For this vision to become reality and not just another evanescent illusion, the theory must be grounded in reality, appropriate policies must be formulated and effectively implemented, and the theory itself as well as the implementing policies must be successfully tailored to regional and country circumstances, a particular problem for Africa, since experience from its recent democratic initiatives has yet to be incorporated in the ongoing development and testing of the theory's central propositions.

The purpose of this chapter cannot be to test the validity and applicability of democratic peace theory in contemporary African settings, for the necessary research to do so has scarcely been undertaken. In particular, there has been very little research in contemporary sub-Saharan Africa testing whether the findings of the democratic peace literature in the international arena are applicable and valid in domestic settings. Rather, its modest and much more limited purpose is to identify and preliminarily explore the range of issues that must be addressed for the theory to not only be properly tested in African settings, but for the results of those tests to add to and modify the theory as needed so that its empirical research is more truly global. First, this chapter will briefly review the state of the democratic peace literature. Second, it will examine the assumptions upon which that literature generally builds concerning the domestic character of democratic regimes. It will argue that progress in seeking answers to the elusive, central question in the democratic peace literature—how and why democratic structures and/or democratic cultural norms produce foreign policies that support peace between and among democratic regimes—hinges at least in part on closer articulation between democratic peace theory, empirical democratic theory, and democratic transitions theory. This enlargement of democratic peace research may then yield insights into how democracy may promote domestic conflict mediation. Third, this chapter explores the possible reverse impacts of international relations upon the domestic structure and functioning of democracies, including, specifically, international assistance to countries undertaking transitions to and consolidation of democratic regimes. Fourth, even more than other aspects of contemporary democratic theory and democratic transitions theory, democratic peace theory has evolved and been tested without reference to sub-Saharan African experience with democratization, in part because that experience is still of such recent origin. The final section of this chapter will explore some of the important, distinctive contours of African democratic initiatives and their socioeconomic and cultural contexts which must be addressed in order to test, and potentially modify, democratic peace theory in the cause of rendering its empirical foundations more truly global in scope.

DEMOCRATIC PEACE THEORY

The democratic peace literature has established persuasively and almost unanimously that over the modern history of democracy, since 1815, democracies have rarely if ever fought one another. The key proposition is that there is something in bilateral relationships between democracies (or democratic dyads) that almost unfailingly influences them to resolve their differences without resorting to violence. Democratic dyads are significantly less likely to go to war with one another than are authoritarian regimes or mixed dyads consisting of a democracy and authoritarian state. Nils Peter Gleditsch, for example, has asserted that a democracy dyad is a "near perfect condition for peace."[3] Zeev Maoz and Nasrin Abdolali have argued that democracies rarely clash with one another and never fight one another in war.[4]

The hypothesis that democracies do not fight one another is based upon more than a generation of macro-level historical research, which substantially qualifies this school's original philosophical premise: Democracies are inherently more peaceful in international relations generally, not just in relationship to other democracies. Immanuel Kant argued as such in his *Perpetual Peace*.[5] Woodrow Wilson's vision was to prevent interstate war through democratization, but he may have believed the broader claim as well. Rudolph Rummel gets some of the credit for reviving the democratic peace hypothesis in its most general form.[6] But scholarship since his early writings has generally rejected the hypothesis that democracies are intrinsically more peaceful in their international behavior, generally settling instead on the narrower proposition that democracies are most reliably peaceful in relationships with each other.[7]

That democracies do not fight each other does not necessarily mean they are pacific in their foreign policies. Indeed, democratic peace research suggests that democracies historically have not been significantly less war prone than nondemocracies.[8] But when democracies do go to war, the evidence indicates that they tend to prevail and not infrequently their defeat of authoritarian regimes in war has led to postwar replacement of those authoritarian regimes with new democratic ones.[9]

The democratic peace theory has appeared to challenge the realist and neorealist orthodoxy of the Cold War years in its contention that domestic political structures and/or norms help explain how states seek power and security in international relations. But John Mearsheimer, while not specifically attacking the narrower proposition that war does not erupt within democratic dyads, retorts that democracies are as likely to fight wars generally as nondemocracies.

He contends that other realities such as nationalism and religious fundamentalism can potentially shred the bonds between democracies. He contends that democracies will experience a security dilemma in that the risk always exists that democracies will backslide into authoritarianism and, thus, must worry about each other's relative power as a hedge against such reversion. "Lamentably," he concludes, "it is not possible for even liberal democracies to transcend anarchy."[10] Stephen Krasner, writing even as the post–Cold War era dawned, argued that it is the power structure of the international order, not features of domestic regimes, that explains the absence of war even between democracies. "Nuclear weapons," he argues, "have raised the costs of war for major powers to such unambiguously high levels that the balance of terror, not the character of internal regimes, is what precludes wars among the major states."[11]

Others have argued that the democratic peace hypothesis is not necessarily incompatible with realist and neorealist theory. The founder of Cold War era realism, Hans Morganthau, allowed generously for the role of democratic structure and democratic belief systems as components of power.[12] Ray argues that democratic peace theory is as state centric, as reliant upon states functioning as unitary actors in the international arena, and as consistent with a power-centric conception of interstate relations as realism and neorealism.[13] To the extent that democracies have historically tended to prevail in the wars they have fought, clearly they have been more powerful than their adversaries and/or they have used their power more shrewdly than their enemies. Democracies may also be more powerful because democratic regimes cultivate or mobilize war-making resources more successfully than authoritarian regimes. If democracies use their power more effectively, it may be at least in part because democratic processes of leadership recruitment and selection are superior to those of autocracies, and/or because the deliberative processes of democratic regimes produce more realistic decisions than do their opposite numbers.

Significant for purposes of this chapter is the related observation that stable democracies are less likely to become involved in interstate wars than democracies of more recent origin.[14] This finding has invited the hypothesis that regime stability is an important intervening variable in the relationships between democracies, and even that it is regime stability rather than the stability of democratic regimes that is responsible for war being avoidable between states in the international arena.[15] The research has tended to establish that although wealth, economic growth, and trading linkages are clearly important to the consolidation and sustainability of democracy, these variables have appeared not to explain peaceful interdemocracy relations more successfully than those variables related to democratic political structure and culture.[16] Thus, it appears to be democratic institutions and political cultures per se, not their supporting socioeconomic structures, that explain democratic foreign-policy behavior.

An interesting and potentially important subtheme in contemporary democratic peace research has been the observation that democratic states tend not only not to initiate war with each other, but to be less likely to be the targets of warlike initiatives by nondemocracies than are other nondemocracies.[17] Autocracies, in short, tend to pick on each other. The reasons why this should be so have themselves been less the subject of empirical research than the core proposition they support. Scholars have speculated that autocrats are sufficiently canny to recognize that, given their relatively complex and extended decision-making processes, democracies are more likely to exhibit a propensity to negotiate rather than fight than are other authoritarian regimes. This hypothesis, however, appears on its face to sit uneasily with a finding that democracies are likely to fight autocracies where they would not fight other democracies, precisely because autocracies do not generate the respect of policymakers and citizens in democracies as other democracies do.[18]

Two particular problems arise as a result of this research. First, contributors to the democratic peace literature have wrestled, but by their own admission have not really satisfactorily dealt, with the question of why the contours of democratic regimes should dispose them to deal peaceably with similar regimes and at the same time impel policy makers to differentiate between democratic and nondemocratic regimes in their foreign relations. It is at best awkward to both hypothesize that democratic structures and political cultures naturally induce particular patterns of behavior and say that those same variables also enable and encourage democratic decision makers to differentiate between democratic and nondemocratic regimes.[19] There is no necessary logical incompatibility between these two propositions, but plausible, testable explanatory hypotheses do not leap to mind, nor have they to those toiling in this particular vineyard.

The other problem lies in operationalizing the two variables in the equation: democracy and war. Operationalizing democracy for purposes of this research is the subject of the next section. With respect to the other term, what kinds, levels, and degrees of interstate conflict are to be specified and differentiated from each other? And does the proposition that democracies do not fight one another hold equally for all levels of violent conflict? Gleditsch argues that the finding that democracies do not fight one another "should be tempered with an appreciation that it applies only where a relatively high threshold is set for both 'democracy' and 'war.'"[20] But there would appear to have been too little research to pronounce conclusively on this point.

In short, macro-level historical, empirical research impressively supports the proposition that democracies do not fight one another but has yet to isolate the reasons why this should be so. But if democratic regimes can be, and often are, the keys to conflict resolution, both domestically and internationally, it is essential that scholarship on democratic peace center more directly on why democracies have these properties, what aspects of democracy are most important in this relationship, and how they operate to achieve these desirable, much-sought-after results. The limited progress to date in addressing these questions is considered in the next section.

DEMOCRATIC PEACE THEORY'S DOMESTIC FOUNDATIONS

Democratic peace theory relies for its validity on clear, empirically supportable hypotheses concerning how specifically democratic institutions, processes, and culture function domestically. Addressing this issue implies a linkage between the macro-level character of contemporary democratic peace research and more meso- and micro-level research that is required to understand the connections between regime structure and foreign-policy behavior. The same research may then also shed light on whether and how the democracy facilitates domestic conflict resolution and, by extension, its transformation into constructive public debate.

Two hypotheses have dominated democratic peace research on how and why regime contours influence interstate relations between democracies. The *democratic culture* hypothesis holds that democratic norms embedded in a country's political culture influence the behavior of leaders in democratic countries toward each other. The *democratic structure* hypothesis rests broadly on definitions set forth by Gurr and Jaggers in their Polity III data. They find explanatory power in [1] "institutions and procedures through which citizens can express effective preferences about alternative political policies and leaders . . . through regular and meaningful competition among individuals and organized groups, and a level of political liberties sufficient to ensure the integrity of democratic participation, [2] institutionalized constraints on the exercise of executive power [and 3] the guarantee of civil liberties to all citizens in their daily lives and in acts of political participation."[21]

The strength of the democratic dyads proposition may depend upon how one defines both "democracy" and "conflict." Charles Kegley and Margaret Herman have argued that democracies may be found to be more likely to initiate "interventions" (not necessarily wars) against each other if reliance is placed upon the democratic culture hypothesis than if one relies upon the structural hypothesis.[22] The relative explanatory power of the two hypotheses has been hotly contested in the contemporary democratic peace theory literature. Randall Schweller, for example, has argued in support of the democratic culture hypothesis that "Democratic public opinion generates an institutional heritage of openness and division of power that inhibits the preventive motivation for war. . . . Citizens of government founded on the enlightenment principles of individual liberty and the pursuit of happiness are naturally repulsed by the unethical and immoral aspects of preventive war."[23] Melvin Small and J. David Singer find the structural hypothesis more persuasive if the key elements of "democratic structure" (free elections, the vote, and a parliament that enjoys at least parity with the executive branch) are present.[24] Some, however, question the credibility of both hypotheses, finding circularity in the democratic culture hypothesis and doubtful validity in a perceived assumption in some formulations of the structural hypothesis that citizens in democracies are essentially pacifist.[25]

These two hypotheses are neither logically nor empirically necessarily antithetical to one another. In essence, both hypotheses depend ultimately on the judgments of democratic citizenries: the democratic cultural norms they may uphold and the restraints upon executive leaders that they impose via the ballot box.[26] Moreover, these two hypotheses may be valid collectively only when other variables are imported.[27] The case has been made that the relationship between democratic regimes and the peace they share is reciprocal, not unidirectional. Thompson and Tucker argue that "domestic actors interact with changing environments; they do not simply project their preferred strategies on a featureless external environment. The causal arrows are more likely to be reciprocal than unidirectional—from the inside out or the outside in."[28] In short, after nearly three decades of investigation, there appears to be no clear consensus on why and how democratic culture should influence the foreign-policy behavior of democracies.[29]

The inconclusiveness of current research on whether, why, and how the domestic contours of democratic regimes contributes to interstate peace among democracies sharply restricts the capacity of democratic peace theory to explain whether and precisely how democracy per se may explain and create domestic conflict resolution and humane public order. It follows that the scope of democratic peace research may require enlargement to incorporate more of the perspectives and insights of other political-science subdisciplines, specifically those of empirical democratic theory and—in the interests of enhanced relevance to the circumstances of new democracies in less-developed countries—its derivative, democratic transitions theory.

Empirical democratic theory addresses domestic conflict resolution in ways that depart markedly from democratic peace research. First, empirical democratic theory has tended to center less upon why and how democratic regimes engender peaceful resolution of potentially violent conflicts than on the constitutional context, or prerequisites, for conflict resolution processes that stable democracies are assumed to facilitate.[30] Second, democratic peace research has found that democratic institutions and/or political culture cause peaceful interdemocracy relationships independently of levels of socioeconomic development. But empirical democratic theory has generally suggested that, for democracy to perform the peaceful conflict resolution it is assumed to assure, there is a high degree of interdependence between the consolidation of democratic constitutional principles and a viable market economy, healthy economic growth, high levels of prosperity, and functioning checks and balances within society among ethnic communities and interest groups. The implicit hypothesis here is that if these are not intervening variables between democratic regimes and their foreign policy behavior, they may well be antecedent variables influencing the capacities and viability of democratic regimes themselves. Third, democratic peace research conceptualizes interchanges between democracies in ways quite distinct from how empirical democratic theory defines domestic exchanges. Democratic peace theory centers almost exclusively on the absence of violent conflict between democracies, while empirical democratic theory celebrates the articulation of competing conflict interests and preferences as well as processes democracies provide for resolving them peacefully. In this respect, democracies differ from autocracies, which tend to sublimate, suppress, diffuse, or ignore conflict. Moreover, empirical democratic theory highlights the achievement of consensus and cooperation among conflict interests, not simply the absence of war or forms of violent conflict. Fourth, empirical democratic theory tends to place a considerable degree of emphasis upon pact making among rival parties to establish the rules of the game as a foundation for peaceful articulation and mediation of conflicting interests and preferences.[31] Democratic peace theory research has speculated upon but done little to test the proposition that democracies do not fight one another because they share comparable political value systems. It has given little consideration to whether and/or how democracies may structure their relationships with each other in order to regularize cooperation and mediate conflict in ways they find it more difficult to do with autocracies.

This brief juxtaposition of the regime-behavioral assumptions of democratic peace theory and of empirical democratic theory suggests the outlines of a broadened cross-disciplinary research agenda directed to understanding how and why democracies successfully mediate conflict and strengthen the foundations of humane political order. On the one hand, democratic peace theory invites research on why and how democracies avoid war and violent conflict over their differences with each other. In its contention that answers to this question lie in the distinct character of domestic democratic regimes, democratic peace theory also invites attention to the interconnections between democracies' capacities to resolve international conflicts among themselves peacefully and to do likewise domestically. Neither question has been addressed adequately by empirical democratic theory.

On the other hand, disarticulation between the premises of empirical democratic theory and those of democratic peace theory invites research on whether and/or in what ways the conflict-mediating properties and processes of democracies differ internally from those obtaining between democracies. Equally important is the related issue of whether, how, and why between-democracy and within-democracy conflict-resolution processes and propensities interact with, reinforce, conflict, and or mutually influence each other. For example, Uganda, Kenya, and Tanzania have recently resolved to reestablish formal regional cooperation following the collapse of the old East African Economic Community and more than a generation of often tense and occasionally hostile relations with one another. All three countries have at the same time recently embarked on domestic democratic transitions, each of which are in their individual ways problematic and facing somewhat uncertain long-term prospects. Cases such as this deserve research on how conflict mediation processes of embryonic democracies at international and domestic levels influence each other. How might the consolidation, or failure of consolidation, at one level influence processes at the other level? How might international processes of conflict mediation and cooperation among the three countries influence and/or be influenced by democratic reversals in one or more of the participating countries? Democratic peace theory suggests that democracies tend to prevail over and force democratization upon authoritarian regimes with which they go to war. It does not consider what influence, if any, patterns of peaceful conflict resolution and cooperation among democracies may exert to forestall or mitigate erosion of democracy in one party to a democratic dyad or a larger group of democracies.

To the extent that there is an interface between the conflict-mediating properties of democracies and conflict mediation, both domestically and within international democratic dyads, empirical democratic theory suggests that the elements and foundations of this peaceful democratic conflict resolution are perhaps more complex than envisaged by democratic peace theory. For example, empirical democratic theory invites deeper inquiry into the possibly distinctive contours of interdemocracy relations. Even where they are not joined for formal democratic institutions, such as those of the European Union, do democracies informally agree to value the articulation of competing interests, establish implicit rules of the game for adjudicating them, mutually recognize the necessity and legitimacy of each other's constitutional foundations, and/or tacitly recognize the interdependence of each other's political and socioeconomic/cultural structures and decision-making processes? In short, empirical democratic theory implicitly suggests the hypothesis that democracies do not fight each other because informally (as well as perhaps formally) they evolve the elements of micro-democratic regimes within their dyads that do not occur, or occur in very different ways, within mixed or authoritarian dyads. Thus, it does not suggest direct answers to the question of how democratic regimes avoid war with another. Rather, it implicitly advances the hypothesis that the eventual answers may be found in more complex political articulation between democracies than democratic peace theory has to date generally tended to contemplate.

INTERNATIONAL IMPACTS ON DOMESTIC DEMOCRATIC TRANSITIONS

Closer articulation of the international and domestic functioning of democratic polities opens an additional frontier research area that requires further exploration in the interests of a more comprehensive and valid theory on the relationship between democracy and conflict resolution. Democratic peace theory departs from the long-prevalent realism and neorealism schools precisely in its acknowledgment that domestic political structures are an important conditioning influence upon state behavior in the international arena. Yet to be articulated in democratic peace theory are the insights of a small but growing policy-focused literature on the impact of external assistance and other international influences on the course of domestic democratization. Democratic peace theory postulates influences of domestic political structure on state foreign-policy behavior but generally not the reverse: the influences of foreign-policy dynamics upon the shape of domestic democratic structures and behavior.

In a 1992 article, Graham Allison and Robert Beschel offered what continues to be one of the most explicit statements on the issue of external promotion of democracy. They are unambiguous in their contention that external engagement in further democratic transitions has occurred and can be constructive to that end. "Not only is it possible for the United States to promote democracy," they argued, "but we believe the evidence suggests that in fact the United States has promoted democracy and is promoting democracy."[32] They identify ten principles for promoting democracy abroad:

1. Demonstrate and communicate democratic society's superior performance.
2. Build an international security, economic, and political order favorable to democracy.
3. Promote pluralization of societies and the development of civil society.
4. Encourage the evolution of a democratic political culture.
5. Strengthen democratic institutions.
6. Assist the development of market economies.
7. Socialize the military and the security forces to respect democratic norms and values.
8. Nurture and support leaders who are building democracy.
9. Provide sustained advice and assistance about critical choices in the transition to democracy, market economies, and cooperative international relations.
10. Differentiate between various regions and countries.

Their thesis that democracies can and should promote democratization in other countries sits uneasily with at least some contemporary formulations of democratic theory. "When I reflect on the conditions favoring polyarchy," Robert Dahl confesses, "I am driven to the conclusion that the capacity of democratic countries to transform non-democratic regimes into stable polyarchies is very limited in the short run."[33] Nonetheless, broadly speaking, post–Cold War democracy promotion by the United States and other industrial democracies has adhered to the objectives set forth by Allison and Beschel.[34] What is most significant about the Allison and Beschel article for purposes of this chapter is its unambiguous implication of external engagement with the development and strengthening of other countries' democracies. While they cannot fairly be accused of prescribing to new democracies how they should conduct their affairs, their article is remarkable for not invoking principles of national sovereignty and self-determination as a cautionary guideline for external engagement in promoting democratization. It is as though they tacitly contend that engagement by one democracy with democratization in another country is by definition a collaborative and cooperative enterprise rather than an exercise of hegemonic stability.

Also noteworthy in the Allison and Beschel argument is its emphasis on the importance of stitching together the elements of an international democratic regime to undergird, underwrite, and support domestic democratization: building "an international security, economic, and political order favorable to democracy" and providing "nurture and support leaders who are building democracy." At the same time, in advocating active support for the development of civil society in support of democratic institutions, Allison and Beschel counsel continuation of a generation of foreign-assistance strategy employing external assistance to build support for other countries' institutions, not only at the government-to-government level but also from below.

What is distinctive about the Allison and Beschel argument is its clarity and comprehensiveness, though its contentions were new or revolutionary then or now. Nonetheless, neither democratic peace theory nor empirical democratic theory has given anything like sufficient attention to the implications of international engagement with domestic democratization for peace promotion. What are its implications for the character and durability of new democracies as vehicles for conflict resolution? For the manner and degree to which such intervention may influence the performance of democracies in supporting peace among democracies? For the forms and impacts of mutual interdependence and influence between democratic regimes, domestically and internationally? For the homogenization of intra- and interdemocracy conflict-mediation processes? For patterns of interdemocracy peaceful conflict resolution, multilaterally among three or more democracies as well as bilaterally between two democracies? Finally, to what extent and in what ways, if any, does international engagement in domestic democratization ipso facto tend to contribute directly to peaceful conflict resolution on either the domestic or interdemocracy level?

AFRICA AND DEMOCRATIC PEACE THEORY

No region of the world is more in need of reliable theory and strategy for transforming violent conflict into constructive public debate. Nowhere are the connections closer between the problems of promoting domestic conflict resolution and strengthening humane public order and those of international conflict resolution. And nowhere have democratic transitions embodied more profound hopes and expectations that their successful consolidation may be the keys to effective conflict mediation. Yet neither democratic peace theory nor empirical democratic theory and derivative democratic transitions theory have taken full account of the distinctive circumstances of sub-Saharan Africa that represent both potential resources and serious obstacles to realizing these objectives. Conversely, as is the case with empirical democratic theory and democratic transitions theory, democratic peace theory will lack true global reach and applicability until its central tenets have been refined to reflect both the distinctive contours specific to regions, and commonalities genuinely shared by all world regions, including sub-Saharan Africa.

At least five fundamental factors common to contemporary sub-Saharan Africa compel refinement of democratic peace theory before its utility to conflict mediation and the strengthening of public order on the continent can be established. First, as some of the democratic peace research has suggested, the theory may have been validated to date principally by the experiences of relative stable, established democracies.[35] The same applies to empirical democratic theory, and even democratic transitions theory continues to incorporate the experiences of the relatively stable democracies of South America. African democracies are almost without exception very new, demonstrably fragile, incompletely consolidated, and in danger of being engulfed by the very domestic conflict they are theoretically expected to pacify. Their domestic fragility impedes their capability to resolve challenges to international peace within the continent that grow out of those sources of domestic conflict, such as ethnic nationalism and the plight of hundreds of thousands of refugees, and the failure to entrench positive foundations for international peace in such forms as economic cooperation.[36]

Second, a corollary to the fragility of African democracies has been that elements of authoritarian ancient regimes, in the form of neopatrimonialism, have continued to function within new formal democratic frameworks.[37] Neither democratic peace research, empirical democratic theory, nor democratic transitions theory have fully come to terms with the behavioral implications of the transitional coexistence of the old and new. It follows that democratic peace theory's capacity to predict and inform domestic or international peace promotion on the basis of democratic regimes remains impaired.

Third, the viability of the African state per se, let alone its democratization, has been called into question sharply by developments in post–Cold War Africa. Carl Rosberg and Robert Jackson recognized the importance of international juridical recognition to the viability of the African state.[38] Now lacking reinforcement by the great powers in the service of their Cold War agendas, this juridical support has proven threadbare in the cases of Somalia, Sierra Leone, Liberia, Rwanda, Burundi, and Zaire, and potentially in places like Kenya, Uganda, and Ethiopia. Democratic peace theory, like empirical democratic theory and democratic transitions theory, has treated lightly the issue of the connections between the formation of democratic regimes and the renewal or reconstruction of the foundations of the polity itself as a basis for its democratization.

Stated another way, they have insufficiently distinguished and addressed different levels of conflict resolution to which democracy may be reciprocally related: (1) over policy matters, (2) over power within the state, and (3) over the existence and bases of the state itself.

Fourth, empirical democratic theory takes account of the importance of viable balances of power among interests, including those of ethnic communities, to the empirical viability of the democratic state.[39] However, a prior issue predominates in contemporary sub-Saharan Africa: How, if at all, and in what ways can democracy facilitate peace and public order by constructing those viable, legitimated balances of power among ethnic communities where those communities have not previously negotiated them? How, if at all, can fledgling sub-Saharan democracies be aided in dealing with the ethnic conflict that has threatened their existence in so many recent instances? Liberal democratic theory has at least on occasion presumed that ethnic communities are rational in pursuit of their interests and thus amenable to democratic institutions' assumed capabilities to resolve conflicts among them on that basis.[40] Or is it the case that in such cases the causal arrow does indeed run in the reverse direction, from peace to democracy, rather than the reverse?[41] Moreover, while all three branches of democratic theory recognize the close and important connections between democracy and economic liberalization and development, the operation of ethnic dynamics as a set of intervening and/or antecedent variables remains underexamined.

Fifth, the close interface between domestic and international peace, or its absence in contemporary sub-Saharan Africa at least partially as a consequence of the fragility of the polity itself, compels closer articulation between the lessons of external democratization assistance and these three branches of democratic theory: democratic peace, empirical democratic theory, and democratic transitions theory. The preceding section considered the insufficient attention of democratic peace and empirical democratic theory to the interface between domestic and international peace in relation-

ship to democracy. However, it is also the case that external democratization assistance has only just begun to devote resources to
the interconnections between the promotion of domestic democracy
and the fashioning of bases for peaceful diplomacy and support for
democratic institutions at the international level.[42] Among the underlying issues requiring attention are whether and how peaceful
diplomacy among sub-Saharan African democracies occurs in situations where (1) natural regional hegemons are themselves democracies, as in the case of South Africa; (2) where they are not, as in
the case of Nigeria; and (3) where the future of the hegemonic polity itself, as well as its domestic structure, are indeterminant, as in
the case of Zaire (or the Democratic Republic of Congo).

CONCLUSIONS

A rich and fundamental research agenda awaits those who would
advance the democratic peace agenda. Of particular interest and
prominence in this agenda is the interface between domestic and
international peace and democracy's roles in this interface. This
chapter has suggested that although democratic peace theory has
been the preserve principally of students of international relations,
its validity and its validation rest on assumptions about the domestic functioning of democracy. It has suggested that elusive answers to the fundamental questions of how and why democracies
achieve peace between themselves internationally, as well as maintain it domestically, may be found sooner to the extent that democratic peace theory is more closely articulated with empirical
democratic theory and its derivative, democratic transitions theory.
Moreover, all three subbranches of democratic theory need to recognize the potential importance, for good and/or for ill, of external
democratization assistance in the quest for answers to these fundamental questions. Finally, democratic peace theory, like empirical democratic theory and democratic transitions theory, must
address and reflect the fundamental and distinctive issues posed
by conflict-ridden sub-Saharan Africa if it is to be truly global in its
empirical research and if it is to facilitate domestic and international peace in that troubled region.

NOTES

1. The key contemporary texts include Robert Dahl, *Polyarchy: Par-
ticipation and Opposition* (New Haven: Yale University Press, 1971);
Samuel Huntington, *The Third Wave: Democratization in the Twentieth
Century* (Norman: University of Oklahoma Press, 1991); and Guillermo

O'Donnell and Philippe C. Schmitter, *Transitions from Authoritarian Rule: Tentative Conclusions about Uncertain Democracies* (Baltimore: Johns Hopkins University Press, 1986).

2. Immanuel Kant, "Perpetual Peace," in *The Philosophy of Kant*, ed. Carl J. Friedrich (New York: Modern Library, 1949); Rudolph Rummel, "Libertarianism and International Violence," *Journal of Conflict Resolution* 27 (1983): 27–71; Rudolph Rummel, "A Test of Libertarian Propositions on Violence," *Journal of Conflict Resolution* 29 (1985): 419–455; Rudolph Rummel, "Libertarian Propositions on Violence Within and Between Nations," *Journal of Conflict Resolution* 29 (1985): 419–455; James Lee Ray, *Democracy and International Conflict* (Columbia: University of South Carolina Press, 1995); Bruce Buena de Mesquita and David Lalman, *War and Reason* (New Haven: Yale University Press, 1992).

3. Nils Peter Gleditsch, "Geography, Democracy, and Peace," *International Relations* 20 (1995): 297–320; Steve Chan, "Mirror, Mirror on the Wall . . . Are Freer Countries More Pacific?" *Journal of Conflict Resolution* 28 (1984): 617–648.

4. Zeev Maoz and Nasrin Abdolali, "Regime Types and International Conflict 1816–1976," *Journal of Conflict Resolution* 33 (1989): 3–35.

5. Kant, "Perpetual Peace."

6. Rummel, "Libertarianism."

7. Nils Peter Gleditsch argued, "After nearly a decade of debate following Doyle's and Rummel's articles, there is now a near-consensus on two points: there is little difference in the amount of war participation between democracies and non-democracies (Rummel being the major dissenter here) but that wars (or even military conflicts short of war) are non-existent (or very rare) among democracies." See "Democracy and Peace," *Journal of Peace Research* 29 (1992): 369–370. Gleditsch and Havard Hegre differentiate between dyad, nation, and system levels of analysis, concluding that "democracies hardly ever fight each other but overall participate in war as much as other countries . . . and the relation the relationship between peace and democracy at the system level must be bell shaped." See "Peace and Democracy," *Journal of Conflict Resolution* 41 (1997): 284.

8. Gleditsch, "Democracy and Peace."

9. David Lake, "Powerful Pacifists: Democratic States and War," *American Political Science Review* 86 (1992): 24–37; Gleditsch and Hegre, "Peace and Democracy"; Kenneth Benoit, "Democracies Really Are More Pacific (in General): Re-examining Regime Type and War Involvement," *Journal of Conflict Resolution* 40 (1996): 638.

10. John Mearsheimer, "Back to the Future: Instability in Europe After the Cold War," *International Organization* 15 (1990): 5–57.

11. Stephen D. Krasner, "Realism, Imperialism, and Democracy," *Political Theory* 20 (1992): 48; Buena de Mesquita and Lalman, *War and Reason*.

12. Hans Morgenthau, *Politics Among Nations* (New York: Knopf, 1948).

13. Ray, *Democracy*, 38.

14. William Thompson and Richard Tucker, "A Tale of Two Democratic Peace Critiques," *Journal of Conflict Resolution* 41 (1997): 428–454, con-

test, largely on methodological grounds, the thesis to this effect of Edward Mansfield and Jack Snyder, "Democratization and the Dangers of War," *International Security* 20 (1995): 5–38.

15. Thompson and Tucker, "A Tale."

16. Zeev Maoz and Bruce Russett, "Alliance, Contiguity, Wealth, and Political Instability: Is the Lack of Conflict Among Democracies a Statistical Artifact?" *International Interactions* 17 (1992): 245–267. Maoz and Russett concede the possible role of stability as an intervening variable, but Ray, *Democracy*, responds that democracy can have positive effects on political stability, perhaps more so than can autocracies. See Huntington, *The Third Wave.*

17. Margaret Herman and Charles W. Kegley Jr., "Ballots: A Barrier Against the Use of Bombs and Bullets," *Journal of Conflict Resolution* 40 (1996): 436–460.

18. William J. Dixon, "Democracy and the Management of International Conflict," *Journal of Conflict Resolution* 37 (1993): 42–68. Buena de Mesquita and Lalman, *War and Reason*, note that democratic states are more constrained in their use of violence against each other than against nondemocratic states. "That evidence," argues Ray, *Democracy*, 31, does suggest that any cultural tendency for democratic states to abhor violence is attentuated when they interact with undemocratic states."

19. Dixon, "Democracy."

20. Gleditsch, "Democracy and Peace," 369–370.

21. Keith Jaggers and Ted Robert Gurr, "Tracking Democracy's Third Wave with the Polity III Data," *Journal of Peace Research* 32 (1995): 469–482. The database includes countries with populations over 500,000.

22. Charles Kegley and Margaret Herman, "How Democracies Use Intervention: A Neglected Dimension in Studies of the Democratic Peace," *Journal of Peace Research* 33 (1996): 309–323.

23. Randal Schweller, "Domestic Structure and Preventive War: Are Democracies More Pacific," *World Politics* 44 (1992): 244–246.

24. Melvin Small and J. David Singer, "The War-Proneness of Democratic Regimes, 1816–1965," *Jerusalem Journal of International Relations* (Summer 1976): 50–69.

25. Scott Gates, Torbjorn L. Knutsen, and Jonathan W. Moses, "Democracy and Peace: A More Skeptical View," *Journal of Peace Research* 33 (1996): 1–10.

26. Alex Mintz and Nehemia Geva, "Why Don't Democracies Fight Each Other? An Experimental Study," *Journal of Conflict Resolution* 37 (1993): 484–503.

27. Arie Kacowicz, "Explaining Zones of Peace: Democracies as Satisfied Powers," *Journal of Peace Research* 32 (1995): 273, finds merit in both positions in combination with other factors. He finds that it is "well established" democracies that do not fight with each other, where satisfied powers are fully fledged nation states without irredentist claims and strong states in relation to their own societies, strong powers in military and socioeconomic terms, sharing a normative consensus of international law and a common institutional framework, whose leaders are "affected by a

domestic institutional constraints." John O'Neal, Frances O'Neal, Zeev Maoz, and Bruce Russett, "The Liberal Peace: Interdependence, Democracy and International Conflict," *Journal of Peace Research* 33 (1996): 17, argue that "the longer a particular system exists without fundamental change, the more like the nonviolent norms of conflict resolution have become established and these will influence a government's foreign policies and conduct."

28. Thompson and Tucker, "A Tale."

29. William R. Thompson, "Democracy and Peace: Putting the Cart Before the Horse," *International Organization* 50 (1996): 171, agrees, concluding, "It is curious that nothing resembling a consensus has emerged on just what it is about democratic regimes that makes them less likely to go to war with other democratic regimes."

30. Dahl, *Polyarchy.*

31. O'Donnell and Schmitter, *Transitions.*

32. Graham Allison and Robert P. Beschel Jr., "Can the United States Promote Democracy," *Political Science Quarterly* 107 (1992): 82.

33. Robert Dahl, *Democracy and Its Critics* (New Haven: Yale University Press, 1989), 317.

34. It can be argued that the U.S. Agency for International Development, at least, has given relatively less emphasis to socializing the military and policy to democratic norms, in large part because of legislative restraints on providing foreign assistance to domestic security forces. Similarly, assisting countries to attune their new democratic institutions to the idiosyncracies of their socioeconomic and cultural environments while adhering to fundamental common democratic principles has received less emphasis than arguably is required.

35. Kacowicz, "Explaining Zones of Peace."

36. Katherine Barbieri, "Economic Interdependence: A Path to Peace or a Source of Interstate Conflict," *Journal of Peace Research* 33 (1996): 42, however, has suggested that economic interdependence need not necessarily promote peace. She contends that "the relationship between interdependence and conflict appears to be curvilinear with low to moderate levels of interdependence reducing *dyadic* disputes and extensive interdependence increasing the likelihood of military conflict, whether the dyadic relationships are symmetrical or asymmetrical" (emphasis added). But she argues that "the greatest hope for peace appears to arise from symmetrical trading relationships."

37. Michael Bratton and Nicolas van de Walle, "Neopatrimonial Regimes and Political Transitions in Africa," *World Politics* 46 (1994): 453–489.

38. Robert Jackson and Carl Rosberg, "Why Africa's Weak States Persist: The Empirical and the Juridical in Statehood," in *The State and Development in the Third World,* ed. Atul Kohli (Princeton, N.J.: Princeton University Press, 1986).

39. Dahl, *Polyarchy.*

40. Milton Esman, *Ethnic Politics* (Ithaca, N.Y.: Cornell University Press, 1994).

41. As suggested by Thompson and Tucker, "A Tale."

42. During the 1990s, the U.S. Agency for International Development has been in the forefront of new initiatives in this area in the Horn of Africa and also in Southern Africa, where southern African states themselves took the initiative in forming the Southern African Development Cooperation Council (SADCC) to reduce their dependence on the South African apartheid regime. Now those states and liberated South Africa wrestle with the problem of how to constructively reincorporate the latter in new forms of regional cooperation.

7

Establishing a Democratic and Stable Constitutional Order in China

Xunda Yu

There are three historic events in twentieth-century China. The 1911 Revolution, the 1949 Revolution, and the reform started from 1979 are three milestones in China's modernization. Politically, they all aimed at the establishment of constitutional order; namely, the establishment of a political order in which the principles and rules prescribed by the constitution became dominant in political life. However, though the three revolutions have greatly moved China toward a constitutional order, they have by no means reached this goal. This accounts for the slowness of political development in China's modernization in the twentieth century. Today, with the carrying out of market reform, whether China can progress to democratic constitutional order will become critical to the sustaining of the reform fruits and the furthering of Chinese modernization. This will be a key issue in the political arena in twenty-first-century China. This chapter will discuss the relation of constitutional order and the three historic turning points in twentieth-century China in the first three parts, and several important theoretical issues on how China moves further toward a constitutional order in the fourth part.

AN ABORTIVE CONSTITUTIONAL REFORM IN THE LATE QING DYNASTY

The government of the late Qing Dynasty (1840 onward) suffered from a pincer attack: Domestically, the late Qing Dynasty had gone to the last phase of its dynastic transmigration; its ruling power was too weak to keep people in compliance with its policies. Rebellions sprouted like mushrooms after a rain. The other problems that plagued the late Qing Dynasty included rampant corruption, a steady decentralization of power, and losing control on too many fronts at the same time. Externally, the Qing Dynasty was defeated by strong foreign powers, forced to open its doors to the outside, and subjected to the terms of unequal treaties. So, the second half of the nineteenth century and the beginning of the twentieth century saw the gradual disintegration of the old imperial order.

The successful aggression of the West made the Chinese clearly understand that there was a big threat to China's existence in the world, which finally led to two historical movements: salvation and enlightenment. The goal of salvation was to make China become a "wealth and power" country and ultimately to relive its old experiences as a world power. The goal of enlightenment was to find the cultural reasons for the rise of the West and the decline of China and to ultimately create a new culture which could lead to the realization of these goals. Politically, to say the least, ideas on democracy and constitutionalism had emerged in China in the 1850s (Luo 1992: 277). During that time, some of China's intellectuals had recognized that one of the reasons for China's failure in conflicts with the West was its autocratic political system, and one of the reasons for the West's success lay in their democratic political systems. Therefore, reforming the political system gradually became a social trend. There were three parts in this social trend at the end of the nineteenth century and the beginning of the twentieth century: the revolutionary democratic movement, the constitutional movement, and the reform for a "new administration" promoted by the government of the Qing Dynasty. After the failure of constitutional monarchy reform in 1898 and the decades of pain and frustration brought about largely by the weakness of the Qing government, the Chinese people, totally disillusioned with the Qing Dynasty, began to take a keen interest in the revolutionary democratic movement launched by Sun Yat-sen, and finally overthrew the Qing government in the Revolution of 1911.

The Revolution of 1911 was the first revolution in modern China. On January 1, 1912, the Revolutionary Alliance established a provisional parliament in Nanking and elected Sun Yat-sen to the provisional presidency of Asia's first democratic-republic, the Republic of China. On March 11, Sun Yat-sen promulgated the provisional constitution, the first constitution in the history of China. The promulgation of the provisional constitution demonstrated the efforts of Chinese people in establishing the constitutional order in China.

But after Yuan Chi-kai replaced Sun Yat-sen as head of the central government, he coerced the new parliament into formally electing him to the presidency. He then dissolved the parliament so that he could assume dictatorial power and finally declared himself emperor on December 12, 1915. The restoration of the monarchy did not have popular support. One after the other, provinces and districts declared their independence from the Yuan government. Faced with intense and mounting opposition, Yuan fell gravely ill and died on July 6, 1916. After that, China had a central government and a constitution in name only; the whole nation fell into turmoil.

Many things contributed to the failure of China's first constitutional government. The weakness of democratic forces was a fundamental one. The force of pushing democratic constitutionalism in modern China mainly came from advanced intellectuals and some enlightened members of the ruling class. Looking at the power structure, with the decline of feudal authority, the socially secular power with commitment to supporting democracy began to emerge. The following are the main evidences: From the end of the nineteenth century to the beginning of the twentieth century there were a number of newly emerging newspapers presenting folk opinions which generally were not controlled by the officials; various independent folk organizations that were of a political nature arose; local autonomy increased; the national bourgeoisie, with certain economic strengths and antiautocracy demands, was also growing. These factors formed a social force which, to some extent, was able to challenge the feudal authority and was conducive to the promotion of democratic constitutionalism. Although there were enlightened persons in the Qing government, as a whole the government was a conservative political group which resisted reform and opposed democracy, and was an obstruction against democratic reform. It was the late Qing Dynasty's resistance to democratic reform that made modern China fail to fulfill its social transition under the leadership of the government. On the opposite side, it created a crack between the government and the people and a break between the traditional and the modern. The old structure was hard to transform gradually, but to be continued, the new structure could not emerge as an agreeable social environment. China was therefore not able to establish a constitutional order through reform as Britain and Japan had. The modernization in China was started and pushed only by foreign forces and a domestic elite that had some government power and modernization ideas in mind. With a short period and a limited involvement, the modernization had not been able to give Chinese society and traditional culture fundamental change, and Chinese society was not able to accumulate a political and cultural force that was, with its economic and social basis, strong enough to challenge the autocratic rule of the Qing Dynasty.

The bourgeoisie revolution of 1911 overthrew the Qing Dynasty. Although there appeared to be a revolutionary force conducive to the promotion of the democratic constitutionalism at the time that the bourgeoisie revolution of 1911 broke out, it could not establish a new ruling order. The reason for the victory of the revolution was not the strength of the revolutionary force, but the weakness of the Qing Dynasty. During 1911, there was no single force which could actually replace the Qing Dynasty with a new ruling order within the society. So, after the collapse of the Qing Dynasty and the collapse of the anti-Qing coalition, China fell into a split and civil war. After the death of Yuan Chi-kai, the Beijing government controlled by the Northern Warlords and the late Nanking National Government promulgated several constitutions. However, those governments themselves were neither democratic governments nor political authorities to effectively govern the nation, and democratic forces in Chinese society at that time were not strong enough to effectively check and restrict the governments; therefore, all those constitutions were nothing but political furnishings.

THE CONSTITUTIONAL CRISES IN NEW CHINA

The revolution led by the Chinese Communist Party (CCP) was the second revolution of twentieth-century China. Some of the biggest positive roles of this revolution on China's development were that it set up political authority, united the country and established order, and terminated the state of disintegration. However, regarding the challenge of how to make and govern the nation, there have been two trends since the beginning of the establishment of the People's Republic of China (PRC): one is to make the nation according to the citizen-state model and to govern the state by the rule of law; another is to make the nation according to the vanguard party–mass model and govern the state by the will of the vanguard party. With some commonalties, these two models are different.

To make the nation according to the citizen-state model and to govern the state by the rule of law was a continuation of the long-term effort that China had made to establish a constitutional government and form a lawful constitutional order. On September 21, 1949, the Chinese People's Political Consultative Conference promulgated the Common Program, which served as a provisional constitution and showed that the People's Republic of China had started to govern the state by the rule of law. After then, a handful of laws and legal regulations, the Law of Marriage and the Law of the Land, for instance, were gradually made and promulgated, which played an important role in protecting citizens' basic rights, and especially farmers' rights. Held on September 15, 1954, the First National People's Congress proclaimed the Constitution of the People's Republic of China. This was the first constitution of PRC. The work of drafting the constitution was started on January 15, 1953, when the central government of the PRC set up the Constitution Drafting Committee headed by Mao Ze-dong. After it was made, the draft of the constitution was put into discussions, first among more than 8,000 people who were from the democratic parties, people's organizations, and other groups, then among 150 million people, which lasted more than two months (Yang 1997: 20). It was an unprecedented move in China's history. The 1954 Constitution affirmed the basic rule that everyone is equal under the law. Mao Ze-dong also pointed out that the constitution was "the basic law of the nation," and "must be carried out" (Mao 1977: 129). Liu Shao-qi made it more clear. He said, "The Constitution must be carried out by every Chinese person and every governmental institute [and] the Chinese Communist Party members must become the models in abiding the Constitution and any other laws" (Liu 1985: 168). Therefore, we can take the promulgation of the 1954 constitution as a historical starting point to move forward to when the state was governed by the rule of law and constitutional order.

To make the nation according to the vanguard party–mass model and govern the state by the will of the vanguard party is an extension of the rules and methods that the CCP used in leading the Chinese communist revolution. Compared with the citizen-state model, the vanguard party–mass model has its own features.

1. In the citizen-state model, legislation and legal enforcement are the basic methods of governing a state. The will of the party cannot be the will of the state and cannot be forced upon the citizens of the nation, except as it is translated into the will of the people through legislation of the National People's Congress. However, in the vanguard party–mass model, the party directly makes policies that are the guidelines of all activities and announces the documents that are the carriers of the policies, then puts the documents into effect nationwide through party organizations.

2. In the citizen-state model, the content of democracy applies to the state system, and the form of its realization is the system of the People's Deputy Congress. But in the vanguard party–mass model, democracy exists mainly as an institution or a method for leadership, and the form of its realization is "democratic centralism."

3. In the citizen-state model, the basic method of organizing the society is to equally allocate rights with corresponding obligations among

people, to insist on the rule that everyone is equal under the law, and to have the aid of the government to ensure the realization of the lawful relationship of rights and obligations. But in the vanguard party–mass model, administrative hierarchy is the method of organizing a society, which focuses on the relationship between command and obedience.

4. In the citizen-state model, citizens can establish a systematic mechanism of restriction to restrain the behavior of officials and prevent the government from disobeying the will of the citizens. In the vanguard party–mass model, the vanguard party also wants to accept supervision from the masses. However, the majority of the masses are not the party members. Therefore, it is hard to have a systematic mechanism for ensuring effective supervision and restriction over the party's decision-making procedures.

The fact that these two models exist simultaneously is determined by specific historical reasons. The constitutional movements in modern Chinese history emerged during the process of learning to govern the state from Westerners in order to save the nation. The aim of the movement was to make the state stronger and to improve the legitimacy of the government's authority and the centripetal force of the government among the people. This was, of course, not born from the social basis, the political structure, and the cultural tradition of China itself, and was therefore totally different from Western constitutional movements that were under the background of "Natural Law" or "Super Law" (Corwin 1928). As its logical consequence, when the CCP won power through revolution and founded the state, it made and promulgated the constitution and laws on one hand; on the other hand, it simply put the organizing and controlling methods that were formed and used during the revolution into the practice of making and governing a nation, which was the only method it was familiar with.

While there was a great difference between these two models, it was clear that the CCP itself, as a ruling party, tried to make the nation according to the citizen-state model and to govern the state by the rule of law. Therefore, these two trends were not completely mutually exclusive in China's circumstances. However, the following reasons interfered with the operation of the citizen-state model. First, beginning in 1956, a planned economic system was formed in China, and the government became the center of domination, individuals lost freedom of choice, the citizen's rights that were supposedly given by the constitution were actually false. Second, Mao Ze-dong became a utopian socialist after 1956 in many respects. He viewed citizens' rights that the constitution stipulated as so-called "bourgeoisie rights," "which was equal in form but unequal in nature," and advocated restraining these rights "under the dictatorship of the proletariat," which obviously placed restrictions on applying a relationship of rights and obligations to organizing the society and governing the state. Third, due to the mistake on the class-struggle theory, Mao Ze-dong and the central committee of the CCP retook class struggle as the main contradiction in Chinese society, gave the main focus to class struggle in Chinese politics, and resolved the class-struggle problem and its relevance without any consideration of constitutional procedure, which separated the constitution from the nation's political life. Fourth, after the promulgation of the 1954 Constitution, the National People's Congress did not create any concrete legal mechanisms and regulations to ensure the citizens' rights that the constitution stipulated, and also did not set up corresponding institutes to supervise and examine the implementation of the constitution and to correct actions that disobey the constitution. Under all these circumstances, the constitution had symbolic meaning only. From 1956 to 1966, no act was promulgated in the National People's Congress (Zhao 1990: 96) and the vanguard party–mass model dominated China's social and political procedures.

From the viewpoint of the citizen-state model, the Cultural Revolution was actually a serious constitutional crisis. First, the Cultural Revolution negated the basic political system that the constitution approved. During that period, the People's Delegation Congress closed for nine years, from 1966 to 1974. Second, during the Cultural Revolution citizens' rights were rudely trampled on. From the chairman of the nation to ordinary society members, all were unable to protect human dignity and political freedom for themselves. Third, all practices of the Cultural Revolution went outside the constraints of the constitution, which had no effective methods to restrict and correct those practices. Therefore, the Cultural Revolution could be considered negative to the citizen-state model.

China promulgated three constitutions within seven years: in 1975, when the Cultural Revolution came to its end, in 1978, and in 1982. This phenomenon not only reflected the dramatic change in the Chinese political situation and the change of viewpoint of CCP leaders toward concepts of development and developmental objectives of Chinese society, but also showed the intention of CCP leaders to restore or rebuild the constitutional order in China. Among these three constitutions, the 1982 Constitution listed many more citizens' rights than others. But without a fundamental change in organization and governance models at the time when all three constitutions were promulgated, the vanguard party–mass model still played the dominant role. Therefore, the promulgation of the constitutions only showed that there was a tendency to transform to the constitutional order in China. The accomplishment of the transformation is still underway.

FUNDAMENTAL CHANGES IN CHINA TODAY

The failures of the "Great Leap Forward" and the Cultural Revolution demonstrate the severe malpractice of the original institutions. The contacts and communications with developed countries show the backwardness of China in the world. The joint forces of these two things push China toward reform.

The reform that started in 1979 has continued to emerge for more than eighteen years. The practice of reform has fully proved itself to be a great social revolution which has led to fundamental changes within China in almost every respect. Economically, the most impressive turnabout has been the separation between the government and economic enterprises and the rapid development of a nonstate sector. In 1996, the nonstate sector contributed 72 percent of China's industry growth, 76 percent of China's industry profit (Xue and Ma 1997: Preface), and continues to grow at a rate much higher than that of the state sector. It has become the main source of employment, and 84 percent of total employment was in the nonstate sector. In Guangdong, Jiangsu, Shandong, and Zhejiang, more than half of investment came from the nonstate sector (Xue and Ma 1997: 746, 531, 488, 497, 508). More and more commodities were sold at their market value. Markets of merchandise, capital, foreign currency, and labor have either already been fully established or are in the process of formation. The economy has also been greatly internationalized. In 1995, China's international trade reached about $278 billion, comprising 40 percent of total GDP (World Bank, 1997: 242, 236). In 1996, 47 percent of international trade came from foreign-invested enterprises (Xue and Ma 1997: 751).

Important progress has been made in the construction of democracy and a legal system based on the rule of law during the past eighteen years. After the abolition of the People's Commune, village peoples' autonomy was established in the countryside as of 1987; the work of the National People's Congress has been normalized; the leadership of the CCP has been defined political, and it must exercise its activities under the constitution; many acts have been promulgated since 1979; the jurisdiction of the law has covered most parts of the nation and the law replacing the documents of the party is now becoming the basic means of governing the nation; and competitive elections for government officers have been held in some provinces. By establishing this practice as the sole criterion for testing the truth, China has broken the constraints of bookish ossified Marxism in the people's minds. Concepts that lead reform go beyond the assumption of the socialism–capitalism dichotomy. In the field of human rights, China has joined more than ten international Human Rights Covenants. Hong Kong has returned to China according to the pattern of "one country, two systems," which is the first time a Chinese government has governed a place based on basic law.

With the emergence of the market economy after 1979, China has gradually transformed from a traditional, closed, and centralized society into a modern, open, and diversified one, and citizens have enjoyed much freedom. The planned economy forced people to depend on the government, almost all Chinese were subordinated into one unit, and most of them did not have any freedom to choose jobs, working places, or living places. Now, peasants can work in cities, students can find a job based on their own choices, and officers in government and workers in the state-owned sector can resign their jobs and work in the nonstate-owned sector. People can flow from one place to another one. All these changes could not have been imagined without reform.

While recognizing the positive changes in China, we should fully realize there are also social and political problems that are byproducts of economic reform coupled with a lack of political reform, some of which may become more problematic with a further development of the economy. Corruption, polarization between the rich and the poor, severe losses in some state-owned enterprises, unemployment, crime, differentiation in economic and income levels among different districts, and weakening governability are some obvious problems. Politically, there are still others. The emerging middle class is asking for more reforms to protect their interests. Intellectuals are appealing for more freedom in their professional pursuits and ordinary people are complaining about almost everything that affects their daily lives. Because there is no compatible political system which would allow for more popular participation in state affairs and policy-making processes, all these problems could cause potential political instability in the future.

In spite of all these problems, reform has indeed caused profound change in China, which is historically meaningful. No doubt, the CCP still grasps the main political resources in China, its leading status is stable, and the vanguard party–mass model is still a method of organizing and governing the nation. However, reform not only makes the citizen-state model become an important method of organizing and governing the nation again, but also makes governing the nation by the rule of law a common requirement, owing to the tremendous changes it has created in China's economy, politics, culture, and social life. Reform has diminished the restrictions on personal identity which were formed during the period of planned economy, lessened the dependence of the Chinese people on the government and enhanced the independence and self-reliance of individuals, and heightened people's awareness of their own rights. In the market economy and daily life, it becomes a common requirement for people to have the aid of law to protect their constitutional rights, especially property rights, the rights of development, and the rights of political freedom and to normal competitive and transactional behavior, along with the popularization of democratic culture. The worship of an individual leader, which was very popular during the Cultural Revolution, has now almost disappeared. To remove corruption and to control and restrict government power by law has become a common goal. In the party and government, it has been difficult for the government to use the traditional governing model that relies on administrative control as its main tool to effectively manage a society based on a market economy. The traditional governing model, characterized as governing by man and being influenced by individual inclination, causes distrust of the reform policy and harms the performance of the party and the government. The lack of transparency in the administrative system that China practiced before the reform hinders the unifying of the Chinese international trading system with international practices. All these problems create demands that the party and the government change their leading methods. The law, with many strengths such as reliability, popularity, predictability, structural complementarity, and state enforcement, can adjust not only individual conduct, but also important relationships among interests in the whole society and other customary social relations. It also maintains the order of social life, democratic politics, and market economics; improves the legitimacy of political ruling; and becomes the basic tool for realizing the functions of the state and pushing the development of society. Therefore, moving from "rule by man" to "rule by law," protecting the dignity of the constitution and the law enhancing people's consciousness of abiding by the law, and ensuring people's identification of the law are basic requirements of the party and the government to lead and govern the state. The changes mentioned provide China from top to bottom and from bottom to top with a new impetus to transform to the constitutional order in a fundamental way consistent with the requirements of a moral order.

China is still in the process of reform. By 2010, the nonstate sector will not only become the main part of China's economy, but also the main source of China's taxation, which will cause a fundamental change in the relations between state and society. By that time,

China's market institutions will be established and stabilized, which will finally make China a plural society. By that time, China's legal institutions will be established and stabilized too, which will become the guarantee of social order. The Chinese people, as a whole, will bid farewell to poverty, will enjoy more education, and will have stronger interests in political participation. All these will certainly lay a stronger groundwork for China in the transition to a true constitutional order.

HOW TO ESTABLISH A DEMOCRATIC AND STABLE CONSTITUTIONAL ORDER IN CHINA

Democracy and Constitutional Order

Generally speaking, democracy is the core and foundation of constitutional order, while constitutional order is the manifestation and safeguard of democracy. However, though democracy and constitutional order share commonalities, there are differences between them. From the historical point of view, the constitutional state emerged before the democratic state. It is true that constitutional monarchies existed in Europe as well as constitutional states before democratic institutions were introduced in a complete fashion (Lane 1996: 263–264). In regard to their content, democracy stresses people's sovereignty and majority rule, while constitutional order stresses the respect of citizens, and especially government, for a constitution, and the creation of a social structure in which government and citizens can function independently and limit themselves and each other. A good constitutional order is able to secure the authority of the government as well as effectively limit the power of the government (to prevent "ills of government"). It is also able to ensure the rights of citizens as well as protect social interests and the rights and freedom of other people (to prevent "ills of citizens") (Ostrom 1997). Thus, it encourages both government and citizens to act according to rationality and rules. In this way, constitutional order stabilizes the development of democratic politics. As a matter of fact, in countries of successful democratic development, large-scale democratic development always happened after the formation of constitutional order. Without constitutional order, aspirations for democracy provoke irrational activities of citizens. China's Cultural Revolution is a typical example. Therefore, after building a basic system of democracy in China, the urgent task of political reform should now be the establishment of a stable democratic constitutional order. Only after carrying out this task can we try further reform to introduce large-scale democratic politics into China and to stabilize constitutional order. It has been proven by experience that such a reform sequence will encourage the healthy development of Chinese democratic politics (Grey 1997: 111–140).

Constitution, Constitutionalism, and Constitutional Order

The constitution is the basic law of a nation, a collection of principles and rules by which a nation organizes and rules itself. There are common or similar parts in terms of the constitutive elements of constitutions among all modern nations; namely, they all include prescriptions about basic citizen rights and duties, major institutes of government and their relations, and the power distribution between central, regional, and local governments. On the other hand, differences in cultural traditions, histories, and ways of organizing and ruling society will produce different constitutions for different nations. As the collection of principles and rule of organizing and ruling a nation, a constitution is the theoretical representation of a nation's constitutional order. Constitutionalism is a theory on the politics of contracts or the politics of duties, which also means a special arrangement of institutions and political practices. The starting point of constitutionalism is to make the adherence to a constitution the prerequisite of all political activities. Its focus is to set up a system of rules to manage and limit government, so as to ensure the control of executives by the constitution without dissipating government's power so far as to make for weak and unresponsive government (Ball, Farr, and Hanson 1989: 64). Modern constitutionalism originated in the West. However, the institutions and practice which Western nations have carried out are particular to their own national situations. They cannot be imitated without changes by other nations. The basic ideas in constitutionalism, by contrast, have universal significance. All institutions, including constitutions, will become powerless if their workings are not monitored and transgressions punished. In a nation, transgressions of the constitution by individuals or groups can be corrected by the government. But if the transgression comes from the government, and if necessary arrangements of institutions and powerful social forces are lacking, correction will be impossible. Both a constitution and constitutionalism are important for establishing a constitutional order. And the latter is more important than the former, because a constitution without constitutionalism will not be respected. In some nations, such as England, there is no written constitution, and legislation, judicial opinions, and political customs have served as a constitution. Since there is successful constitutionalism, a stable constitutional order gradually developed (Lipson 1989: 232–250). China needs a good constitution to move toward a stable constitutional order. Though some improvements need to be made, the current 1982 Constitution fits the national situation of China. What China lacks is constitutionalism and the culture of constitutionalism, the necessarily institutional arrangements and effective political participation of all citizens which ensure the carrying out of the constitution and constitutional documents. Therefore, the construction of constitutionalism should be one of the focuses in efforts to establish constitutional order in China.

Political Authority, Patterns of Rule, and Constitutional Order

What a constitution prescribes or endorses forms a kind of political order. Nonetheless, the document of a constitution cannot be transformed automatically into reality. The formation and sustenance of political order presuppose the existence of certain political authority. This is especially true for constitutional order. The 1911 Revolution, the first revolution in twentieth-century China, has shown that once revolutionaries lost political authority, the constitutional order they had built up lost the ability to exist and function. In this sense, we can say that the existence of legitimate political authority is the prerequisite of carrying out and protecting constitutional order. Of course, not all kinds of political authority are in harmony with constitutional order. Where does the legitimacy of political authority come from? It is critical, for a constitutional order to exist and work, that effective leaders adhere to a rule of law. The history of the People's Republic of China has shown that constitutional order is incompatible with the rule by man's will instead of by lawful means. Mao spent a long time fighting against tyranny and trying to solve social contradictions in a socialist society by means of democratic ways. But even a man like him led China into constitutional crisis, because he used the pattern of rule by man. Constitutional order exists only under the political authority of democracy combined with the pattern of rule by law. The Chinese Communist Party is the ruling party in China. In China, to ensure that the political authority of the CCP conforms to the rule of law is the basic condition for building constitutional order peacefully. Whether the party rules the state according to the law and constitutionality, and whether it insists on the development of Chinese democratic politics and finally sets up the ultimate political authority of a constitution will be critical to the construction of a constitutional order.

The Creation of Constitutional Order Is a Historical Process

Since the Wuxu Reform in 1898, it has been one hundred years since the Chinese began to pursue the goal of a constitutional order. During this period, the Chinese political situation has changed greatly. Now, constitutional authority is emerging and the rule of law is expanding. However, there is still a long way to go for China to have a constitutional order in which the boundary of state power is clear, the division of labor is rational, the freedom and rights of citizens are fully realized, transgression of the constitution can be corrected in time, and the principles and rules that the constitution prescribed can prevail in sociopolitical life.

In countries like America, France, and England, it took a long time to achieve a constitutional order. France is somehow similar to China. From the time of the 1789 Revolution and the first constitution of 1791, France has undergone eleven political regimes: Five of them were republics, and the remainder comprised three monarchies, two empires, and one fascist puppet state (Safran 1991: 2). Sixteen constitutional formulations have been issued (Wang and Li 1997: 141). However, constitutional order was not stabilized until 1957, the formation of the Fifth Republic. The reason that it always takes a long time to form a constitutional order is that it takes a long time to develop conditions necessary to support constitutional order, such as democratic political authority; legal rules; autonomous society; right relations between central and local government and among different religions and ethnic groups; the correspondence of rights and duties of citizens or what Saton (1962) referred to as the mastering of "technology of liberty"; and the formation of democratic politics and consensus about the necessity of the authority of constitutions.

China has had a long tradition of feudal tyranny. The majority of the country's population is peasant. Besides, it is in a new historical process of paradigm shift and cultural transformation. It would be unrealistic to expect that constitutional order will emerge after one political revolution or dramatic political action. For the Chinese future, the crucial thing is to look in the right direction. Once the direction is clear and meets the true test of experience, the goal will finally be reached.

REFERENCES AND BIBLIOGRAPHY

Ball, T., J. Farr, and R. L. Hanson. 1989. *Political Innovation and Conceptual Change*. New York: Cambridge University Press.

Corwin, E. S. 1928. "The 'Higher Law' Background of American Constitutional Law." *Harvard Law Review* 42: 1–93 (Chinese language edition).

Grey, R. D. 1997. *Democratic Theory and Post-Communist Change.* Englewood Cliffs, N.J.: Prentice Hall.

Lane, J. E. 1996. *Constitutions and Political Theory.* New York: Manchester University Press.

Lipson, L. 1989. *The Great Issues of Politics: An Introduction to Political Science.* Englewood Cliffs, N.J.: Prentice Hall.

Liu Shao-qi. 1985. *Selected Works of Liu Shao-qi.* Beijing: People's Press.

Luo Rong-qu. 1992. *The Quest for the Process of China's Modernization.* Beijing: Beijing University Press.

Mao Ze-dong. 1977. *Selected Works of Mao Ze-dong.* Beijing: People's Press.

Ostrom, V. 1997. *The Meaning of Democracy and the Vulnerability of Democracies.* Ann Arbor: University of Michigan Press.

Safran, W. 1991. *The French Polity.* White Plains, N.Y.: Longman.

Satori, G. 1962. "Constitutionalism: A Preliminary Discussion." *American Political Science Review* 56: 100–120 (in Res Publica, 1995).

Wang Bang-zhuo, and Li Hui-kang. 1997. *Socio-Ecological Analysis on the Western Political Party's System.* Shanghai: XueLin Press.

World Bank. 1997. *World Development Report 1997* (Chinese translation). Beijing: China Financial and Economic Publishing House.

Xue Muqiao, and Hong Ma. 1997. *1997 Almanac of China's Economy.* Beijing: China Economic Almanac Publishing House.

Yang Lei-yu. 1997. "The First Socialist Constitution in China's History." *The Party's Literature* 1: 20–23.

Zhao Zhen-jiang. 1990. *The Forty Years of China's Legal Institutions.* Beijing: Beijing University Press.

8

Democratization and the State in the Third World

Sushil Kumar

Since the end of the Cold War, democracy has been gaining a global context. An aspect of it is the emphasis on the prospect which democracy holds out for peace; the idea is that peace requires democratization as a global phenomenon. This idea draws its inspiration from Kant's *Perpetual Peace*. Its centrality to post–Cold War international-relations theory is evident from the copious literature which has of late appeared on the subject. The focus is different from that of peace discourse during the Cold War—a discourse "between non-conformist free-trade liberalism that saw global capitalism as creating a new warless world, and socialism, which saw capitalism as the engine of a highly militarized, exploitative and centralized state system of enormous destructive capacity."[1]

David Held conceptualizes the post–Cold War democratization as "cosmopolitan democracy."[2] It serves as the context for restructuring and reorienting domestic political and social institutions so that an impact is felt on state goals and preferences, in opposition to what the realist theory postulates about state behavior. Democratization in this sense implies a departure from the state-centric approach with a view toward synthesizing it with rival approaches which seek to imbue the state with a measure of moderation in its drives for preservation and dominance. In short, post–Cold War state discourse aims to pose a "counter-challenge to the existing paradigms of thought and action."[3]

During the Cold War, there was also a movement away from the Westphalian model to the U.N. model.[4] This was a consequence of the tension

between claims made on behalf of individual states and those made on behalf of an alternative organizing principle of world affairs: ultimately a democratic community of states, with equal voting rights in the General Assembly of nation-states, openly and collectively regulating international life while constrained to observe the UN Charter and a battery of human rights conventions.[5]

The U.N. model modified, at least partially, an international order based on sovereign states, an order which was buttressed by an international law which treated states as its only subjects and in its scope did not go beyond interstate relations. Alternative approaches to international law and relations were no doubt pioneered, but they were not given much attention. Since the end of the Cold War, the situation has changed. The U.N. model is now being transformed into the global model and is in tension with it.[6] Hence, the problem of U.N. reforms is not merely one of organizational adjustment with an emerging distribution of power or that of adequate representation of the Third World, including India's permanent membership on the Security Council—though these are important for continued viability and representativeness of the world body—but that of resolving its tension with the tenets of the global model. These tenets are the following:

- The reference point for democracy in the contemporary world is the cosmopolis, or the world as a whole; it is no longer the state. This means that political systems should seek legitimacy at the global level for the interests they serve and the value they hold. This means that "internal affairs" are now a business of the world community also. The existing international law is anachronistic and the states, grounding their legitimacy on the fact of recognition, are just "judicial entities," clinging to juridical myths for the exercise of authority (which often amounts to perpetration of violence to dam the tide of democracy). The globalist democracy goes beyond such legal and juridical fictions.
- The issues which escape the control of the state should be subjected to regional or global regulating agencies.
- The democratic process is critically advanced by embedding the state and other political institutions into a global civil society and its widening area of public concerns. Democracy within a statist framework is understood in terms of free press, competitive politics, and elections. But democracy within a globalist context is transnational in character and works through an expanding circle of multilateral institutions, value-

based networks, and social movements, which concern themselves with issues of peace, justice, and morality, heretofore solely a business of the state.[7]

- An attribute of democratization is its potential for transforming hierarchy and eroding hegemony, both within and between nations (the hierarchy and hegemony in relations among nations and communities).

In short, democratization both at international and domestic levels puts humane governance at the center of policy concerns. Its strategy is predicted on growing distrust of government: of state elite, bureaucracy, civil, and military. The institutions of representative democracy, parliaments and legislatures, are regarded as not adequate in realizing good governance. Hence, political and social conditionalities to trade and aid are emphasized. Similarly, in domestic politics, direct action and direct democracy through referendum and plebiscite are considered helpful. Such forms of participation enable the people to articulate their normative perspectives and express moral judgments on controversial and contested issues. The considerations of democratic accountability are expected to compel governments to shape their action on these issues in line with the expressed preferences of the people. Such a democratic process is now being extended to the conduct of international relations also. The globalist democracy thus aims to arouse and channel popular aspirations in the hope that it will eventually bring about a convergence of national interest with the goals which the international community sets for itself.

The operational dynamics of the global model in specific contexts is targeted on leadership and organizational issues. The result is a combination of international and domestic strategies for restructuring state institutions and public policies to effect a transition in favor of global norms. As this convergence extends to an ever wider arena of policy processes, the issues cease to be either purely domestic or purely international. More and more issues are viewed as of a mixed nature. They are described as "intermestic" issues and are supposed to be judged by citizens, not in terms of such categories as sovereignty, nationalism, or patriotism, but in terms of the impact on their personal well-being.[8] As such, the global model treats these issues as a fit case of decision making within a pluralistic framework, comprising elements drawn from multilateral institutions and domestic interest groups.

The scope of democratic decision making in international relations is widening.[9] The emphasis is on bringing more and more issues of foreign policy within its fold. The demands for national self-determination—seeking autonomy, secession, or integration with a larger, regional setup—affecting relations between two or more states are considered appropriate for such decision-making processes. For example, the road to the European Union was laid by national referenda. Referenda on issues of self-determination likewise led to the breakup of the former Soviet Union, and later of Yugoslavia and Czechoslovakia. The democratic process is believed to demystify state boundaries and open them to change under popular pressure.

The other issues amenable to participatory impact pertain to counterinsurgency types of military action or production and deployment of nuclear and other weapons of mass destruction. It is believed that popular initiatives such as declaration of localities as "nuclear free zones" would attract world attention and have effects on policy making.[10] Such an explication of cosmopolitan democracy is, no doubt, a good statement of mankind's deeply felt aspirations for a world order based on freedom and peace. Many Third World statesmen have been emphasizing it, including those in India, such as Gandhi and Nehru, and, more or less, all the successive prime ministers.

But the question is, how can such a world order be realized? The structure of the international system gets in the way. It was so during the Cold War, and it is so even after the end of the Cold War. The end of bipolarity did not result in a fundamental restructuring, in basic features, of the system, a system which had caused and nurtured the East–West conflict during the Cold War. That is, as long as the impact of the systemic structure on state goals and preferences is felt, the liberal emphasis on domestic change in the direction of cosmopolitan democracy as a sufficient condition of peace is unreal. Kant also thought likewise: "The problem of the establishment of a perfect constitution depends on the problem of a lawful external relationship of the states and cannot be solved without the latter.[11] This is also Gourevich's "second image revered" argument.[12] The role of the state in peace and war is the issue. It has been a subject of debate between the realists and the liberals. The problem is not settled yet. Mearaheimer says, "The relational power of systemic versus domestic level explanations for international politics has not yet been determined by empirical research."[13] Such a conclusion is reinforced by the experience of countries like India, which are democratic and engaged in optimization of social development, economic liberalization, and political democracy, but, in external relations, are faced with insecurities arising from irredentist claims, sponsored terrorism, and tension on the borders. When democracy within national boundaries does not lead to international peace and stability, policy is forced to address the systemic variables. Policy goals and strategies appear not as much as functions of state attributes, but as international constraints arising from the policies of other states. Such policies may, of course, be rooted in the lack of democracy in these states, but the likelihood of their being rooted in geopolitical and strategic perceptions of these states is much greater. In any case, the democratization wave may take a long time to sweep across these states and make them peace oriented in terms of the democratic peace hypothesis. And so, in the short run, the compulsions of making policy in a geopolitical context remain.

The importance given to structure by Third World states in such situations may not signify acceptance of realist assumptions in international relations. Far from it. Democratic countries of the Third World—India, again, is an illustrative example—have been opposed to power politics. The emphasis on structural variables largely focuses on the limited objective of democratizing the state system with a view to incorporating it into efforts for enlarging the area of liberal peace. This is evident from the faith these countries put in cooperative and multilateral initiatives for mitigating the impact of power politics on relations among states. Their policy stance is close to the understanding of Robert Keohane when he says, "Realist assumptions about world politics are consistent with the formation of institutionalized arrangements containing rules and principles, which promote cooperation."[14] The support for the U.N. model among the countries of the Third World is a case in point. This model marks a departure from the realist worldview, as it prescribes international cooperation for promoting norms and rules needed for a democratic and just states system.[15] The Third World emphasis on state security, stability, and autonomy should thus not be interpreted as a design for reproducing states of realist denomination; that is, states engaged in building themselves in response to international insecurity, inequality, and perceived injustice, without any regard to a normatively conceived teleological notion of a world order guiding their relations with other states or with their domestic societies.

Hence, the neo-Weberian and neo-Marxist critique of contemporary state structures is relevant only for drawing attention to some of the deviant aspects of public policy in Third World states.[16] To regard it as negating the political content of societal aspirations in erstwhile colonial countries is tantamount to delegitimizing their independent statehood.[17] Is such a reconceptualization of the state necessary for realizing global norms? Obviously not. On the contrary, it is likely to hamper cosmopolitan synthesis and promote uncertainties consequent on turbulence and instability in domestic politics which are likely to be counterproductive for peace and

freedom in interstate relations. Any thoughts of negating Third
World statehood are thus misplaced.[18] Third World countries do
not deny the ontological primacy of world order. In fact, they regard a
just and democratic world order as a necessary source of support for
their state-building projects, and as essential for achieving their na-
tionalist aspirations and developmental goals. These countries can
easily be attributed with an all-pervasive understanding that, in a
hierarchical and stratified system, they stand to gain nothing by
committing themselves to the principles of interstate relations as
rooted in the realist theory. Yet, for the same reason, they realize
that their only sheet anchor against international and regional
caprice is state stability as an instrumental mechanism of national
self-determination in political, social, and cultural development.

The departure of the U.N. model from the realist understand-
ings of state behavior needs further elaboration to underline that
the Third World perspective on globalization is basically not negative. In fact, there is no practical alternative to be positive. During
the Cold War, domestic peace and development in the Third World
was disturbed when foreign-policy objectives of the great powers
were looking for piggyback rides there and discovered social dis-
satisfactions along class, gender, and ethnic lines to mount on. Why
did such a situation come about? Why did the Third World become
an arena of East–West conflict? Could the Third World put the boot
on the other foot? The answer is no. The vulnerability of the Third
World has to be seen in the context of status hierarchy in the international political system. It was clearly underlined that Third World
states should work in cooperation, especially on the floor of the
U.N. General Assembly, to realize, in a consensual manner with
the developed part of the world, a just and democratic world order
as an essential condition for their survival, and the purposes which
gave them legitimacy in the eyes of their own people. This was the
U.N. model in operation. This was how the U.N. model was making
history. The most significant thing was that developed Western
countries went along with the effort, except when they perceived it
as a cover for Cold War politics. Hence, the commitment on the
part of the Third World to the U.N. model implies their continued
commitment to a post-Westphalian global order. Such a commitment clearly contrasts with the realist prescriptions for state behavior, and is consistent with post–Cold War emphasis on
cooperative security, arms control and disarmament, and, above
all, good governance.

In the realist view, the state is inner directed. Paraphrasing
Machiavelli, one can say that the state's control over its own international role was so complete that it could, and should, be the ar-

chitect of its own moral code. In these terms the only "good" the state served—that is, the supreme value of foreign policy—was the accomplishment of its own ends. This is very close to the notion of raison d'état (the logic that governs state action): "Whatever the regime decides to do in world politics is transformed by the very fact of decision into a moral goal." Within such a state-centric realist view, international relations are conducted within a framework characterized by the absence of any agreement on values, goals, and policies. As such, interstate relations are situated on a continuum of harmony, cooperation, and hostility, according to a subjectively perceived and evaluated profile of particular interests.[19] The states keep moving one way or the other on this continuum as national interests converge or diverge. And for the same reason, the convergence of interests when it occurs does not constitute a supranational constraint on the primacy of the self-defined national interest.[20] An international normative process directly linking a desirable world order to state action is absent. The emphasis is on interest, power, and necessity, evaluated by a trained elite and actualized through a foreign policy formulated within the rational-actor model of the state.

The state, for realists, represents the underlying society, not only in relation to the outside world but also in terms of the values to be realized in society. For this reason, international relations are supposed to stop at the border, so that other states or social forces located therein are not able to interfere with the social values within the state. An implication of such an approach is a framework of state–society relations in which the state tries to mold the society after its own interests, through politicization and, if necessary, militarization of the economy and civil society. This results in international and domestic conflicts, which tend to rob the society of its traditional values of tolerance, human sensitivity, and concern for the future.

Such a construction of the state idea corresponded to the European (Franco–Prussian) model, which reached its fullness in Germany at the beginning of the nineteenth century. This model emerged as a defensive response to expanding imperialism. But in the twentieth century, the nations which sought escape from imperial dominance did not undertake state building and political reconstruction in line with its imperatives. This was not so with the socialist states, which had sought their raison d'être in their declared opposition to capitalism, colonialism, and organized religion. The subsequent marriage of socialist ideology with anticolonialism was, however, critical to the diffusion of the European model in the Third World. The strategy of the Western powers to harness internal social tensions to their international objectives was also in no small measure a contributing factor. The characteristic feature of this model is its amenability to articulation with ideological worldviews, as opposed to the immanent working out of a value-based autonomous political process through debate and interest-group activity.

So great has been the impact of this model of the state that the political landscape in the Third World has come to be characterized by different ideological reproductions of it. The trend in political analysis and public-policy making in these states has been first and foremost to figure out international and domestic allies and enemies of the state by situating it in a matrix of social forces, national and international. This has pushed the art of governance into a mode where the search for allies and coalition partners, both within and outside the state, has become a major strategic objective. Pointing an accusing finger at foreign and domestic enemies and holding them responsible for all the problems of the people has emerged as the dominant style of governance and political thinking. The elite groups, in their power-seeking strategies, compete among themselves for harnessing the might of the state to crush the alleged domestic enemies and external opponents.[21]

The post–Cold War opposition to these models of statehood in most parts of the Third World targets the state–society relationship and articulates two parallel approaches, one of reform and the other of transformation. The reform strategy favors constitutional democracy characterized by institutional checks on the exercise of state power, and the existence of a robust civil society capable of autonomous interaction with the state. Lessons are drawn from Anglo-American constitutional history (well analyzed by Carl J. Friedrich).[22] In the context of democratization, this Anglo-American model emerges at the center of political discourse because constitutionalism and democracy provide an escape from the depredations of domestic and foreign policies of power-seeking states, whose intellectual antecedents lie in the European model.[23]

The transformation strategy calls for a paradigm shift. The globalists reject the goals which the state seeks to achieve: power, wealth, and order. They regard these goals as opposed to liberty, equality, and fraternity. While taking this position, the globalists of this orientation imply (often much to the amazement of political theorists) that there is no possibility of realizing these values in state-led societies. In international relations, they deny the possibility of the state role in nonrealist terms, and so they contest the realist construction of international relations. They point to the empirical reality on the ground—at the societal level—where the

inability of the state in addressing the problems of the people effectively is all too evident.

The starting point of the globalist argument is the postbehavioral
call to scholars "to be relevant and meaningful," "to be aware of the
value premises" of a theory, and "to engage in reshaping society."[24]
Some postbehavioralists adopt the approach of methodological ho-
lism, and take analysis beyond the level of the state to that of world
society. These scholars very rightly deconstruct the structural features of the international political order with a view to understand
their impact on state goals and behavior patterns. Such external
determination of the state is juxtaposed with a counterreality at
the societal level, a reality consisting of a complex web of interdependence illustrated by cooperative action of transnational networks. Such nonstate competence is generally situated in issue areas
of global concern calling for local action. For this reason, it is regarded as complementary to state jurisdiction. As such, these issue
areas are common to both domestic and foreign spheres of state
activity, and so the counterreality is one in which state actors, to
quote Rosenau, "compete, cooperate, interact, or otherwise coexist
with counterparts in a multicentric world comprised of a vast array of diverse transnational, national and subnational actors."[25]

This world-society approach to theory building has its roots in
the theoretical innovations made during the Cold War under the
banner of peace research, with the sole objective of advancing normatively oriented strategies of reform.[26] The world-society approach
also shares space in its antistatist discourse with postmodern and
poststructural social-science theories. They offer a strong critique,
not so much of economic and financial globalization (because they
focus on communities not incorporated into these processes that
now, under the impact of neoliberal economic reforms, are being
increasingly excluded from the priorities of the state), as of political and cultural homogenizing tendencies. They criticize the situation which offers to mankind a "singular alternative."[27] They
celebrate "difference," especially identity difference, with a view
"to stress the possibility of new forms of political community and
political practice that are open to a variety of peoples' experiences
and histories, not closed off by the claims of the state or the claims of
hegemonic universalism."[28] Peace research also assumes certain global values, treats them as sui generis, and seeks to realize them through
alternative strategies and rationalities which are culturally rooted,
aesthetic, and environmentally friendly. Freed from structuralists
thinking, this implies a direct approach to problems defined as obstacles to peace, development, and democratization. The academic
focus is on discursive consciousness, which puts the state at the

center of attack from the perspective of value-based narratives. Such an approach to these problems is contesting the structuralists for space in domestic politics and international relations.

In the context of globalization, it is a contest with both old and new globalists. The old globalists had posited North–South conflicts and sought to resolve them through demands for a new international order. The emphasis of these demands was on state action in international relations, though the limitations of such action in the context of social and material conditions governing North–South relations was realized. The new globalists also emphasize state action, but in the domestic sphere. "They think that the state should not act on its own." Nor can it be successfully pressured by its own people unless they are networked into the ever-widening concerns of a global civil society. The only way out is through deepening the processes of democratization. The globalist agenda therefore puts emphasis on necessary adjustments to extend the democratic procedures to important areas of policy making. It also includes strategies for pushing these adjustments through aid–trade linkages. In the Third World, this agenda is seen as paving the way for global social and economic forces to penetrate autonomous centers of community power and mobilize popular classes for the benefit of global capital and against the state. Such fears of Third World states are compounded by recent cases of state failure and collapse. Hence, the post–Cold War discourse on the state increasingly points to a recursive relationship between domestic and international spheres and to the constituted nature of statehood and the global order, each constraining the evolution of the other, through the mediating influence of democratizing processes.

Globalization is likely to be self-limiting unless the gap between policies and popular preferences, consequent on competitive bidding for global capital, is narrowed by political pressure to democratize the organization and functioning of the international institutions which are increasingly taking over the policy-making functions of national governments. The accountability of these institutions to the people, premised on the U.N. model of international relations, is imperative for the long-term health of the emerging global order. It will also give relief to states from a deepening legitimacy crisis arising from the loss of control by the public domain of production, markets, and money flows, and also from their defective structure and wrong priorities. Hence, an interactive relationship between democratization processes and states in the Third World is expected to generate win–win outcomes for policy development.

NOTES

1. Nigel Young, "Peace Movements in History," in *Towards a Just World Peace: Perspectives from Social Movements*, ed. Saul H. Mendlovitz and R.B.J. Walker (London: Butterworth, 1987), 143.

2. David Held, ed., *Prospects for Democracy* (Cambridge: Polity Press, 1992), 27.

3. Rajni Kothari, "Masses, Classes and the State," in *Towards a Just World Peace*, 398.

4. Antonio Cassese, *International Law in a Divided World* (Oxford: Clarendon Press, 1986). Cassese contrasts the U.N. Charter system with the Wesphalian system. See also R. P. Anand, *New States and International Law* (New Delhi: Vikas, 1972).

5. Held, *Prospects for Democracy*, 29.

6. These processes of transformation focus on increasing validation of external claims on the shape and substance of domestic governance. In this context, the international relations (IR) discourse on the concept of the state is addressing the tension between normative aspiration and political constraint. A retreat of the state and its restructuring is considered necessary for advancing global norms and policy objectives.

7. Multilateralism, by definition, constrains unilateral action on a range of issues. Such expectations were aroused when the U.S. world-order agenda emphasized multilateralism. It was expected that growing multilateralism would limit the freedom of action even of a great power like the United States, and the expectations were high when President Clinton assumed office as a self-proclaimed multilateralist.

8. For the concept of "intermestic" issues, see Bayless Manning, "The Congress, the Executive and Intermestic Affairs," *Foreign Affairs* 57 (1979): 308–324.

9. The linkages between public opinion and foreign policy have been a subject of debate in IR theory. The earlier approach is embodied in such writings as Gabriel Almond, *American People and Foreign Policy* (New York: Praeger, 1950), and Walter Lippmann, *Public Opinion* (New York: Macmillan, 1922). There is now a shift away from this approach. See O. R. Holsti, "Public Opinion and Foreign Policy: Challenges to Almond–Lippmann Consensus," *International Studies Quarterly* 36 (1992): 439–466.

10. Kusuma Sorab, "People's Movement against Nuclear Projects: The Kaiga Case," in *Nuclear Energy and Public Safety*, ed. Vinod Gaur (New Dehli: INTAC, 1996), 154–162.

11. Immanuel Kant, "Idea for a Universal History with Cosmopolitan Intent," in *The Philosophy of Kant*, ed. and trans. Carl Friedrich (New York: Random House, 1949), 123.

12. Peter A. Gourevitch, "The Second Image Reversed: The International Sources of Domestic Politics," *International Organization* 32 (1978): 881–913.

13. John J. Mearaheimer, "The Author Replies," in "Correspondence: Back to the Future," Part 2, "International Relations Theory and Post–Cold War Europe," *International Security* 15 (1990): 195.

14. Robert Keohane, *After Hegemony* (Princeton: Princeton University Press, 1984), 67.

15. The Third World demands for a new world order were embodied in U.N. resolutions adopted during 1974–1975. See also Mahboob-ul Haq, "Intellectual Self-Reliance" (speech delivered to inaugurate Third World Forum in 1975), *International Development Review* 1 (1975): 8–13.

16. See David Lake, "Power and the Third World: Towards a Realist Political Economy of North–South Relations," *International Studies Quarterly* 31 (1987).

17. Political content has been central to the aspirations of emancipatory, anticolonial, and counterhegemony movements everywhere, not only in the Third World. These movements have always been preoccupied with political units defined in juridical, cultural, and geographical terms. The effort has been to synthesize this emphasis with the Marxian understanding of world capitalist systems. The post–Cold War globalizing tendencies and the integrationist imperatives of global capital call for a retooling of the synthesis and launching of a new political project.

18. T. Bierstaker, "Reducing the Role of the State in the Economy: A Conceptual Exploration of the IMF and World Bank Prescriptions," *International Studies Quarterly* 34 (1990): 477–492.

19. Robert Axelrod and Robert O. Keohane, "Achieving Cooperation Under Anarchy," *World Politics* 38 (1985): 226–254. See also other articles in this special issue of *World Politics*, edited by Kenneth Oye.

20. Kenneth Thompson, while discussing the role of ethics in IR, quotes Hans Morgenthau: "The purpose of foreign policy is not to bring enlightenment or happiness to the rest of the world but to take care of the life, liberty and happiness of the American people." See Kenneth Thompson, "The Ethical Dimensions of Diplomacy," *Journal of Politics* 46 (1984): 380.

21. The liberals have therefore been critical of international military assistance and of arms transfers, and also of domestic efforts to augment defense production or growth in the ranks of internal security forces. These are seen as instruments of repression. The liberals maintain that a state which is politically exclusionary in distribution of power, rewards, and benefits is prone to build institutions and instrumentalities of centralized control and pursue the logic of superior might in relation to decentralized centers of power. When a state pursues such a strategy, it subverts not only democracy but also, when the exclusionary policies are based on social and communal bias, the secular nature of the polity immanent in the concept of territorial nationalism and citizenship. (This concept was espoused by the Indian National Congress during the movement for national independence and has been the basis of one-nation theory, a concept which has been opposed and rejected by almost all of India's neighboring states.) The state, by departing from this approach to nationalism, increasingly narrows the social basis of its power, and is driven to modalities of governance which are authoritarian, a strategy which in the long run is counterproductive and self-defeating. But the liberals commit the error of treating such policies as units of analysis without situating them in the dynamics of conflict at the global level.

22. Carl J. Friedrich, *Constitutional Government and Democracy: Theory and Practice in Europe and America,* Indian ed. (Boston: Ginn, 1950).

23. The difficulty, however, arises when even within the framework of this Anglo-American model the state coopts certain interests in the society and cooperates with them, often to the disadvantage of other interests. The need to have institutional safeguards against such policy options cannot be overemphasized.

24. David Easton, "The New Revolution in Political Science," *APSR,* December 1969, 1051–1052.

25. James N. Rosenau, "The Relocation of Authority in a Shrinking World," *Comparative Politics* 24 (1992), reprinted in *The Theory and Practice of International Relations,* 9th ed., ed. William Clinton Olson and James R. Lee (Englewood Cliffs, N.J.: Prentice Hall, 1994), 37.

26. Peter Lawler, "Peace Research and International Relations: From Divergence to Convergence," *Millennium: Journal of International Studies* 15 (1986): 367–392.

27. This was the thrust of Rajni Kothari's presentation on "marginalization of the state" to a seminar organized by the School of International Studies, Jawaharlal Nehru University, New Delhi, 3–4 January 1993.

28. Ramashray Roy, R.B.J. Walker, and Richard Ashley, "Dialogue: Towards a Critical Social Theory of International Relations," *Alternatives* 13 (1988): 88.

9

Globalization and Democracy in Latin America

He Li

The 1980s and 1990s have witnessed a wave of democracy in Latin America. The region underwent a far-reaching process of political transformation that resulted in the largest and most extended series of competitive elections in its entire history. Not only did every Latin American democracy survive the 1980s, but the number of democracies steadily increased over the course of the decade (Remmer 1991, 1993; Kelly 1998; Diamond 1993; Diamond, Linz, and Lipset 1989). Much more than in other developing regions—Asia, Africa, the Middle East—democracy has become the norm in Latin America. On the political front, the authoritarian governments so prevalent in Latin America at the end of the 1970s have become a distant memory. Today, all countries have democratically elected governments. The democratic process has been extended to local governments as well: Mayors in seventeen countries are now elected by popular vote, while in seven others these officials are appointed by elected municipal councils. Meanwhile, Latin American countries have opened up their economies to the global market. Many countries in the region have privatized and deregulated their economies and opened them up to foreign trade and investment.

Recent developments in Latin America raised new questions and posed new challenges for the scholarly community. A major concern, for many, is the problematic relationship between globalization and democratization. Does globalization lead to democracy? To what extent is globalization related to democracy? Are rising levels of trade, capital flows, and deregulation forcing Latin American countries to move toward democracy? These are the major questions to be examined in this chapter.

Though our focus is on Latin America, the conclusion of this chapter will have broader implications for other developing areas, where economies are experiencing similar fundamental transformation. This chapter is organized into four parts. The first section briefly reviews previous research in the area. The second section discusses the research design. The third section summarizes the empirical results. Finally, the fourth section offers some concluding remarks.

LITERATURE REVIEW

The global economy is undergoing rapid and fundamental changes that are reshaping political and social relations in many nations around the world. In many respects, these changes have encouraged the spread of democratic values and practices. In other ways, these changes may have hindered the spread of democracy. Democracy and globalization have been under a great deal of scrutiny in recent years. The comparative-politics literature is replete with analyses of the relationship between economic conditions and democratic politics. Social scientists have explained of problems of democratization from many perspectives and have come to different conclusions on the impact of globalization on democratization. This section will review the contending perspectives on democracy and globalization; namely, Marxist, dependency, bureaucratic–authoritarian, and neoliberal interpretations.

Neoliberals believe that globalization has been the inevitable result of technological change, and democracy is strengthened by global economic liberalization. The neoliberals believe their preferred form of globalization is the single best strategy for promoting stable and high-quality democracies throughout the world. The leading proponent of this view is Francis Fukuyama (1989, 1992). He renders his argument in terms of the inevitability of global political and economic homogenization, which forces liberal democracy as the only choice for modern states. Couched in terms of a prophesy, Fukuyama affirms that history has become one for all of humankind and that liberal democracy constitutes the end of societal evolution. Whatever unfinished business of history still remains will, according to him, soon be achieved with liberal democracy and the market economy, coupled together as a permanent arrangement for all societies the world over, within which human beings can pursue their desires and aspirations. The empirical results of Williamson (1996) lead to the conclusion that there is an unambiguous positive correlation between globalization and convergence in standard of living. He finds that when the pre–World War I years are examined in detail, the correlation turns out to be causal: Globalization played the critical role in contributing to the convergence.

In addition, neoliberals believe that globalization would open up society to democratic tendencies, while economic liberalization would provide the material bases (across a wider spectrum of society) for democratic consolidation. Spokesmen for several U.S. administrations have also seen the expansion of global capitalism as positively linked to democracy. In a similar vein, Samuel Huntington (1991) claims that with increasing levels of globalization the world is now undergoing a "third wave" of democratization in which the spread of democratic norms and practices is replacing authoritarian ones in many countries around the globe.

In contrast, dependency scholars challenge the assumptions of the neoliberals. According to dependency theories, global capitalism was the cause of underdevelopment in Third World countries and, implicitly, the lack of democracy (Dos Santos 1993; Wallerstein 1982, 1993). They maintain that democracy can be realized only by achieving economic and political autonomy and that integration with the international economy is negatively related to democracy (Frank 1984; Amin 1987). Dependency theory argues that such integration is the principal reason for underdevelopment of the developing countries. Osvaldo Sunkel (1973) proposed that transnational integration and national disintegration go hand in hand as the process of globalization goes on and deepens, thus threatening the stability of transnational projects of integration. However, as Tatu Vanhanen (1997) argues, it is difficult to test the assertions of the dependency theorists because their hypotheses are never clearly stated.

Many Latin American experts are committed to the bureaucratic–authoritarian thesis proposed by O'Donnell (1973). They argue that the breakdown of democratic or semidemocratic regimes in Brazil and Argentina in the mid-1960s was triggered by economic crises caused by the exhaustion of the "easy" stage of import substitution industrialization (ISI) and the inability of these countries to "deepen" their economies and thus undertake the "hard" state of ISI under "incorporating" regimes. According to their analysis, these bureaucratic–authoritarian governments sought to revive economic growth by consolidating ties with international economic forces. Leaders of these regimes often forged alliances with multinational corporations. To establish credit and gain time, they also need to come to terms with their creditors. Tasks of this kind have commonly been delegated to the most internationalized members of the original coalition, frequently young economists trained at U.S. institutions, and often identified by derisive nicknames, such as the "Chicago boys" in Chile (Kaufman 1979).

Marxists suggest that neoliberal globalization as a whole would dilute and weaken democracy. The Marxists believe that globalization can only be understood by investigating such factors as state, class, the power relations underpinning institutions, the sources of values and norms, the rules of international society, and the power politics of the supposed transnational civil society (Wood 1997; Tabb 1997).

Some Marxist analyses deal with effects of globalization on equality. According to them, international economic integration under neoliberal rule will tend to concentrate power and wealth in the hands of those who already have it eroding the quality of democratic politics, and with it the legitimacy of democratic political institutions. Where equality and legitimacy are already low, further erosion threatens to undermine the stability of democratic institutions as well. As an article in *Monthly Review* ("Globalization" 1992a) put it as follows: "Although a handful of third-world countries, benefiting from the globalization process, have made noteworthy progress in industrialization and trade, the overall gap between core and periphery nations has kept on widening."

In sum, current analyses of globalization can be seen as the successors to earlier theories which explained the world as encompassed by a single system. In spite of the potential importance of examining democracy and globalization in Latin America, empirical research on the subject has been scare. Explanations for the recent surge in the processes of democratization and economic liberalization, and for the forms they have taken, remain fragmentary. In this chapter we want to fill this void by including variables of international trade and foreign capital in our analysis of democracy in Latin America.

RESEARCH DESIGN

This cross-sectional survey is a cross-national empirical study of the relationship between democracy and globalization, which will explore the impact of globalization on democratization in Latin American countries.

The Sample

Our sample consists of Latin American countries as defined by the U.N. Economic Commission of Latin America and the Caribbean (with the exception of Cuba). This chapter looks at the case of Latin America, since the countries in this region share similar economic, social, historical, and cultural backgrounds. Within the common background of the former Spanish and Portuguese colonies, a great variety of types of government are observed. There are leftist and rightist regimes, and liberal governments as well as authoritarian ones. As Wiarda and Kline (1996) point out, "It is both the differences and the commonalities among the countries of the area that make Latin America such a fertile laboratory for studying comparative economic, social and political change."

Variables

As we mentioned earlier, there are few careful cross-national empirical analyses on the relationship between democracy and globalization (Gasiorowski 1995; Diamond, Linz, and Lipset 1989). One of the problems encountered is how to quantify the variables. Political rights (PR) and civil liberties (CL) will be used as indicators for the dependent variable (i.e., democracy). The term "democracy" has different meanings in different contexts, as the burgeoning debate about "Asian" versus "Western" models of democracy attests (Rowen 1995). To measure the Western liberal democracy, Freedom House annually assesses the actual status of political and civil rights in every nation of the world. By the Freedom House's (1996) definitions, political rights "enable people to participate freely in the political process," and civil liberties "are the freedoms to develop views, institutions, and personal autonomy apart from the state." By combining PR and CL, the Freedom House constructs a variable, PRCL. This variable indicates the aggregate level of political rights and civil liberties, running from 1 (most free/democratic) to 7 (least free/democratic) (see Table 9.1). The following is a list of the Freedom House index classifications of countries in Latin America (Freedom House 1996):

Average rating 1.5	Costa Rica
Average rating 2	Chile, Uruguay
Average rating 2.5	Argentina, Ecuador, Panama
Average rating 3	Bolivia, Brazil, El Salvador, Honduras, Venezuela
Average rating 3.5	Dominican Republic, Paraguay
Average rating 4	Colombia, Mexico, Nicaragua
Average rating 4.5	Guatemala, Peru
Average rating 5	Haiti

Table 9.1
Freedom House Index for Measuring Democracy

Classification	Political Rights and Civil Liberties Combined average ranking
Free	1–2.5
Partly Free	3–5.5
Not Free	5.5–7

Note: Countries with a 5.5 average are classified as either partly free or not free depending on which raw scores the overall ranking summarizes.

Globalization has been made possible by means of the establishment of worldwide information and communication networks. New telecommunications computer networks are overcoming the barriers of time and space, allowing corporate and financial interests to operate on a twenty-four-hour basis across the planet. Many see globalization in terms of the new possibilities opened up by global communications, global travel, and global products. Cultural globalization—associated with flows of media and communication, but also with flows of migrants, refugees, and tourists—has brought to the fore questions of cultural identity (Kuper and Kuper 1996).

In both academic and popular discourses, "globalization" has become one of the catch words of the 1990s. In fact, globalization is a short form for a cluster of related changes. Economic changes include the internationalization of production, the harmonization of tastes and standards, and the greatly increased mobility of capital and of transnational corporations. Ideological changes emphasize investment and trade liberalization, deregulation, and privatization. New information and communications technologies that shrink the globe signal a shift from goods to services. Finally, cultural changes involve trends toward a universal world culture and the erosion of the nation-state (Laxer 1995).

There are at least five different dimensions of globalization that need to be distinguished: economic globalization, political globalization, common ecological constraints, cultural values and institutions, and globalization of communications. The focus of this study is on the relationship between economic globalization and democratization.

Multiple indicators are used to measure economic globalization. The first indicator is openness to international trade (percentage of export/import in GNP). The second indicator is inflow of foreign capital (i.e., aggregate net resource flows [% of GNP]), which is the sum of net flows on long-term debt (excluding use of IMF credit), plus official grants (excluding technical assistance), net foreign direct investment, and net portfolio equity flows. The third indicator for globalization is the freedom to engage in capital (investment) transaction. In the rating, countries with fewer restrictions on this freedom are rated higher; 0 represents the most free and 10 the least free (Gwartney, Lawson, and Block 1996).

In addition to these three factors, economic development and education variables are included in our multivariate analysis because significant relationships have been found between the level of per capita income and education on the one hand and political development on the other (Lipset 1959). Data on economic development are readily available from different sources. Gross national product per capita and illiteracy rate will be used as indicators for economic development and education. We lagged the dependent variable one year/two years to reduce the problem of simultaneity and account for changes over time.

Hypotheses

Given the interrelationship between the economy and politics, globalization will produce significant political consequences and make the change of the political system inevitable. We may hypothesize that the globalization contributes to the closer integration of Latin American economies with international economies and hence has opened Latin American countries more widely to the impact of Western democratic values. This study will test some hypotheses in that regard. They include the following:

1. Increased level of foreign trade contributes to democracy.
2. Increased flow of foreign capital contributes to democracy.
3. Freer movement of foreign capital contributes to democracy.

The outcomes of the test will provide some answers in the controversy over the relationship between democratization and globalization.

Methods of Analysis

Although the hypotheses sound theoretically plausible, they must be tested on the basis of reliable evidence and a scrutiny of relevant historical experience and political theories. Concretely, the following research methods will be adopted to test the hypotheses: First, we utilize a multiple correlation model to explore the linkage between democracy and globalization. Correlation analyses are used to indicate the strength of hypothesized relations between democracy and indicators of globalization. Second, given various competing theories regarding globalization and democracy, and that globalization alone is not an explanatory variable for democracy, a multiple regression analysis is used to examine the hypothesized relationships.

RESULTS

Available data allowed us to establish the following crucial variables (by country): (1) political rights and civil rights, (2) openness, (3) foreign investment, (4) freedom to engage in capital transactions with foreigners, (5) GNP, and (6) education. Table 9.2 presents these data and documents the sources used. We conducted the tests of the hypotheses by calculating multiple correlation statistics. Our results appear in Table 9.3. An examination of the data reveals there are several statistically significant relationships.

Foreign Trade and Democratization

It is a common notion that integration with the international market often brings about social and political changes with it, because an open economy cannot avoid the persistent inflow of foreign ideas and trends. Technology that is being introduced and trade that is being exchanged carry democratic values with them. It appears that an open trade system is important to promote democracy in the region. Yet our review of the multiple correlation statistics suggests the lack of a statistically significant relationship between democratization and free trade.

As Barber (1992, 1996) has written, multinational corporations sometimes seem to prefer doing business with local oligarchs, inasmuch as they can take confidence from dealing with the boss on all crucial matters. Despots who slaughter their own populations are no problem, as long as they leave markets in place and refrain from making war on their neighbors. In trading partners, predictability is of more value than justice. In their recent studies on NAFTA and Mexico, Heredia (1994) and Barkin, Ortiz, and Rosen (1997) did not find any correlation between increasing percentage of foreign trade and increasing level of democratization in Mexico.

Foreign Investment and Democratization

Latin America has been one of the major investment areas of the international order. The relationship between direct foreign invest-

Table 9.2
Data for Selected Variables (by Country)

	PRCL	Openness	FI	FT	GNP	ED
Argentina	2.5	14.8	3.2	10	8860	4
Bolivia	3.0	40.4	9.0	5	2410	19
Brazil	3.0	16.5	1.8	0	5240	17
Chile	2.0	60.0	8.2	5	8410	5
Colombia	4.0	35.3	2.3	5	5480	9
Costa Rica	1.5	82.0	0.3	5	5480	5
Dominican Rep	3.5	64.5	1.0	5	3280	18
Ecuador	2.5	59.2	5.3	2	4350	10
El Salvador	3.0	42.8	1.9	5	2250	29
Guatemala	4.5	45.0	1.9	8	3330	44
Haiti	5.0	34.4	37.2	2	1046	55
Honduras	3.0	65.3	14.7	5	2000	27
Mexico	4.0	30.7	4.6	5	7300	10
Nicaragua	4.0	65.2	27.4	0	2790	34
Panama	2.5	75.6	8.4	10	5600	9
Paraguay	3.5	61.7	2.3	5	3390	8
Peru	4.5	22.4	7.7	8	3300	11
Uruguay	2.0	42.7	3.3	10	6070	3
Venezuela	3.0	54.3	0.9	5	8520	9

Sources: Freedom House, *Freedom in the World: The Annual Survey of Political Rights and Civil Liberties, 1995–1996* (New York: Freedom House, 1996). Ranking system was developed by Dr. Raymond Gastil and has been modified by current Freedom House staff. World Bank, *World Development Report, 1996* (Washington, D.C.: World Bank, 1997), and James Gwartney, Robert Lawson, and Walter Block, eds., *Economic Freedom of the World, 1975–1995* (Vancouver: Fraser Institute, 1996).

ments and the political, social, and economic conditions found in developing countries is one of the most hotly contested and frequently debated topics in the field of international political economy. Contrary to what neoliberals hold, the prediction that increased flow of foreign capital leads to democracy is not supported. Political and civil-rights violations increase along with the inflow of foreign investment ($r = 0.454$). There are at least two possible explanations for this fact. First, according to a recent study (Rothgeb 1996), the penetration of developing countries by multinational corporations leads to increased levels of domestic political conflict because it creates a degree of deprivation that at least some members of the local population find intolerable. Further, several studies (Heredia 1994; Rothgeb 1996) show that corporations' primary

Table 9.3
Multiple Correlation Coefficients (n = 19)

	PRCL	OP	FI	FT	GNP	ED
PRCL	1.000	-0.388	0.454*	-0.227	-0.496*	0.660**
OP	-0.388	1.000	0.029	-0.059	-0.124	-0.066
FI	0.454*	0.029	1.000	-0.402*	-0.483*	0.669**
FT	-0.227	-0.059	-0.402*	1.000	0.339	-0.375
GNP	-0.496*	-0.124	-0.483*	0.339	1.000	-0.713**
ED	0.660**	-0.066	0.699**	-0.375	-0.713**	1.000

Key: PRCL: Political Rights and Civil Liberties; OP: Open trade (exports + imports)/
GNP (Gross National Product); FI: Aggregate net resource flows (% of GNP) are
the sum of net flows on long-term debt (excluding use of IMF credit), plus official grants (excluding technical assistance), net foreign direct investment, and
net portfolio equity flows; FT: Freedom to engage in capital transactions with
foreigners; GNP: Per capita gross national product; ED: Illiteracy rate.

*Significance LE 0.05, one tailed-test; **significance LE 0.01, one tailed-test.

interest is in the markets, the work force, and the natural resources
that may be acquired in any particular country. For a long time,
external forces have been on the side of repression, both directly
and indirectly. Where democratic elections produced governments
that were hostile to Western interests, as in Guatemala and Cuba
in the 1950s and Chile in the 1970s, Western powers were quick to
subvert them and sustained their authoritarian successors. In sum,
driven by a preoccupation with maximizing returns, multinational
corporations are the primary agents of globalization, working
through control of information, markets, investment, final flows,
and employment practices. However, these multinational corporations are not the forces of democratization in Latin America.

Capital and Foreign Exchange Control
Liberalization and Democratization

Financial globalization has been proposed as the single most
important characteristic of the contemporary international political economy. Conventionally, this means that financial markets of

different nation-states are more integrated than ever before (Li and Smith 1997). In recent years, Latin American countries have removed various restrictions on capital movement across their borders. Contrary to neoliberal theory's predictions, our review of the multiple correlation statistics suggests the lack of a statistically significant relationship between democratization and freedom to engage in capital transactions with foreigners (FT).

Multiple Regression

Clearly, democracy and globalization also depend on other factors, such as education and economic development (Lipset 1959; Gasiorowski 1995; Muller 1988, 1995). As one can see from Table 9.3, income (r = –0.524) explains variations in democracy better than foreign trade and inflow of foreign capital. It is found that education was the most important variable in promoting democracy (r = 0.664). Of course, correlation may mask a spurious causal relationship, and variables other than ones we chose may be more powerful in explaining relationships among our variables. We utilize a regression model to explore the linkage between democracy and globalization. The following is the result of our multiple regression, with beta (standardized regression coefficient) in parentheses.

$$PRCL = a - 0.0187 \ OP + 0.0201 \ FT + 0.0017 \ FI - 0.00097 \ GNP + 0.297 \ EDU$$
$$(-0.398) \qquad (0.0657) \qquad (0.0185) \qquad (-0.250) \qquad (0.471)$$

The equation has a R^2 of 0.59972, and an F-ratio of 3.895, which is statistically significant at the 0.022 level. About 60 percent of improvement of political rights and civil liberties are explained by this equation. Technically speaking, a standardized regression indicates the relationship between independent and dependent variables in standard deviation units. In our model, a coefficient of 0.471 would indicate that for every increase of one standard deviation in education (X), PRCL (Y) increases by a 0.471 standard deviations when all other independent variables are held constant. With an increase of one standard deviation in open trade (OP), PRCL (Y) increases by a 0.398 standard deviations. With an increase of one standard deviation in GNP, PRCL (Y) increases by 0.25 standard deviations. It is clear that education, trade, and GNP explain more of the variation in democratization than FT (0.0657) and inflow of foreign capital (FI) (0.0185). It appears that the higher the level of socioeconomic development, the more popular support there is for a democratic change, and the more favorable social conditions are for democracy or consolidation of democracy (see Table 9.4).

Table 9.4
Results of Estimation

Independent Variable	Regression Coefficient	t
Intercept	3.883	0.0016
Open	-0.398071	-2.181
FI	0.018542	0.076
FT	0.065765	0.337
GNP	-0.250390	-0.966
ED	0.471201	1.548

Note: Dependent Variable: PRCL; Sample size: 19; F-Value: 3.89543; R^2: 0.59972; Adjusted R^2: 0.44546.

CONCLUSION

Democratization and globalization characterize Latin America in the last two decades. The potential interplay among democracy (political rights and civil liberties), globalization (increased level of foreign trade, foreign investment), economic development (GNP per capita) and human development (level of education) is great. Our study indicates that there is no significant relationship between free trade and democracy. Free and open market systems can coexist with authoritarian regions; countries such as Chile, Argentina, and Brazil under military control point to this conclusion. The multiple correlation results show that foreign private investment (the prime mover of globalization) and democracy are inversely related; that is, an increase of inflow of foreign investment tends to undermine democracy. Freedom to engage in capital transactions with foreigners has no association with political freedom. In other words, financial liberalization has no effect on the spread of democracy.

The analysis of regression modeling brings out an important conclusion: Economic globalization has little to do with democratization unless there is a high level of economic development and education. For a developing country, the key to democratization is economic development and education. Generally speaking, after the country becomes economically prosperous and its people become well educated, democratization will tend to grow naturally and stand firmly. In other words, integration with international markets can only add a helping hand if some of the preconditions, such as high level of economic development and education, are already there. Many studies (Coll 1997) have shown that the United States is no longer the same hegemonic power that it was during the most of the Cold War, when it was able to coerce and dictate the fate of many small Latin American and Caribbean nations. In short, that path to democracy was in the past, and today democracy is mainly shaped by internal factors and does not have much to do with globalization.

This study aims to be preliminary analysis on the complexity of the interactions between democratization and globalization. It incorporates only six main variables. The conclusions drawn here could be used as broad guidelines for further studies. Future studies could further investigate the relationships among other aspects of globalization, especially the effects of global communications and global travel on democratization.

APPENDIX:
OPERATIONAL DEFINITION OF ANALYTICAL VARIABLE

Dependent variables

1. PRCL.

Independent variables

2. Open openness (exports + imports)/GNP.
3. FI Aggregate net resource flows (% of GNP) are the sum of net flows on long-term debt (excluding use of IMF credit), plus official grants (excluding technical assistance), net foreign direct investment, and net portfolio equity flows.
4. FT (freedom to engage in capital transactions with foreigners).
5. GNP.
6. ED (illiteracy rate).

NOTE

The author acknowledges financial support from a Faculty Development Grant of Merrimack College in the completion of this project.

REFERENCES AND BIBLIOGRAPHY

Amin, S. 1987. "Democracy and National Strategy in the Periphery." *Third World Quarterly* 9: 1129–1156.
Barber, Benjamin. 1992. "Jihad vs. McWorld." *The Atlantic* 269 (3): 53–55, 58–63.

―――. 1996. *Jihad vs. McWorld: How Globalism and Tribalism Are Re-shaping the World.* New York: Ballantine Books.

Barkin, David, Irene Ortiz, and Fred Rosen. 1997. "Globalization and Re-sistance: The Remaking of Mexico." *NACLA Report on Americas* 30 (4): 14–27.

Bergsman, Joel, and Xiaofang Shen. 1995. "Foreign Direct Investment in Developing Countries: Progress and Problems." *Finance and Development* 21 (3) (December): 6–8.

Coll, Albert R. 1997. "United States Strategic Interests In Latin America: An Assessment." *Journal of Interamerican Studies and World Affairs* 39: 45–58.

Diamond, Larry. 1993. "The Globalization of Democracy." In *Global Transformation and the Third World*, ed. R. R. Slater, B. Schutz, and S. Dorr. Boulder, Colo.: Lynne Rienner.

Diamond, Larry, Juan J. Linz, and Seymour Martin Lipset, eds. 1989. *Democracy in Developing Countries.* Boulder, Colo.: Lynne Rienner.

Dos Santos, T. 1993. "Structure of Dependence." In *Development and Underdevelopment: The Political Economy of Inequality*, ed. M. A. Seligson and J. T. Passé-Smith. Boulder, Colo.: Lynne Rienner.

Feng, Yi. 1995. "Regime, Policy and Economic Growth: The Latin American Experience." *Growth and Change* 26: 77–104.

―――. 1996. "Does Economic Freedom Cause Political Freedom, Or the Other Way Around?" Paper presented at the annual meeting of the American Political Science Association, San Francisco, August 31, 1996.

Frank, A. G. 1984. *Critique and Anti-Critique: Essays on Dependency and Reformism.* Westport, Conn.: Praeger.

Freedom House. 1996. *Freedom in the World: The Annual Survey of Political Rights and Civil Liberties, 1995–1996.* New York: Freedom House. (This survey was started in 1973 by Gastil Raymond and updated annually by Karatnycky and the Freedom House Survey Team.)

Fukuyama, Francis. 1989. "The End of History." *National Interest* 16: 1–18.

―――. 1992. *The End of History and the Last Man.* New York: Penguin.

Gasiorowski, Mark J. 1995. "Economic Crisis and Political Regime Change: An Event History Analysis." *American Political Science Review* 89: 882–895.

"Globalization—To What End?" 1992a. Part 1. *Monthly Review* 43 (9): 1–18.

"Globalization—To What End?" 1992b. Part 2. *Monthly Review* 43 (10): 1–18.

Gwartney, James, Robert Lawson, and Walter Block, eds. 1996. *Economic Freedom of the World, 1975–1995.* Vancouver: Fraser Institute.

Heredia, Carlos A. 1994. "NAFTA and Democratization in Mexico." *Journal of International Affairs* 48: 13–38.

Huntington, Samuel. 1991. "A New Era in Democracy: Democracy's Third Wave." *Current*, September, 27–39.

―――. 1992. "How Countries Democratize." *Political Science Quarterly* 106: 579–616.

Huntington, Samuel, Myron Weiner, and Gabriel Almond. 1987. *Understanding Political Development: An Analytic Study.* New York: HarperCollins; and Boston: Little, Brown.

Inter-American Development Bank (IDB). 1997. *Economic and Social Progress in Latin America*. Baltimore: Johns Hopkins University Press.

Johnson, Bryan T., and Thomas P. Sheehy. 1996. *1996 Index of Economic Freedom*. Washington, D.C.: Heritage Foundation.

Kaufman, Robert R. 1979. "Industrial Change and Authoritarian Rule in Latin America: A Concrete Review of Bureaucratic–Authoritarian Model." In *The New Authoritarianism in Latin America*, ed. David Collier. Princeton: Princeton University Press.

Kelly, Janet. 1998. "Democracy Redux: How Real Is Democracy in Latin America." *Latin American Research Review* 33: 212–225.

Kennedy, Paul. 1996. "Globalization and Its Discontent." *New Perspectives Quarterly* 13 (4): 31–33.

Kuper, Adam, and Jessica Kuper, eds. 1996. *The Social Science Encyclopedia*. 2d ed. London: Routledge.

"Latin America's Backlash." 1996. *Economist*, 30 November, 19–20.

Laxer, Gordon. 1995. "Social Solidarity, Democracy and Global Capitalism." *Canadian Review of Sociology and Anthropology* 32: 287–313.

Li, Quan, and Dale L. Smith. 1997. "Liberalizing Capital Controls: Economic Pluralism or Political Institutions?" Paper presented at the annual meeting of the International Studies Association, Toronto, Canada, March 19, 1997.

Lipset, S. M. 1959. "Some Social Requisites for Democracy: Economic Development and Political Legitimacy." *American Political Science Review* 53: 69–105.

Mainwaring, Scott, and Timothy R. Scully, eds. 1995. *Building Democratic Institutions: Party Systems in Latin America*. Stanford, Calif.: Stanford University Press.

Messick, Richard, ed. 1996. *World Survey of Economic Freedom, 1995–96: A Freedom House Study*. New Brunswick, N.J.: Transaction Publishers.

Muller, Edward N. 1988. "Democracy, Economic Development, and Income Inequality." *American Sociological Review* 53: 50–69.

———. 1995. "Economic Determinants of Democracy." *American Sociological Review* 60: 966–983.

O'Donnell, G. A. 1973. *Modernization and Bureaucratic–Authoritarianism: Studies in South American Politics*. Berkeley: Institute of International Studies, University of California.

———. 1993. "The Browning of Latin America." *New Perspectives Quarterly* 10 (4): 50–54.

Osorio, Jaime. 1993. "Latin America: For a New Reinsertion in the World Economy." *Social Justice* 20 (3–4): 24–32.

Owens, Edgar. 1987. *The Future of Freedom in the Developing World: Economic Development as Political Reform*. New York: Pergamon Press.

Payne, Leigh A. 1994. *Brazilian Industrialists and Democratic Change*. Baltimore: Johns Hopkins University Press.

Pinkney, Robert. 1994. *Democracy in the Third World*. Boulder, Colo.: Lynne Rienner.

Remmer, K. 1991. "The Political Impact of Economic Crisis in Latin America in the 1980s." *American Political Science Review* 85: 777–800.

————. "Democratization in Latin America." In *Global Transformation and the Third World*, ed. R. R. Slater, B. Schutz, and S. Dorr. Boulder, Colo.: Lynne Rienner.

Robinson, Ian. 1995. "Globalization and Democracy." *Dissent* 43: 373–380.

Rothgeb, John M. 1996. *Foreign Investment and Political Conflict in Developing Countries*. Westport, Conn.: Praeger.

Rowen, Henry. 1995. "The Tide Underneath the 'Third Wave.'" *Journal of Democracy* 6: 52–64.

Silva, Eduardo. 1966. *The State and Capital in Chile: Business Elites, Technocrats, and Market Economics*. Boulder, Colo.: Westview Press.

Sunkel, Osvaldo. 1973. "Transnational Capitalism and National Disintegration in Latin America." *Social and Economic Studies* 22: 132–176.

Tabb, William. 1997. "Globalization Is an Issue, the Power of Capital Is the Issue." *Monthly Review* 49 (2): 20–30.

United Nations Development Program (UNDP). 1994. *Human Development Report*. New York: Oxford University Press.

Vanhanen, Tatu. 1997. *Prospects of Democracy: A Study of 172 Countries*. London: Routledge.

Wallerstein, I. 1982. "The Rise and Future Demise of the World Capitalist System: Concepts for Comparative Analysis." In *Studies on a Just World Order*. Vol. 1, *Toward a Just World Order*, ed. R. Falk, S. S. Kim, and S. H. Mendlovitx. Boulder, Colo.: Westview Press.

————. 1993. "Present State of the Debate on World Inequality." In *Development and Underdevelopment: The Political Economy of Inequality*, ed. M. A. Seligson and J. T. Passé-Smith. Boulder, Colo.: Lynne Rienner.

Wiarda, Howard J. 1995. *Latin American Politics: A New World of Possibility*. Belmont, Calif.: Wadsworth.

Wiarda, Howard J., and Harvey F. Kline, eds. 1996. *Latin American Politics and Development*. 4th ed. Boulder, Colo.: Westview Press.

Williamson, Jeffrey G. 1996. "Globalization, Convergence, and History." *Journal of Economic History* 56: 277–306.

Wood, Ellen Meiksins. 1997. "Globalization and Epochal Shifts: An Exchange." *Monthly Review* 48 (9): 21–31.

World Bank. 1996. *World Development Report, 1996*. Washington, D.C.: World Bank.

PART III

DECENTRALIZATION

Decentralization Politics and Policies

Dora Orlansky

DECENTRALIZATION: THE APPEAL OF A CONCEPT

Throughout most of this century, the general tendencies have been to invest increasing decision-making responsibility in the public sector and—during the first decades—to expand the centralization in the national government. But after the 1950s, the federal government's share of total government expenditures declined, mainly in relation of local governments; nevertheless, the network of grants or subsidies from higher levels of government to lower has made the situation more complex (Olson 1969; Oates 1977: 299–308). Proposals to shrink the scope of government activity have emerged in two broad ways: calls for decentralization and calls for privatization. The call for decentralizing responsibility promotes the shifting of power from the national government to cities and states, shrinking the scope of government activity by putting decision-making responsibility in the hands of smaller units of government. Advocates of privatization go farther, arguing that government authority should be reduced in the aggregate, not simply shifted among levels (Henig 1985).

With the 1970s' reversal in economic fortunes, critics of government became more numerous and their tone more strident. In the intellectual arena, the most potent were Hayek and Friedman, both of whom were economists with a grand vision for society. Hayek raised the issue of the centralized nature of socialism (collectivism, planning) against the decentralized nature of the competitive-market process. The fundamental point made by Hayek with regard to availability of economic information is its dispersion.[1] Hayek, who was perhaps the first to describe the competitive process as decentralized, believed that central planning was both politically dangerous and economically inefficient. It was politically dangerous because it reduced individual liberty, increased the power of the state, weakened the role of parliament, and undermined the rule of law by investing government officials with considerable discretion. Planning was economically inefficient because it dampened competition, increased the prevalence of monopolies, and suffocated entrepreneurialism. Friedman argued that slow economic growth and declining productivity called for a fundamental reassessment of the role of government in economic activity, and that continued government intervention at the expense of market competition threatened not only to destroy economic prosperity but also to reduce human freedom (Hurwicz 1969; Zifcak 1994).

Partly by fiscal concerns, partly by a strategy of conflict displacement, the configuration of subsystems (regions, Länder, states, departments, municipalities, etc.) and national government has attracted research attention, since the reallocation of tasks, financial resources, and political power between center and subsystems became a political issue. In this respect, parallelism in decentralization policies can be found between New Federalism in the United States as well as decentralization policies in unitary states like France, stressing both modernization goals and regional resistance as determinants of "changes in the vertical configuration." New Federalism policies of the 1980s redefined relationships between federal and local governments, including less national funding and a greater emphasis on local resources to meet the local needs; the number of services privatized by local governments increased sharply (Derlien 1992; Pouder 1996).

Prud'homme (1994: 2) attempted to give operational content to the concept of decentralization: "An ambiguous concept, its border not well defined; perhaps this ambiguity contributes to the appeal of the concept." *Spatial decentralization*, commonly called regional policy, is defined as a process of diffusing urban population and activities geographically away from large agglomerations. *Market decentralization*, or economic liberalization, is defined as a process of creating conditions in which goods and services are provided by market mechanisms rather than by government decision. *Administrative decentralization* is defined as the transfer of responsibility for planning, management, and the raising and allocation of resources from the central government and its agencies to field units of government agencies, subordinate units or levels of government, semiautonomous public authorities or area-wide corporations, regional or functional authorities or nongovernmental private or voluntary organization, and so on (Prud'homme 1994). On the other hand, administrative decentralization has taken a number of forms: *deconcentration* of functions within different offices of the central bureaucracy, *delegation* of semiautonomous or quasipublic corporations, *devolution* to local governments, and the transfer of functions to nongovernment organizations. Even decentralization may be implicit in the concept of *debureaucratization*; that is, decisions are allowed to be made through political processes that involve larger numbers of special interest groups, rather than exclusively or primarily by governments through legislation, executive decree, or administrative regulation (Rondinelli, Nellis, and Cheema 1984).

As Bennett (1994) pointed out, decentralization as a common theme crosscuts a wide variety of more specific processes. Chiefly, two different topics are included: (1) decentralization of government and (2) decentralization of decision processes to market and quasimarket solutions. These two subjects outline a twofold conceptualization of decentralization processes.

Decentralization in both market and government terms means grasping the opportunities of reform for all levels. Although not all services can be decentralized in administration, or charged for, or removed from local political decision, there is considerably greater scope in most countries than is used at present. It could be defined rather as a complex mix of private and public–private relationships that do not need representation (or government) in a formal sense, but instead need to focus on customer choices (Bennett 1994).[2] It is becoming clear that the greater the extent of decentralization to the market, the less need there is for complex government and representative structures. Generally, the higher the degree of market decentralization, the fewer tiers are required and the more government at local level can be consolidated into functions that can be performed by individual (unitary) local authorities. For example, this underlies the move in the United Kingdom toward unitary councils. It can be further encouraged by removing the finance of some functions to central government (especially education), giving other functions to districts, and allowing the market a greater role in other functions (Bennett 1994).

What determines the demand for centralization or decentralization of the government service and policy complex in different countries? The dimension in which a decentralization of the government complex is desired seems to be determined basically by the following conditions: (1) The larger the population, the smaller will be the demand for centralization; (2) the degree of centralization varies inversely with the geographical extension of a country; (3) the higher the wealth of a country measured in per capita income, the more likely is a marked decentralization; (4) the higher the degree of income inequality, the stronger the demand for decentralized choice; and (5) political and institutional constraints are factors in the sense that less demand for decentralization is to be expected insofar as autonomous groups are integrated or accepted in the political arena (Oates 1977: 299–308).

THE CENTRALIZATION–DECENTRALIZATION CONTINUUM

Decentralization represents both a reaction from below to a previously strong political control from the center, and a quest from above to advance the privatization of the economy and to alleviate the intricate fiscal situation of the central government. How services and goods are provided by various levels of government and who pays for them are questions that have an impact throughout the economy. Thus, political decentralization has been paralleled by decentralization of fiscal responsibilities. The basic underlying idea is obviously an attempt to free local governments from central control, based on the hypothesis that this would promote local democracy and make for more efficient local government. From that perspective, one of the main objectives of decentralization is increased efficiency and effectiveness of economic and social development programs. Technical arguments in favor of decentralization normally emphasize such benefits as reduction of overload and congestion in the channels of administration and communications, timely reaction to unanticipated problems that inevitably arise during implementation, improved technical capacity to deliver services at field levels, and improved administrative and managerial capacity. Decentralization is also seen as having potential to improve the efficiency of local government by subjecting its actions to the scrutiny of the local electorate by both the articulation of demands and responses for public services (Bird and Wallich 1994; Silverman 1992).[3]

But increased efficiency is only one reason behind the demand. In some countries, decentralization may be part of the political strategy of ruling elites to keep most of their power by resigning some of it. For instance, free elections may be held at the local level before they are held at the national level in an attempt by new political forces to consolidate a still fragile power (Prud'homme 1994). In Poland and Hungary, for instance, the local governments were established in their present form in 1990, in Romania, Bulgaria, and

Russia in 1991, and in Albania in 1992. Although the extent to which real decentralization now taking place in the transitional countries of Eastern and Central Europe differs from country to country, the process of political and fiscal decentralization affects almost all of the crucial aims of reform, including macroeconomic stabilization, the effectiveness of the social safety net, private-sector development, and—as in the case of Russia—even nation building (Bird and Wallich 1994).

How taxing, spending, and regulatory functions are allocated among governments and how intergovernmental transfers are structured are questions of fundamental importance to the efficient and equitable provision of public goods (Shah 1994). There seems to be a consensus (the "New Fiscal Federalism")[4] on the proposition that the primary responsibility for macroeconomic stabilization policies and for the redistribution of income and wealth must rest with the central government; decentralization makes redistributive policies, whether interpersonal or interjurisdictional, more difficult if not impossible.[5] The federal government should concentrate on a particular set of missions, including interaction with the rest of the world, strengthening social insurance, and contributing to national saving by running a surplus in the unified federal budget.[6] States should have much clearer responsibility for most kinds of public investment, especially for improving the skills of the labor force and upgrading public infrastructure. This line of reasoning suggests devolution to the states of federal spending programs for education, housing, training, and most other types of investment, a move that clarifies which level of government is accountable for performance in these areas and makes a federal surplus easier to achieve (Rivlin 1991). The presumption in favor of the federal solution— that is, the decentralized provision of public services in response to local demands (not uniform among different communities)—is based on two necessary conditions: the absence of spillover effects and of any economies of scale (Oates 1977).

The Tiebout model, in contrast to Samuelson's allegations concerning the inefficiencies resulting from decentralized choice for public goods, showed that for a particular class of public goods (those whose consumption is restricted to a specific geographical area) individual choice can, at least in principle, generate an efficient outcome: "The economic rationale for a federal system is to be found in the capacity of decentralized government units to improve resource allocation in the public sector through the diversification of public outputs in accordance with local tastes" (Oates 1977: 9).

On the contrary, a unitary form of government (i.e., a single or multitiered government in which effective control of government functions rests with the central government) facilitates centralized decision making to further national unity objectives. It places a greater premium on uniformity and equal access to public services. In China during the 1980s, subnational governments secured a significant degree of autonomy from the central government; as a result, China maintains the legal structure of a unitary form of government but is considered a decentralized federation (Shah 1994; Kuo 1994).

The need for centralization based on economic and administrative rationales has been emphasized more often in the case of Korea than in other countries, because the Korean government has stressed national security and economic growth as ultimate national goals. To achieve national security and economic growth effectively, it has been argued that it is necessary to centralize the direction of the economy and coordinate at the national level the development of extremely scarce resources, especially capital technology and skilled personnel. Thus, the greater the involvement of the national government in the economy and in security, the less the decentralization in Korea (Jung 1991).[7]

FROM UNITARY TO DECENTRALIZED STATE— AND VICE VERSA

Decentralization is both a process by which organizations move power from the center to subunits and an attribute which shows the degree of autonomy exercised by the subunits. Decentralization describes the process of change to a new decentralized (or more decentralized) system of government and refers also to the state that results from this process (Prud'homme 1994; Bennett 1994).

Political interest in the issue of decentralization (as against centralization) entered the eighteenth-century debate concerning laissez-faire versus state-imposed restrictions, as well as the nineteenth-century controversies concerning the feasibility and desirability of socialism (Hurwicz 1969). An increasing centralization results from the extension of the spatial limits for costs and benefits of public activities, the growing demand for a more active redistribution policy (especially in more economically developed countries), and the mandate (often a constitutional mandate) for the central government to guarantee the provision of certain goods and services all over the country (Oates 1977: 299–308): "Centralization goes on in a spirit of progress over the putative recalcitrance, corruption, and prejudice of the traditional local authorities" (Meyer and Scott 1983: 205). Changes in this spirit are often designed to maximize legitimation problems; they are accompanied by bureaucratic regulations designed to conflict with other levels of authority. For example, American centralization in recent decades has been built around the assumption that local authorities have exercised their authority illegitimately to mistreat minorities and the poor (in education, employment, social services, police administration, and so on), to succumb to illicit special interest (in air and water pollution), to ignore the collective good in a host of ways, and to display general incompetence (Meyer and Scott 1983). Central government's involvement is justified to ensure horizontal equity and minimum standards of service (health, education, social insurance) in all jurisdictions (Shah 1994).

Ideological opposition to regional government has historically come from a variety of sources. One of the most ubiquitous, the Jacobin philosophy, is a French invention, a "nineteenth century caricature of the spirit of the revolution" based on the idea that democracy, far from demanding decentralization, requires centralized government. Diversity and pluralism are seen as corroding the national sovereignty. From a universalistic perspective of citizenship, the provinces have been seen as bastions of archaic social order (Keating 1988).

The recent regional devolution process in France (1981–1986) transferred executive powers to locally elected representatives, reduced those of the prefects (since the time of Napoleon Bonaparte), and abolished referral procedures for Paris approval of local decisions.[8] Mayors and other regional authorities were empowered to commit funds and make policy (Claisse 1989). According to Fortin (1989), as a result of decentralization, the French administrative system appears very complex, even overloaded. There are cumbersome multilayered administrative systems: the central administration, their field services, the prefectures, the regions, the departments, and the communes, and each of them has a head with his own powers. "The proliferation of new *de jure* and *de facto* powers sometimes savors of a new feudal system" (Fortin 1989: 106). Furthermore, experience shows that by emphasizing the elective nature of local leaders, decentralization has accentuated the politization of career officials.

In fact, distinction between federalism and regional devolution is of little more than formal significance, since regional government serves to create a new locus of political power. Moreover, in both federalism and regional devolution, the independent exercise of constitutionally separated functions have brought about interdependence, collaboration, and conflict patterns.

Whereas other countries in Western Europe responded to the turbulence of the environment since the mid-1970s by decentralization—as in France, Spain, and Italy—the United Kingdom experienced centralization. In effect, the central–local network began to deteriorate in the political context of economic and fiscal pressures. The 1979 Conservative government centralization policy toward local government emerged partly as the unintended by-product to control public expenditure, and the result of a succession of measures seeking to curb local government spending and other resistance from local government (i.e., to shift the boundaries between public and private, to promote market processes over planning techniques, and to assert the principle of consumer sovereignty).[9] The collective character of local services was seen as an obstacle to the government's objective of expanding the sphere of market relations. Thus, the status of local government in the British polity has been deeply changed by the central government's increased power over local governments' expenditures and taxation, the elimination of elections and of councils, and the transference of local government functions and their reallocation either to appointed boards or, even better, to the market.[10] "What was new was the government's interpretation of the meaning of the term unitary state. It changed its meaning to governmental supremacy not parliamentary" (Jones 1988: 168). Parliament has traditionally viewed local government as a policy-making institution and not as an executive agent of central government. But conventional precepts and practices ("folk law") were supplanted by positive law ("jurist law"). A process of juridification associated with a shift toward redefining the central–local government relationship has restructured the central–local relationship as being a formal, rule-determined relationship of superior and inferior (Jones 1988; Loughlin 1996).

THE SUBSIDIARITY PRINCIPLE

Federalism has historically been a centralizing measure to draw together different territories, and not the shifting away from a central government. In the case of European Union (EU) membership, based upon the principle of subsidiarity, the assignment of responsibilities—taxing, spending, and regulatory functions—should be exercised by lower levels of government unless a convincing case can be made for assigning these to higher levels of government. Subsidiarity is controversial, because it not only strikes at the heart of the most pressing, intricate, and interrelated issues and dilemmas of cooperation between political and administrative institutions of local, national, and supranational governments, but also pertains to perceptions of the relationship between political authority and civil society. The concept of subsidiarity is linked to important debates in political theory dealing with the relationship between the state and the individual, between different levels of government, and between state and society (Shah 1994; Blichner and Sangolt 1994).

The concept of subsidiarity comes from at least three main roots (Blichner and Sangolt 1994). First, in Catholic social doctrine, Pius XI, in the early 1930s, defined subsidiarity as the state delegation of social functions inside a perfect structured hierarchical polity (Encíclicas Papales 1991). As early as 1891, Leo XIII (in *Rerum Novarum*) had given the first indications of a Catholic approach to subsidiarity against the background of both a "threatening socialism and rampant economic liberalism." Furthermore, "though social philosophy and natural law both condemn as false these basic principles of liberalism, this should not lead us," Leo XIII wrote, "into the opposite error defining society as part of the state and letting the state submerge society" (Blichner and Sangolt 1994: 286–287). Subsidiarity as a key concept in a continental and Catholic model of the welfare state is at odds with the Scandinavian conception of the welfare state (Blichner and Sangolt 1994).

Second, in a wider European utilization, the concept has been deconfessionalized and also related to the discussion of federalism. British conservatives have seen the principle of subsidiarity as a way of avoiding detailed and unnecessary EC regulations. The basic argument is that at any level of government centralization should only take place if a task cannot be accomplished by lower levels.

Third, neoconservatives have used the concept of subsidiarity in their critique of the welfare state.[11] From this perspective, the concept of subsidiarity is connected to liberal philosophy accentuating individual freedom and minimal state intervention. The state should only act in situations where the market fails, because of the core argument that state provision of welfare intrudes on and suffocates the institutions of civil society. The charge that unresponsive government bureaucracies displace the mutual-aid activities of families and communities has long been a favorite of conservatives. However, the problem of intrusive and aggrandizing state bureaucracy has moved to the forefront of left concerns as well, and a "sloganized problem has produced a sloganized solution": decentralization of programs and incorporation of schemes of community participation in their administrations (Fox Piven 1993).

NEW FEDERALISM AS A CONSERVATIVE PANACEA

The subsidiarity strategy has been the fiscal counterpart of the fundamental conservative opposition and hostility to redistributive policies. Based on skepticism about government activism, it basically leaves to private initiative all the functions that individuals can perform privately, and only adversely turns to the levels of government closest to the community (localities and states) to address public needs, with federal action as a last resource; federal government should be reserved for those needed functions that only the national government can undertake.

But federalism and decentralization reform agendas could be very different in both their aims and their political outcomes. A crescendo path in state retrenchment can be found from Eisenhower to the Bush administration, which coined the phrase, "confusing banner of empowerment to increase local participation" (Fox Piven 1993). The Eisenhower sorting-out strategy consisted of the decentralization shift to state and local governments of certain functions along with the resources to finance them. Nixon viewed his federalism approach as a means of improving and strengthening government, especially at the state and local levels. It was a shifting course of conservative ideology, a decentralizing approach, but not an intended antigovernment path toward dismantling it. By the Nixon consolidation (blocking) fiscal policy, resources would remain centralized, but would be used to finance decentralized functions. The notion was to have the federal government do what it does best (levy taxes) and to have state and local governments do what they do best (administer local spending). New Federalism reforms were needed to close the gap between promise and performance. Yet if the goal of improved performance required nationalizing certain shared or local functions such as welfare or environmental regulation in order to rationalize the financing and delivery of public services, Nixon accepted that conclusion (Beer 1988; Conlan 1988).

Reagan, in a different way, conceived New Federalism as part of a broader strategy to cut the federal budget and to reduce the role of government in society at every level. The major focus of this retrenchment program, of course, was the federal government, and his eloquence on this subject was often extreme. By the devolution (turnbacks) strategy of Reagan, functions would be discontinued and in that sense decentralized, but would not get federal financial assistance. The reduced role for the federal government would by itself mean an enhanced role for state and local government. The Reagan administration gave concrete expression to the emerging theory of "competitive federalism" being developed by conservative "public choice" economists, a theory that applauds interjurisdictional competition in a federal system as an instrument for controlling governmental activism. This vision, though heavily localistic, lacks a strong role for government of any kind. This quest for com-

munity emphasizes "voluntarism, the mobilization of private group-
ings to deal with our social ills" (Conlan 1988).

According to Massey (1993), the subnational government refor-
mation in the United Kingdom and the United States was based on
the creed that the private sector is intrinsically dynamic and superior to public institutions for the delivery of goods and services,
and that market efficiency is the appropriate principle of social
performance in practically all spheres of community activity. President Reagan and an administration opposed to government per se
began an era of New Federalism. The president sought to give back
to the states matters best left to them, and his budget proposal for
fiscal year 1982 included federal program cuts that limited central-
government intervention in subnational issues. In the United Kingdom, the election of Mrs. Thatcher meant a concerted effort to
transform the culture of local government through the concept of
leverage (imported from America).

Thus, public–private partnership, local capacity building, citizen empowerment, deregulation, and so on are concepts that were
carried across from the United States to Britain and other countries. The policy-borrowing process may sometimes be no more than
the borrowing of a general idea, not the specific design (Wolman
1992). Yet in contrast to the United States—although an analogue
decentralization discourse—there was in Britain a centralization
of control.[12] The different approaches partly reflected the different
political cultures; America's separation of powers and the federal
principle make centralization and executive dominance parts of a
political reflex of the policy-making elites (Massey 1993). Liberalization reforms took place upon the subnational governments giving the central government powers to order local authorities to sell
land and property, forcing through a major policy of privatization.
Political arguments were based on the importance of consumers'
empowerment, free business as a remedy against unnecessary bureaucracy, and the promotion of greater accountability onto
subnational governments. The conservative policy panoplia reduced
the "role and importance of the state as the guardian of community
interests" (Barnekov, Boyle, and Daniel 1989: 11).

DECENTRALIZATION WAVE IN PUBLIC ADMINISTRATION

Decentralization is one of the recurrent notions in New Public
Management (NPM) discussions and it covers at least three different types of transfer of authority and power. There are basically
two types of vertical decentralization: hierarchical decentralization
(deconcentration), which implies the passing of decision making

down to lower levels; and the process of devolution or delegation, both "more radical" insofar as the decisional authority is given to a separate and previously subordinate or an independent agency, respectively. On the other hand, horizontal decentralization is defined as "the extent to which non-managers—professionals, clerks, and even customers—control decision processes" (Mintzberg 1979; see also Prud'homme 1994; Pollitt 1995). In addition, functional decentralization, a more complex administrative reform process, implies the splitting of different functions into core services, support services, and commercial services, and the delegation of certain functions to the private sector, ad hoc boards, nongovernmental organizations (NGOs), and so on. It brings about delegating budgetary control, responsibility, and accountability down the organizational hierarchy.

Since bureaucratic rigidity and inefficiency are often attributed to excessive centralization, decentralization reforms in the public sector have become a worldwide instrumental trend in both developed and developing countries for liberating managerial potential. They took place for a decade in the United Kingdom after the election of the Conservative government to power in 1979. Thus, delegation was one of the topics of the British program of Financial Management Initiative, though decentralization in government is a difficult task because "administrators at top levels fear a loss of control." They perceive conflicts between the implications of increased delegation of authority and the requirements of public accountability.[13] The publication of *Improving Management in Government: The Next Steps* (Efficiency Unit 1988) and *Beyond Next Steps: A Civil Service for the 21st Century* (Kemp 1993) indicated the determination of the British government to persist in the purpose. In the United States, the move to decentralize the public service originated from the legislation of the 1978 Civil Service Reform Act. The most extensive devolution of human-resource management has occurred in New Zealand (State Sector Act in 1988 and the Public Finance Act in 1989) and Sweden, where the policies are to minimize the involvement of central-management bodies in the human-resource management activities of departments and agencies. There has also been substantial devolution in Australia, where more central control has been retained (over pay and conditions of service, employment structures, etc.) than in the cases of New Zealand and of Sweden, and keeping basically the same personnel-management principles across the Australian public service. Significant devolution has also taken place in Denmark, The Netherlands, and the United Kingdom. Elsewhere, decentralization and devolution are more limited, and for several other Organization for Economic Cooperation and Development (OECD) countries (e.g., Japan), these reforms do not appear to be a priority (Metcalfe and Richards 1990; Lam 1996; OECD 1996).

Based on different authors (Massey 1995; Overman and Boyd 1994; Pollitt 1990; Dunleavy and Hood 1994; Hughes 1994; Osborne and Gabler 1994) Lam (1996) summarized the most significant aspects of reforms in public administration in the following items:

1. Reforms have to be analyzed as the expressions of a turning point in the paradigm of public administration from a classical Weberian to a "post-bureaucratic model."

2. The traditional spirit of public service has been replaced by a suggestive managerialism.

3. The post-bureaucratic paradigm of public administration consists of "entrepreneurial, customer driven, market oriented; supported on managerial rather than political leadership; results directed, strategic and anticipatory."

4. Thus, "administration" has transformed into management in the public sector.

5. A set of similar administrative doctrines dominate the agenda of public administration in many countries and introduce innovations coming from practice and from the private sector, through a consultant- and practitioner-driven movement.

6. The essential components of New Public Management innovations include the reduction of bureaucratic hierarchies and rules, the identification of the costs of inputs and outputs, the use of contracts for the provision of public services, the introduction of purchaser/provider distinctions through desegregating organizations and their functions, the increase of provider competition, and the increase of consumer power through enhanced scope for exit and redress.

Decentralization in public administration is an important issue under NPM. And "it is not only an administrative matter but a political issue as well" (Lam 1996). On the one hand, it involves more empowerment of subunits of the government or subgovernment levels—regional, state, or municipal devolution—or delegation to other agencies outside the government (deregulation, privatization, contracting out, etc.). On the other hand, the elected government members are expected to exercise closer scrutiny and to exert greater political pressure (i.e., politization) over the administration.

As the principle of delegation of authority means more power and autonomy given to subunits (territorial or functional), it might imply lesser control and lesser responsibility assumed by the central government (Lam 1996). But according to Peters and Savoie (1995: 77), "While several ideological and theoretical forces appear to be thrusting government organizations toward greater autonomy and diminished control from the center, others at the same time appear to be demanding a reassertion of that control." The "coordination and empowerment conundrum" refers to the two alternative and conflictive dimensions of administrative reform: (1) NPM leads to the fragmentation and decentralization of ministerial structures into smaller agencies and the empowerment of lower-echelon employees, a "deregulated" government, while (2) the increasing fiscal problems press for much more central control and coordination of public policies and programs across a diversity of ministries and agencies.[14]

FINAL COMMENTS:
THE CASE OF LATIN AMERICAN COUNTRIES

In contemporary territorial politics, the relations between national and subnational governments can no longer be seen in terms of hierarchical subordination (as in an absolute unitary setting), or indifference (as in a "pure" federal system); rather, they must be understood as reciprocal exchange of possibilities for action, just as in functional politics.[15] Centralization and decentralization in organizational design can be mixed in ways that do not require a rigid division between policy on the one hand and operations on the other, with the former centralized and the latter decentralized. Rather, there can be a "tight–loose configuration," whereby mutual adjustments constitute the norm for decision making and thus organizational coordination (Aucoin and Bakvis 1988).

But in fact, a mixed-motive game based on both conflict and cooperation develops within intergovernmental interactions; negotiating and compromising therefore become the only possible modus vivendi (Parri 1990). As Sbragia (1996: 219) pointed out for the federal system, in a decentralized setting, "roles and responsibilities can never be completely fixed or defined. They are constantly being challenged by one governmental unit or another. The options available to any single government are typically unclear enough so that officials from any unit may find it worthwhile to push against the boundaries." Decentralization goes on in a spirit of suspicion and delegitimation of the center. In the long run, such processes are certainly absorbed in routinized institutionalization. In the short run, they originate large numbers of legitimation conflicts (Meyer and Scott 1983). Decentralization as federalism, "far from being a static property, packages the conflict between governments. Governments *qua* institutions must be thought of as political actors— as politicians. Territorial units rather than functionally organized interests are central to the analysis" (Sbragia 1996: 220).

By the late 1970s, decentralization gained widespread support around the world as the proposed solution to longstanding problems of public-sector efficiency and equity. Throughout Latin America, there have been numerous experiences of decentralized governments giving specific meaning to the phrase "closer to the people" (Peterson 1997). In effect, the World Bank has been engaged in the decentralization movement, based on the widely held assumption that bringing government decision making closer to the citizenry increases public-sector accountability and therefore effectiveness (Prud'homme 1994: 3). "This influential approach considers decentralization to be the appropriate mechanism for reforming the provision of public goods such as health, education, and targeted poverty reduction programs."

The move toward decentralization of government responsibilities as well as resources through fiscal transfers to provincial and local governments has not been restricted to countries such as Argentina and Brazil, which operate under federal structures. Chile and Colombia, unitarian structures, have also pursued decentralization programs. The objective is to strengthen service delivery at the local level, and to increase participation in the development process (Rowat 1996). Since benefits accrue mainly to residents of separate jurisdictions, such services would be better provided by subnational governments (Shah 1994).[16]

"The wave of enthusiasm for decentralization has been encouraged by its conceptual compatibility with decentralized mechanisms of productive resource allocation associated with free markets" (Fox and Aranda 1996: 1). However, just as many kinds of market failure can inhibit the private sector's productive efficiency, authoritarian and/or bureaucratic concentrations of power at local and state levels can hamper decentralization from accomplishing increased public-sector efficiency and accountability.

How to avoid heightening interregional inequalities as a result of decentralization is another important question. So is ensuring that decentralization does not result in capture of benefits by local elites or in devolution with power retention by central elites. This and related political-economy questions—for example, the relations of local governments to local community organization and/or NGOs—loom large in this area (Rowat 1996; Prud'homme 1994).

The international development-policy mainstream increasingly accepts that governance issues must be taken into account to make development-policy reforms effective. But decentralization as a framework for governance cannot by itself ensure more effective citizen participation in civil life or higher standards of public accountability. Where local administrative capacity and institutions are weak, decentralization alone cannot be expected to incorporate the voice of the citizenry and to provide the institutional, political, and economic basis for future regional growth and development. Frequently, not enough attention has been paid to the needs (and process) of strengthening institutional capacity at the local level in order to accomplish newly devolved responsibilities; little is known about what happens if decentralization precedes the institutional changes required at the state and local levels.

Decentralization in the public sector is conceived as a sign of decreasing commitment. It implies the loss of control over subgovernments or subunits in the implementation of policy and allocation of resources. As administrative and financial autonomy is granted to subunits, the center might have less influence over the subunits and be less able to account for their performance. As a consequence, the problems of administrative confusion, irrational use of resources, conflicting or redundant policies, and poor coordination might arise (Lam 1996). Proliferation of government agencies has led to compartmentalization and lack of complementarity, which have further weakened the administrative capacities of local agencies.

There is still an absence of coordination between revenues and responsibilities, and countries need to explore what further efforts would be required to ensure that local governments have the resources proportionate with the new responsibilities assigned to them. Instances abound where innovative decentralization programs were centrally created, but not linked to established local organizations and sources of political and financial support. Authority is commonly delegated to local organizations, but they are not given the resources to perform their new functions. Another serious problem has been the untimely and inadequate release of allocated funds. Often the funds that are allocated to local governments are not all distributed. Finally, care must be taken to avoid overlending by state banks that undermines central governments' efforts at budget discipline (Rondinelli, Nellis, and Cheema 1984); it makes macroeconomic stabilization more difficult to achieve, because subnational government fiscal policies can run counter to national policies.

More local is not always better.[17] Insofar as local structures are not indeed democratized, decentralization is one of the means for local political elites to become more powerful via patronage and clientelism. The goal is to decide the most adequate level of government for social-policy decentralization (regional, state, municipality, etc.), and taking into account the heterogeneity of the subgubernmental units. The cases of small and rural local governments are especially difficult, because of different issues (institutional weakness, economies of scale involved in many activities, authoritarian *caciquism*, etc.) (Fox and Aranda 1996).

Another crucial point is that although many observers see the need for generating vastly increased local revenues (through taxation, charges, user fees, and sales), the prospects for this seem rather uncertain, or at least long term. Some of the more common arrangements are portions of national taxes, or the whole of certain nationally imposed and collected taxes are specified for the exclusive use of state and (or) local governments. Frequently, the central Ministry of the Interior directly subsidizes budget deficits of the subnational units and central ministries provide grants for local infrastructure development. Banks or quasibank authorities contribute with loans and grants for capital projects. Funds derived from international assistance agencies are channeled toward subnational units of greatest need or potential. The usual transfer of resources rather than the real power to self-generate resources has been the rule (Rondinelli, Nellis, and Cheema 1984).

The benefits of decentralization in allocative efficiency are not as obvious as suggested by the standard theory of fiscal federalism, and might carry a cost in terms of production efficiency. Moreover, the problem is not so much whether a certain service should be provided by a central, regional, or local government; the real challenge is how to organize the joint production of the service since it has to be cooperatively provided. The incapacity of local agencies to coordinate and integrate their activities with those of central ministries has been one of the main factors that has dramatically hindered the successful implementation of decentralization policies (Prud'homme 1994; Fox and Aranda 1996). In sum, the empirical evidence and the perspectives of local governments in Latin American countries to improve development outcomes has certainly fallen behind the enthusiasm for the decentralization credo.

NOTES

An earlier version of this chapter was prepared for presentation at the Seventeenth World Congress of the International Political Science Association, 17–21 August 1997, Seoul, Korea.

UBACYT CS003 Research Grant and René H. Thalmann (UBA) Research Fellowship. Instituto de Investigaciones Gino Germani, Facultad de Ciencias Sociales, Universidad de Buenos Aires, Junin 1431 #9/A, 1113 Buenos Aires, Argentina. Tel & Fax (+541) 806 7327. dora@orlans.fsoc.uba.ar

1. "A simple way of visualizing this dispersion is to assume that, at least, at the beginning of the allocative process, each economic unit has perfect information concerning itself" (Hurwicz 1969).

2. The most common cases are refuse collection, direct building and maintenance works, public housing, college-based training, primary health care, and some fields of education and personal social services (Bennett 1994).

3. It might be inferred from rational-choice theory that smallness in numbers would encourage participation. The political situation would have to be such as to permit the rational, calculating citizen to believe, for instance, that his or her vote might well break a tie or that the circle of acquaintances whom he or she could influence was large enough to swing an election. The evidence, however, does not support this hypothesis that smallness encourages participation. On the contrary, the turnout for local elections is generally very low when compared with the turnout for national elections (Beer 1977).

4. New Fiscal Federalism is defined as the political economy of multi-level government in both its financial and nonfinancial aspects, based on the need for a separate government institution for every collective good with a unique boundary, so that there can be a match between those who receive the benefits of a collective good and those who pay for it (Beer 1977; FIEL 1993; López Murphy 1995).

5. Among political economists, it is a commonplace to say that in a modern society the redistribution function must be performed by the central government. As Oates (1977) points out, an aggressive policy of income redistribution from rich to poor in a particular locality will very probably chase away the relatively few wealthy and attract the less prosperous.

6. It should also be emphasized that the term "federalism"—territorial allocation of authority secured by constitutional guarantees (Beer 1988)—is not to be understood in a narrow constitutional sense. In economic terms, all government systems are more or less federal; even in a formally unitary system, for example, there is typically a considerable extent of de facto fiscal discretion at decentralized levels. Instead of being dichotomously federal or nonfederal, governments vary along some multidimensional spectrum in the degree to which fiscal decision making is decentralized. In a *cooperative federalism* model, various levels of government have overlapping and shared responsibilities, and all levels are treated as equal partners in the federation; in *dual federalism,* fiscal tiers are organized so that national and state governments have independent authority in their areas of responsibility and act as equal partners (Oates 1977; Shah 1994).

7. According to Jung (1991: 15), "Centralization in Korea, therefore, may be seen as a product of the coalition between the state and the emerging economic forces that benefit from expansion of the central state machine."

8. "Ces consensus en faveur d'une décentralisation politique et administrative contraste nettement avec la situation britanique" (Mazey 1994: 232).

9. Paradoxically, the Conservative Party has been seen as the traditional defender of decentralization by opposition to the Labour Party focused on national priorities and central planning.

10. From 1986 onward, local authorities were to be compelled, whether they wanted to or not, to put out to competitive tender contracts for activities usually carried out by their own employees, such as refuse collection, the cleaning of streets and buildings, catering (especially school meals), the upkeep of public parks, and vehicle maintenance, with provision for future "privatization" of architectural, engineering, surveying, and computing services.

11. The principle of subsidiarity was one of the premises of the neoliberal economic model of Chile's military junta under Pinochet (1973–1990), as well as Argentina's military process while Martinez de Hoz (1976–1980) was the minister of economy. In both cases, the concept of subsidiarity encompassed both the Catholic and the neoconservatist background; ideological roots might likely be found in the German and the Austrian affinities to Catholic theology and social philosophy.

12. However, Kettl (1983: 171) pointed out that, in the United States, "especially through Nixon's and Reagan's reforms, and nevertheless a powerful rhetoric advocating state and local autonomy, there has been a growing tide toward a stronger federal role, even in decisions that once were the predominant province of state and local governments."

13. British ministers are personally responsible to Parliament for what happens in their departments.

14. Administrative reforms such as Next Steps agencies in the United Kingdom and Special Operating Agencies in Canada promote not only decentralization but the inclusion of the private sector to provide public services. "Every recent effort to enhance decentralization however has foundered in the centralization maelstrom, the turbulent whirlpool of national politics that draws power to Washington. Most often that maelstrom is fed by the irresistible lure of federal grants and the assumption, based on old prejudices, that state and local governments have neither the administrative capacity nor the political will to serve their citizens on their own" (Kettl 1987).

15. In the words of Ashford (1982), even the French subsidy system and the U.S. categorical grant system could not be considered the "oppressive system of an overcentralized government, . . . but the cement which holds the system together," allowing, through the connected "territorial political exchange," the partial satisfaction of both the national and subnational policy desiderata.

16. In 1922, Webb defined the "the cash nexus" (Loughlin 1996).

17. The case of decentralization rests on the basic principles of U.S. fiscal federalism, its institutions, and its practices, which are not necessarily suitable for all developing countries. Many studies (Gershberg [1993] in Mexico; Graham [1994] in West Bengal and Nepal) suggest that devolving project-funding decision making to local governments is not likely by itself to promote increased accountability and efficiency (Fox and Aranda 1996).

REFERENCES AND BIBLIOGRAPHY

Albo, G., D. Langille, and L. Panitch, eds. 1993. *A Different Kind of State? Popular Power and Democratic Administration*. Toronto: Oxford University Press.

Ashford, D. E. 1982. *British Dogmatism and French Pragmatism*. London: Allen and Unwin.

Aucoin, P., and H. Bakvis. 1988. *The Centralization–Decentralization Conundrum: Organization and Management in the Canadian Government*. Halifax, Nova Scotia: Institute for Research on Public Policy.

Barnekov, T., R. Boyle, and R. Daniel. 1989. *Privatism in Britain and the United States*. Oxford: Oxford University Press.

Beer, S. H. 1977. "A Political Scientist's View of Fiscal Federalism." In *The Political Economy of Fiscal Federalism*, ed. W. E. Oates. Lexington, Mass.: Lexington Books.

———. 1988. Introduction to *New Federalism: Intergovernmental Reform from Nixon to Reagan*, by T. Conlan. Washington, D.C.: The Brookings Institution.

Bennett, R., ed. 1994. *Local Government and Market Decentralization: Experiences in Industrialized, Developing, and Former Eastern Bloc Countries*. Tokyo: United Nations University Press.

Bird, R. M., and C. I. Wallich. 1994. "Local Government Finance in Transition Economies: Policy and Institutional Issues." In *Institutional Change and the Public Sector in Transitional Economic Dictatorships*. Washington, D.C.: World Bank.

Blichner, L. C., and L. Sangolt. 1994. "The Concept of Subsidiarity and the Debate on European Cooperation: Pitfalls and Possibilities." *Governance* 7: 284–306.

Claisse, A. 1989. "Rolling Back the State in France." *Governance* 2: 7–237.

Conlan, T. 1988. *New Federalism: Intergovernmental Reform from Nixon to Reagan*. Washington, D.C.: The Brookings Institution.

Derlien, H.-U. 1992. "Observation on the State of Comparative Administration Research in Europe—Rather Comparable than Comparative." *Governance* 5: 279–286.

Dunleavy, P., and C. Hood. 1994. "From Old Public Administration to New Public Management." *Public Money and Management* (July–September): 9–16.

Efficiency Unit (Ibbs Report). 1988. *Improving Management in Government: The Next Steps*. London: Her Majesty's Stationery Office.

Encíclicas Papales. 1991. *Rerum Novarum y Quadragesimo Anno*. Buenos Aires: Ediciones Paulinas.

Fortin, Y. 1989. "Country Report: Reflections on Public Administration in France." *Governance* 2: 101–110.

Fox, J., and J. Aranda. 1996. *Decentralization and Rural Development in Mexico: Community Participation in Oaxaca's Municipal Funds Program*. San Diego: Center for U.S.–Mexican Studies.

Fox Piven, F. 1993. "Reforming the Welfare State: The American Experience." In *A Different Kind of State? Popular Power and Democratic Administration*, ed. G. Albo, D. Langille, and L. Panitch. Toronto: Oxford University Press.

Fundación de Investigaciones Económicas Latinoamericanas (FIEL). 1993. *Hacia una Nueva Organización del Federalismo Fiscal en la Argentina*. Buenos Aires: FIEL.

Gershberg, A. Y. 1993. "Fiscal Decentralization and Intergovernmental Relations: An Analysis of Federal versus State Education Finance in Mexico." *Review of Urban and Regional Development Studies* 7: 33–68.

Graham, C. 1994. *Safety Nets, Politics, and the Poor: Transitions to Market Economies.* Washington, D.C.: The Brookings Institution.

Henig, J. R. 1985. *Public Policy and Federalism: Issues in State and Local Politics.* New York: St. Martin's Press.

Hood, C. 1994. *Explaining Economic Policy Reversals.* Buckingham: Oxford University Press.

Hughes, O. 1994. *Public Management and Administration: An Introduction.* Basingstoke: Macmillan.

Hurwicz, L. 1969. "Centralization and Decentralization in Economic Systems: On the Concept and Possibility of Informational Decentralization." *American Economic Association* 59: 513–519.

Jones, G. W. 1988. "The Crisis in British Central–Local Government Relationships." *Governance* 1: 163–183.

Jung, Y. D. 1991. "The Territorial Dimension of the Developing Capitalist State: Measuring and Explaining Centralization in Korea." In *A Dragon's Progress: Development Administration in Korea,* ed. G. F. Caiden and B. W. Kim. West Hartford, Conn.: Ku Press.

Keating, M. 1988. "Does Regional Government Work? The Experience of Italy, France and Spain." *Governance* 1: 184–204.

Kemp, P. 1993. *Beyond Next Steps: A Civil Service for the 21st Century.* London: The Social Market Foundation.

Kettl, D. F. 1987. *The Regulation of American Federalism: With a New Epilogue.* Baltimore: Johns Hopkins University Press.

Kuo, C. T. 1994. "Privatization within the Chinese State." *Governance* 7: 387–411.

Lam, J.T.M. 1996. "Decentralization in Public Administration: Hong Kong's Experience." *Public Policy and Administration* 11: 30–44.

López Murphy, R., ed. 1995. *La Descentralización fiscal en América Latina: Problemas y Perspectivas.* Buenos Aires: Red de Centros de Investigación Económica Aplicada.

Loughlin, M. 1996. "Understanding Central–Local Government Relations." *Public Policy and Administration* 11: 48–65.

Massey, A. 1993. *Managing the Public Sector: A Comparative Analysis of the United Kingdom and the United States.* Aldershot, England: Edward Elgar.

———. 1995. "Civil Service Reform and Accountability." *Public Policy and Administration* 10 (1): 16–33.

Mazey, S. 1994. "La France saisie par la decentralization: aperçu britannique." In *Le Territoire pour Politiques: Variations Européennes,* ed. R. Balme, P. Garraud, V. Hoffmann-Marinot, and E. Ritaine. Paris: Éditions L'Harmattan.

Metcalfe, L., and S. Richards. 1990. *Improving Public Management.* London: Sage.

Meyer, J. W., and W. R. Scott. 1983. "Centralization and the Legitimacy Problems of Local Government." In *Organizational Environments: Ritual and Rationality,* ed. J. W. Meyer and W. R. Scott. Beverly Hills: Sage.

Mintzberg, H. 1979. *The Structuring of Organizations: A Synthesis of the Research*. Englewood Cliffs, N.J.: Prentice Hall.

Oates, W. E. 1977. "An Economist's Perspective of Fiscal Federalism." In *The Political Economy of Fiscal Federalism*, ed. W. E. Oates. Lexington, Mass.: Lexington Books.

Olson, M., Jr. 1969. "Strategic Theory and Its Applications. The Principle of 'Fiscal Equivalence': The Division of Responsibilities Among Different Levels of Government." *American Economic Association* 59: 479–487.

Organization for Economic Cooperation and Development (OECD). 1996. *Integrating People Management into Public Service Reform*. Washington, D.C.: OECD.

Osborne, D., and T. Gabler. 1994. *La Reinvención del Gobierno*. Barcelona: Paidós.

Overman, E., and K. Boyd. 1994. "Best Practice Research and Postbureaucratic Reform." *Journal of Public Administration Research and Theory* 4 (1): 67–83.

Parri, L. 1990. "Territorial Politics and Political Exchange: American Federalism and French Unitarianism Reconsidered." In *Governance and Generalized Exchange: Self-Organizing Policy Networks in Action*, ed. B. Marin. Boulder, Colo.: Westview Press.

Peters, B. G., and D. J. Savoie. 1995. "Managing Incoherence: The Coordination and Empowerment Conundrum." Research paper no. 16, Canadian Centre for Management Development, Ottawa.

Peterson, G. E. 1997. *Decentralization in Latin America: Learning through Experience*. Washington, D.C.: World Bank.

Pollitt, C. 1990. *Managerialism and the Public Services: The Anglo-American Experience*. Oxford: Basil Blackwell.

———. 1995. "Management Techniques for the Public Sector: Pulpit and Practice." Research paper no. 17, Canadian Centre for Management Development, Ottawa.

Pouder, R. W. 1996. "Privatizing Services in Local Government: An Empirical Assessment of Efficiency and Institutional Explanations." *Public Administration Quarterly* (Spring): 103–127.

Prud'homme, R. 1994. "On the Dangers of Decentralization." Policy research working paper no. 1252, World Bank, Washington, D.C.

Rivlin, A. M. 1991. "Distinguished Lecture on Economics in Government: Strengthening the Economy by Rethinking the Role of Federal and State Governments." *Journal of Economic Perspectives* 5: 3–13.

Rondinelli, D. A., J. R. Nellis, and G. S. Cheema. 1984. "Decentralization in Developing Countries: A Review of Recent Experience." World Bank staff working papers no. 581, Management and Development series no. 8, World Bank, Washington, D.C.

Rowat, M. 1996. "Public Sector Reform in the Latin American and Caribbean Region: Issues and Contrasts." *Public Administration and Development* 16: 397–411.

Sbragia, A. M. 1996. *Debt Wish: Entrepreneurial Cities, U.S. Federalism, and Economic Development*. Pittsburgh: University of Pittsburgh Press.

Schiavo-Campo, S. 1994. "Institutional Change and the Public Sector in Transitional Economies." Discussion paper no. 241, World Bank, Washington, D.C.

Silverman, J. M. 1992. "Public Sector Decentralization: Economic Policy and Sector Investment Programs." World Bank technical paper no. 188, Afrika Technical Department Series, World Bank, Washington, D.C.

Shah, A. 1994. "The Reform of Intergovernmental Fiscal Relations in Developing and Emerging Market Economies." Policy and Research series no. 23, World Bank, Washington, D.C.

Wolman, H. 1992. "Understanding Cross-National Policy Transfers: The Case of Britain and the U.S." *Governance* 5: 63–83.

Zifcak, S. 1994. *New Managerialism: Administrative Reform in Whitehall and Canberra.* Buckingham, England: Open University Press.

11

Democratic Decentralization and Institutions of India

Neelima Deshmukh

It is widely recognized that self-governing village communities characterized by agrarian society have been in existence in India from the earliest times. Not only are they mentioned in Rigveda, which dates back to approximately 1200 B.C., but there is also definite evidence available for the existence of village *sabhas* (councils or assemblies) and *gramins* (senior persons of village) until about 600 B.C.[1] These villages bodies were the lines of contact with higher authorities on matters affecting the villages.

In 1947, independent India inherited a local self-government as a small wing of the local level of the government system. The major wing, the district administration, which was a complex of field agencies along with the offices of the existing provincial government, has been evolving structure, powers, and functions since the closing three decades of the eighth century.[2] It now has manifold responsibilities relating to general, regulatory, revenue, and development administration. It is a sort of mini-state government at the local level, with a senior bureaucrat deputy commissioner as coordinator and directly responsible for law and order and general administration. He and various field-office heads are accountable to the state government for the performance of their duties.

The present administrative structure of India emerged from the British colonial systems. As one of the major British interests in India was to use its resources, little attention was given to developing administration as an instrument of economic and social change.

Administration was solely concerned with the maintenance of law and order and the collection of revenues. After attaining independence, instead of being the guardian of law and order, it assumed the role of custodian of welfare and the well-being of citizens, which has led to a greater state intervention in economic and social spheres. The onus for bringing about desired economic or social and political change in India lies upon its government. Development has been the major concern of Third World countries, more so in India after World War II. Almost every branch of knowledge has been affected, and new fields like development education, development economics, development agriculture, and community development have emerged. Like the governments of many countries, India has increasingly turned its attention to development problems. With the initiation of the process of nation building, heavy responsibility is on officials and nonofficials to fulfill welfare goals of the Indian society. They are now called upon to work as a catalyst in the process of social and economic transformation.

The goal of development is therefore not Westernization, modernization, or industrialization alone, but the employment of modern techniques, both mechanical and social, in pursuit of societal objectives through effective public participation that focuses on government-influenced change toward progressive political, economic, and social objectives. One of the major questions faced by developing countries has been the problem of achieving social and economic development through the democratic process. In India, commitment to the democratic process is an important concern for economic development. At the grassroots level, Panchayat Raj institutions were set up to associate village leaders with the administration of planning and development. One of the major issues in Panchayats Raj was decentralization and the degree of autonomy to be enjoyed by *panchayat* bodies.

The local self-government included both urban and rural bodies. The rural local bodies were the village *panchayats* (councils), and the district boards with some organizational linkages between them. The third rural body (local board) was at the intermediate level between those two local bodies and had been established in most places but had been abolished. Subsequently, during the second quarter of the twentieth century, the working record of most such reorganized rural local bodies was by and large unsatisfactory.

PANCHAYATS: PRECOLONIAL PERIOD

In the course of time, these village bodies took the form of *panchayats* (an assembly of five persons) which looked after the affairs of the village. They had both police and judicial powers. Customs and religion elevated them to a scared position of authority. Besides village *panchayats*, there were also last *panchayats* belonging to a particular caste, which adhered to its code of social conduct and ethics. These village bodies had been the pivot of administration, the center of social life, and above all a focus of social solidarity in Indian culture. Although under Mughals their judicial powers were curtailed, local affairs remained unregulated from above and village officers and servants were answerable to the *panchayats*. Sir Charles Metcalfe, the provisional governor general of India (1835–1836), called these Indian village communities "the little republics."[3] During the transition from police to welfare state after India's independence, an acute need was felt to review the performance and redesign the organization and ensure smooth working of these rural local governments, which were basically based on Mahatma Gandhi's Gram Swaraj pattern of making every village a self-sustaining unit. Further, "If the policy of Govt. in giving impetus of panchyat [*sic*] Raj movement is implemented faithfully & fully it will surely bring about the social political & economic revolution which will not only strengthen the democratic character of our society but will also prove the perennial source of energetic honest & competent leaders with potentials to change the entire face of country & guide the destinies of the people most efficiently & effectively."[4] "Nevertheless the Panchayat Raj System has been moving downhill and is only a living caricature of local government.[5] "Villages had been reduced to a focus of frustration. The Gram Sabha is something of Joke."[6]

Due to the interest generated by Panchayat Raj institutions, several state committees were set up to assure their working and to recommend measures for improvement which were based on the basic doctrine of the Shri Balwantrai Mehta committee report. The common critical problem was the domination of Panchayat Raj institutions by economically and socially privileged classes. This was essentially a sociopolitical problem and could have been tackled to a great extent by holding regular elections. Political education of communities oppressed for ages would have certainly changed the scenario with a strong political will. Lack of public participation in developmental programs in the real democratic sense emerged as the crux of the whole problem.

India's development in the early 1950s was planned without taking into account Gandhi's idea of Gram Swaraj. It did not take long to realize the folly of this approach. The community-development projects inaugurated in 1952 soon found themselves hopeless due to ineffective instruments of people's participation. In order to suggest an institutional set up to secure participation in community-development programs, a study of them headed by the Shri Balwantrai Mehta committee was of the opinion that without an agency at the village level which represented the entire community, assumed responsibility, and provided the necessary leadership for implementing development programs, real progress in rural development could not come about at all. Its recommendations was that "public participation in community work should be organized through statutory representative bodies."[7] This gave a fillip to prevailing nationwide sentiments.

The recommendations of the Balwantrai Mehta committee favored democratic decentralization through setting up Panchayat Raj institutions in all states, a three-tier arrangement from the grassroots level of the village block. The district-level national development council also affirmed the basic principles of democratic decentralization enunciated in the Balwantrai Mehta committee report, and left the states to work out the structures suitable to each state. During this stage, the term Panchayat Raj came into vogue, which is a process of governance referring to a system of organically linking people from Gram Sabha to Loksabha.

Thus, the three-tiered Panchayat Raj system was established, with powers, functions, and resources largely devolved upon the intermediate tier, the Panchayat Samiti, to play the primary role in rural development process.

POST-INDEPENDENCE ERA

During the first decade of independence, India's state government was motivated by certain legislative and administrative measures to expand and develop rural local government. This was influenced by three main factors:

1. Mahatma Gandhi's concept of treating the village *panchayat* as a primary grassroots democratic unit.
2. The newly formed constitution of the country, which included concrete provisions about the state's duty to develop *panchayats* as local self-governing units.
3. The viewpoint of the recently launched five-year plan that people's participation should be promoted in management of rural development through local representative institutions.

About the beginning of the 1960s, the network of three-tired rural local self-government, the Panchayat Raj, was set up in most of the states and a few union territories of India. This indicated the enthusiastic efforts of state government, as guided, encouraged, and supported by union government, particularly by the charismatic and dynamic prime minister Pandit Jawaharlal Nehru. However, it began to be realized by the government and Panchayat Raj leadership that both internal and environmental factors were constraining the qualitative standards and tempo of the workings of Panchayat Raj in an egalitarian and largely traditional rural society. The quality of linkages between the Panchayat Raj institutions, cooperatives, and voluntary agencies having an important impact on local development processes were not yet appropriately strong. In reality, the results achieved during the short period of five years were a modest nature. During the next two decades, Panchayat Raj began to stagnate in the first few years (1965–1970) and then started declining in efficacy in its role in promotion and management of development process in rural areas.[8] This trend continued until 1985. Its public image and credibility began to suffer a setback. Its power and functions were reduced by executive orders of the government on grounds of inefficiency, corruption, and political factionalism prevailing within it.

Since the middle of the 1980s, there has been a growing interest within the union government for reviving the role of Panchayat Raj, which has been languishing in many states of the country. Committee after committee were constituted to assess the position of Panchayat Raj institutions and finally the administrators agreed that Panchayat Raj based on the concept of democrative decentralization within the country's government system needed to be revamped suitably to improve its efficacy for accelerating responsive equitable development processes, as well as for contributing to the development of citizen standards. Considering the views of various committees, the union government decided to amend the constitution of the country in order to provide a firm basis for the essential features of Panchayat Raj. This was intended to provide substantial protection for Panchayat Raj against the negligence or the arbitrary action of the state government, which had been contributing to its emasculation in many states over the years. As recently as 1992, the government finally succeeded in getting the amendment approved by the parliament and most of the states have implemented the Panchayat Raj Act.

CONFERRING OF CONSTITUTIONAL STATUS

In recent years, there has been growing serious concern in the country regarding the weak status of Panchayat Raj in most states. It has been widely recognized by the government public leaders, and the intelligentsia that Panchayat Raj institutions have not been able to acquire the status and dignity of viable and responsive people's bodies. The main reasons mentioned by the government and others for this are the absence of regular elections, prolonged supersessions, insufficient representation of weaker sections (e.g., schedule caste, schedule tribes [SC/ST], and women), inadequate devolution of powers, and lack of financial resources. Article 40 of the constitution has directed the Indian state to organize and empower village *panchayats* to enable them to function as the units of self-government. The union government therefore has stated recently the imperative need to enshrine in the constitution certain basic and essential features of Panchayat Raj institutions to impart certainty, continuity, and strength to them.

These provisions of the Panchayat Raj Act can be summarized as follows:

1. A Gram Sabha (village assembly) comprising all registered voters is to exercise such powers and perform such functions as the state legislature may provide as statutory.

2. A three-tier Panchayat Raj system is to be constituted from village to subdistrict and to the district level in a state, but a state with a population of less than 2 million may not have the intermediate tier if it likes the provision for the composition of *panchayat* at each level it is to be made statutorily by the state legislature. Seats in *panchayats* at each level are to be filled by direct election. The state legislature may provide for ex officio membership in the district level and intermediate level for chairpersons of the *panchayats* located at lower levels.

3. Seats are to be reserved for schedule castes and schedule tribes in every *panchayat* in proportion to their population. One-third of these reserved seats are for SC/ST women.

4. At least one-third of the total seats are to be reserved for women. This includes seats reserved for SC/ST women.

5. Seats on a similar basis are also to be reserved in regard to chairmanship of Panchayat Raj at each level.

6. The state legislature may make statutory reservation of seats in the *panchayats* at each level for any backward class of citizen.

7. The normal tenure of the *panchayat* is to be five years. If it is dissolved earlier, elections are to be held within six months.

8. A candidate for election should not be less than twenty-one years of age and should not have been disqualified under any law relating to election to the state legislature.

9. The state legislature may by law empower the *panchayats* to impose taxes, fees, and duties; may assign a share of state government taxes; and may provide for grants in aid.

10. The state legislature may statutorily endow *panchayats* with power and authority to enable them to function as institution of self-governance.

This devolution of powers and responsibilities may include preparation of plans for economic development and social justice.

11. The state government is to constitute an independent finance commission to review periodically every five years the financial position of *panchayats* and to make recommendations for improving them. Further, this commission will make provisions for maintenance of accounts by *panchayats* and necessary audit arrangements.

12. Elections to the *panchayats* are to be supervised, directed, and controlled by the state election commission appointed by the governor.

Schedule 11 of this act contains twenty-nine items, some or all of which may be incorporated into the state acts which are related to the development of the rural economy, infrastructure, social services, poverty alleviation, social welfare, public distribution systems, and the maintenance of community assets. The act came into force in April 1993, and Maharashtra was the first state to implement it.

PRESENT POSITION

The Panchayat Raj system has been statutorily provided fully or partially in twenty-two out of twenty-five states and in six out of seven union territories. In the remaining three states and one union territory, there are traditional tribunal councils. Only in fifteen states is it a three-tiered system. These states are Andhra Pradesh, Arunachal Pradesh, Assam, Bihar, Gujrat, Himachal Pradesh, Karnataka, Madhya Pradesh Maharashtra, Orissa, Punjab, Rajasthan, Tamil Nadu, Uttar Pradesh, and West Bengal. "Total number 2,17,300 village Panchayats existing in 22 states and 3 Union territories covering 96% of about 5.79 million villages and nearly 99.6% of village population. The 4256 Panchayat Samiti/Taluka Panchayat have been provided in 17 states covering about 90% of developed blocks. The Zilla parishad have been provided in 16 states and Union territories."[9]

Political parties are playing an increasingly positive role in the election and workings of Panchayat Raj. This has tended to politicize them a good deal in an increasing number of states. Some relaxations in the statutory control and administrative direction of Panchayat Raj by government is beginning to take place in several states, which, however, still remains quite comprehensive and rather rigid.

ROLE OF NEW PANCHAYAT RAJ
IN AGRICULTURAL DEVELOPMENT

Though India has been a rural country from time immemorial, the process of urbanization has gained momentum in recent years, bringing an imbalanced growth between the urban and rural centers and also polluting the urban areas to the maximum possible extent. "The urban centres proceed on exploding to the extreme level which might be due to the constant and ever increasing migration of rural folks to the urban areas. This type of migration occurs because of two main factors viz. seeking the employment opportunities and sophisticated living conditions because there is no balanced growth between these two areas. Manufacturing and servicing of the sectors of rural economy have not been as adequately represented as that urban economy in the national development objectives since our independence."[10] Moreover, due to the location of government headquarters in urban areas, they have become power centres. "The urban areas have not developed to a greater extent leaving the villages far behind; that is why India has achieved pseudo development for last 50 years of independence creating a handful millionaires and an ocean of paupers."[11] A majority of people have started revolting against these power centers. Mahatma Gandhi's dream of Ramrajya through Gram-Rajya, making villages self-sufficient, self-reliant units with economic, social, and political freedom has not been achieved in any real sense.

This sort of pseudodevelopment has occurred due to the political vacuum in the rural areas created by the absence of appropriate local government. Though it was recommended by Dr. Balwantrai Mehta and subsequently, these Panchayat Raj institutions were established and run for a certain period and all of them were demolished in the latter years. However, through passage and approval of the 73rd amendment to the constitution of India, Panchayat Raj institutions have been accorded constitutional status and have made local self-government as important as that of the state and central governments. Merely declaring them as governments is not sufficient, and they must be provided with responsibility for functions and duties along with the matching authority. For this, they have been provided with a list of twenty-nine sectors in which they can implement various programs and schemes for the development of rural areas. Agriculture is the backbone of the Indian economy, providing employment to 70 percent of the population and contributing a major share to the national income apart from fulfilling the basic needs of food, clothing, and shelter. In a nutshell, without agriculture there cannot be any rural development and national development for which only the Panchayat Raj institutions (PRIs) have been poised. Agriculture has not been declared as a profession as yet and has not been provided with any type of concessions, facilities, or encouragement, as have been attained by the manufacturing and processing industries, whereas the producers of agricultural inputs are flourishing well by exploiting the farmers and farm laborers. However, with the advent of the 73rd constitutional amendment, there would be a facility for the agriculture and its allied fields, since the PRIs, which are closer and answerable to the rural people, would be involved in the agricultural development programs.

Along with various suggestions, such as representation to the farming community, empowerment of Gram Sabha, control of personnel of the development department, creation of agricultural development committees, lead farmer approach, wasteland and dairy development, and supply and distribution of agricultural inputs for achieving the aims and objectives of PRIs, more emphasis should be laid on bringing cooperatives under auspices of PRIs.

Since the *panchayats* have been declared as local governments, they must be made nodal agencies for bringing about development of rural areas in particular. In this regard, these institutions should be given the authority to operate and direct the most important rural economic institutions (i.e., cooperatives) just like the state and central governments. In cases of agricultural development, the cooperative still plays a crucial role. In cases of any discrepancy between agricultural plans of *panchayats*, activities, and allocation of cooperation, the *panchayats* cannot achieve their objectives of sustainable development. This definitely creates problems for *panchayats*, from the designing of cropping patterns to profitable sales of produce by farmers. It also poses a problem for forecasts of inputs to recovery, which hinders the development efforts of PRIs.

SUMMARY

No government can be easily approached by the rural populace except the Panchayat Raj institutions, because they are very near to the rural people who are mostly involved in agricultural and allied occupations. Hence, Panchayat Raj institutions alone can bring real agricultural development, which is essential for rural development and ultimately for national development. Therefore, the new Panchayat Raj system is undoubtedly a fillip to future agricultural development of India.

NOTES

1. Mathew George, *Status of Panchayati Raj in States of India* (New Delhi: Institute of Social Sciences, April 1994), vol. 4, p. 5.

2. B. S. Khanna, *Panchayat Raj in India: Rural Local Self-Government* (New Delhi: Deep and Deep Publications, 1994), 3.

3. M. Aslam, ed., *Evolution of Panchayat Raj and Constitutional (73rd Amendment) Act 1992* (New Delhi: Indira Gandhi National Open University, 1995), 3. Sponsored by the Ministry of Rural Areas and Employment, Government of India.

4. R. Jathar, *Evolution of Panchayat Raj in India* (Dharwar: Institute of Economic Research, Bhartral Books International Publications, Bombay, 1964), 10.

5. Abhijit Datta, "Decentralisation of Local Self Government Reforms in India." *Indian Journal of Public Administration* 33, no. 3 (1987): 562.

6. Thomas Mathai, *Democratic World*, 22 January 1978, p. 6.

7. Government of India, report of the team for the study of community projects and National Extension Service (New Dehli: Committee on Plan Projects, 1957), vol. 1.

8. Khanna, *Panchayat Raj in India*, 21.

9. Ibid., 32.

10. M. Sundaramari, and T. Ranganathan, "Role of New Panchayat Raj Agricultural Development," in *Major Issues in New Panchayati Raj System*, ed. A. Palanithurai and B. R. Dwarki. (New Dehli: Kanishka Publishers and Distributors, 1997), 45.

11. Ibid.

State Human Services as Disciplined Intergovernmental Collaboration

Stephen Page

Social policy, and the human services in particular, confront a variety of pressures in the United States today. Elite political rhetoric is hostile to "big government" efforts to help families who face disadvantages. Simultaneously, many client families and advocates seek more flexibility and responsiveness from the policies and programs intended to assist them. Regardless of the solutions they propose, critics agree that the existing system of human services does not serve families with multiple needs effectively. This chapter describes an emerging attempt to solve this problem through systemic reform at the state and local level.

The current system of human-services policy making in the United States is based on categories of human needs. Legislation and administrative rules specify types of needs and prescribe benefits to address them. A local service provider then supplies each beneficiary with the particular benefit that corresponds to the category into which his or her need falls (e.g., disability, mental health, etc.). Such a system is prone to problems of discretion and administrative accountability. Overly narrow categories may cause inconvenience for clients, as well as difficulties for service providers and administering agencies (e.g., child-care subsidies for parents in job training are usually administered and delivered separately from those for working parents with low incomes). Service providers may even have difficulty placing beneficiaries who need multiple services into the proper category(s) (e.g., single parents who need job training or substance-abuse treatment may also need child care; parents at imminent risk of having children placed in foster care may need substance-abuse treatment in addition to child-welfare services). For a categorical system to work effectively, central policy makers must establish discrete categories of human need and prescribe benefits that address them efficiently, and frontline staff must be able to specify the category(s) into which an individual falls.

As the Great Society and its successor programs have sought to address increasingly complex human needs, and as social conditions have worsened for many families facing disadvantages, these tasks have become increasingly difficult to carry out. The proliferation of categorical programs has produced a situation in which categories of need now overlap for many beneficiaries, especially when the needs of entire families are considered. Under these circumstances, separate services that address each need as a discrete category may help clients less than customized packages of services that address the full range of problems that particular families face. Legislators and administrators in the state capital can never know in advance, however, exactly where and how individual clients' needs will overlap or families' needs will combine at the local level. Legislation and administrative rules therefore cannot specify unambiguous categories of need for many families with multiple social problems—much less distinct, effective benefits to address their complex combinations of needs.

If the array of needs that human services seek to address can only be identified locally for specific clients, then it makes sense to package responsive services and supports at the local level. This logic leads many policy makers to view devolution of policy responsibilities from the federal government to the states, and from the states to the local level, as a promising alternative to the limits of the existing, centralized system.

Devolution can take many forms, however, and some have more potential than others to achieve certain policy goals. Some devolution approaches simply "load shed" policy problems and fiscal responsibilities from one level of government to a lower one. Others may authorize and support decentralized problem solving that may be more creative, flexible, and responsive to local conditions than uniform central policies, without sacrificing basic guarantees of civil rights and an entitlement to some type of assistance. The potential of devolution to improve the effectiveness of human services thus depends on the intergovernmental arrangements that are adopted, and on how responsibilities and relationships are structured among key actors. To offer human services that respond to different families' multiple needs, for instance, services may need to be packaged locally, but funding and monitoring may best come from the state or federal levels. Most recent policy debates, however, have paid scant attention to how some forms of devolution—or divisions of responsibilities among different levels of government—might improve the performance of human services better than others.

In an attempt to fill this gap, this chapter examines a system of partial devolution from the state to the local level that a handful of states are developing in the area of human services.[1] State and local actors share responsibility for providing flexible packages of services that address the particular needs of individual families. I refer to the new system as "collaborative adjustment" for several reasons. It utilizes broad-based, inclusive collaborations among key stakeholders at the state, county, and neighborhood levels to design, deliver, and manage comprehensive, integrated services for children and families. It then disciplines the work of these collaboratives in two ways. It evaluates their accomplishments in terms of the outcomes they achieve for children and families. It also establishes regular occasions for collaborators to convene to assess their accomplishments and to adjust their service strategies and the division of responsibilities among themselves based on those accomplishments.

There are six policy tools of collaborative adjustment which hold the key to its promise of better performance:

1. New models of service delivery.
2. Inclusive collaboration at the state, county, and neighborhood levels.
3. New approaches to allocating funding for human services.
4. Evaluation based on the specific outcomes achieved for children and families.
5. State–local partnership agreements that outline the terms of the working relationship between state and local collaboratives.
6. The master tool of iterative assessment and revision of the other policy tools, which makes possible the collaborative adjustment of state and local responsibilities.

Leading states vary in the extent to which they have adopted each of these tools. This chapter outlines how innovating states are operationalizing each feature, and speculates on the advantages and drawbacks of different approaches. It then suggests how the various tools might work together in synergy to help make human services more effective at assisting families facing disadvantages.

While it is based on actual developments in the states, this chapter articulates a systemic vision that is not yet completely in place on the ground. The vision tracks empirical developments closely, but, as a portrait of what might be, it necessarily goes beyond what has emerged in any one state thus far. Where possible, I provide examples to illustrate the extent to which each part of the vision reflects states' actual accomplishments.

POLICY TOOLS OF COLLABORATIVE ADJUSTMENT

Comprehensive, Integrated Service Strategies

Collaborative adjustment is a way to make policies that support the customization of human services to address the particular needs of individual children and families in the context of their communities.[2] Research over the last two decades indicates that effective programs for children and families offer services that look significantly different from most of those offered by the existing human-services system. Existing services tend to be uniformly designed, distinct from one another, and focused on remediating clients' weaknesses. Effective services, in contrast, are flexible, comprehensive, linked where appropriate, and designed to prevent problems by building on the strengths of each family.[3]

Since effective services can be packaged in various ways, some practitioners refer to new "service strategies" rather than to particular programs or models.[4] Examples include

- home visits by public-health nurses or paraprofessionals to ensure that pregnant women receive adequate prenatal care and that new mothers have basic parenting skills.
- family support and preservation services that seek to prevent child abuse and neglect—and ultimately out-of-home placements of children—by improving parenting skills and family functioning in high-stress, high-risk families.
- school-linked services and pre-kindergarten programs that address the health and well-being of children and families, in addition to children's cognitive development.

Service providers can also build links between these formal services and the informal resources and supports that exist in neighborhoods (e.g., children's play groups, parents' networks, block watches, etc.), to complement their own efforts and limit the need for formal interventions.[5]

Innovating states are using different approaches to foster the local design and provision of new service strategies and informal supports. Some states have dedicated funds to support a particular set of comprehensive, flexible services in specific types of local settings.[6] Some have identified best practices in service delivery from other states and communities and from research findings, and established frontline collaboratives among service providers to adapt them to address local needs and to capitalize on local resources.[7] Some have simply encouraged local service providers and public agencies to work together in designing and delivering new service strategies of their choice.[8] Still other states have set broad goals in a particular area (such as child welfare), convened organizations that provide related services, and urged them to devise and implement their own local service strategies to achieve those goals.[9]

Each of these approaches has advantages and drawbacks for the development of a full system of collaborative adjustment. State-specified service strategies are relatively simple to prescribe and implement, but may not give local service providers much experience addressing larger policy questions and negotiating with state officials. Letting local collaborators pick and choose their own service strategies may help empower them in working with the state. They may have difficulty, however, moving from specific service-delivery projects to taking on planning and administration for all human services for children and families. A more open-ended approach offers service providers the chance to experiment with a range of different service strategies on their own, but may leave them without a concrete initiative on which to focus their energies. It also does little by itself to establish a clear dialogue about service strategies between local actors and the state. Setting broad goals, convening stakeholders, and encouraging the use of various service strategies to achieve the goals are key elements in a system of collaborative adjustment, but developing them takes time and requires considerable capacity building.[10]

Inclusive Collaboration

In the existing system of human services, a separate state agency (or division thereof) is usually responsible for administering a particular type of categorical program. Each agency has line staff, or contracts with service providers, that specialize in a particular discipline and deliver the service(s) associated with its programs. As a result, the children and families who qualify for a variety of services encounter myriad specialists, application forms, rules, and service-delivery processes, none of which may fully address their multiple needs because each deals with only a narrow category of need.

A system of collaborative adjustment, in contrast, utilizes horizontal partnerships among different agencies to bring different kinds of specialists together to serve families in flexible, responsive ways. The organizational entities responsible for delivering, administering, and governing human services are interagency collaboratives at three levels of government: frontline neighborhood service delivery, the county (or region), and the state. In contrast to the existing system, which keeps the delivery and administration of similar or overlapping services separate, interagency collaboration enables service providers to bring a range of services and informal supports together to respond to families' various strengths and needs.

Neighborhood Collaboratives

These include frontline service providers, community leaders, neighborhood residents, and service recipients. Many of the new service strategies require the expertise of several types of service providers working together (e.g., school-linked services may involve public-health nurses, mental-health specialists, child-welfare staff, juvenile corrections officers, and others). Neighborhood collaboratives provide a vehicle for these providers to work jointly with families, community members, and one another to develop customized service plans for individual families, and to coordinate services and informal supports for the entire neighborhood. Frontline collaboration can build on strong interpersonal relationships among service providers, but often requires participants to overcome boundaries and habits created by insular agency work cultures and discipline-specific training. States may or may not assign frontline collaboratives formal decision-making roles in their new system of human services (two that do are Missouri and Washington), but many rely on them to deliver the new service strategies.[11]

Community Partnerships at the County or Regional Level

A community partnership coordinates, convenes, and provides technical assistance to the neighborhood collaboratives within its geographic jurisdiction. Community partnerships are generally responsible for assessing local needs and resources, developing comprehensive service plans based on the priorities of their neighborhoods, submitting these plans to the state, drawing on the resources of their members and of state agencies to implement the plans, and reporting the results to the community at large and to the state.[12] Their comprehensive plans may identify specific outcomes (goals) to be achieved; service strategies to achieve them; the budget and staff necessary to implement the service strategies; requests for waivers, technical assistance, and funds to support implementation; and an evaluation method to measure the achievement of the outcomes.[13]

Depending on the state, communities' comprehensive plans may or may not have a direct impact on how public funds are used to serve children and families. At this point, most states use their community partnerships primarily as planning and management entities for specific programs, with the state still allocating most public resources for human services. With one or two exceptions, the community partnerships in most states have been operating for only a few years, and their comprehensive plans reflect their limited experience and capacity.

The members of community partnerships may be designated in legislation, convened by county or local governments, elected by public ballot, appointed by state officials, or self-appointed. The "partners" in a community partnership may include representatives of county and municipal government, school districts, the county branches of state agencies (or county agencies themselves), service-provider organizations, community groups, the local business and civic community, parents, citizen representatives, and other interested parties. Participation by local governments, school districts, public agencies, service-provider organizations, and community groups gives community partnerships access to policy makers, political influence, financing, expertise, and other resources. A few states have specified that elected county commissioners must approve the members of community partnerships in order to secure local political support for their activities.[14] Service providers and county agency representatives can bring their expertise and, potentially, staff time and funding to the community partnerships. Community partnerships can also gain crucial planning and logistical information from community groups' hands-on perspective on neighborhood needs, and from the voices of local residents who are directly and indirectly affected by their efforts.

The inclusion of "lay participants" (business and civic representatives, consumers, citizens) in making policy and program decisions is a significant departure from the existing human-services system, in which legislatures, public agencies, and service providers have their own final say in making decisions. Including consumers in planning is essential to designing user-friendly, effective systems, and the outside perspective of citizens and business representatives can bring new ideas and pragmatism to decision-making processes. Citizen, civic, and business representatives do not have clear vested interests in decisions about service designs and budget allocations. As a result, community partnerships with lay majorities may be able to avoid the self-interested tendency of service

providers and public agencies to haggle over the allocation of program funds. Discussion can then focus more productively on designing a comprehensive local system of coordinated services and
supports for families and children.[15] Lay participation ultimately
may help build popular support for both systemic human-services
reform and an increase in the overall public commitment to children and families. Several innovating states envision that the importance of lay participants in their state and county collaboratives'
activities will increase over time, as the actors gain experience with
their new roles and responsibilities.[16]

The State Collaborative

Collaboration is necessary across state agencies to set the broader
policy agenda and to coordinate state agencies' operations to support the design and implementation of the community partnerships'
comprehensive plans. A state Children's Cabinet or Family Policy
Council usually makes formal policy decisions and issues mandates
to state agencies.[17] An interagency work team of deputies or an
office of children, youth, and families may staff their work and implement their decisions.[18] In place of an interagency team, some states
have established another complementary body—usually a nongovernmental, state-level entity—to build capacity, train staff, and
otherwise assist the state agencies, community partnerships, and
neighborhood collaboratives.[19]

Regardless of its composition and size, the state collaborative
and its staff usually develop the state's policy strategy for children
and families, including principles and standards for establishing
the local collaboratives and for their planning and service-delivery
activities; identify core results (outcomes) to be achieved, and indicators to measure them; review, revise, and approve the communities' comprehensive plans; develop a budget (jointly or separately
by agency) to support local comprehensive plans and track expenditures; develop statewide data-gathering and evaluation strategies and monitor the results (outcomes) that communities achieve
for children and families; monitor communities' plans and their
implementation to ensure equity and other basic procedural guarantees for families; document and disseminate best practices to
communities (in community planning, service strategies, financing, governance, waiver requests, and other techniques); and provide funding, technical assistance, capacity building, waivers, and
other responses to support the community partnerships' efforts.

The extent to which state collaboratives currently carry out these
responsibilities depends on the level of development of the state's

new system of collaborative adjustment. Most state collaboratives have developed an overall policy agenda for children and families, designated core results to be achieved, and provided technical assistance and capacity building to community partnerships. Even the most innovative states, however, have had only a few years of experience with the process of community partnerships developing comprehensive plans and the state collaborative reviewing and approving them. Best-practice dissemination and waiver assistance generally occur in an ad hoc fashion in most states right now, although a few have established explicit approaches in these areas.[20] A few states are beginning to measure and track data to measure counties' performances.[21] Virtually no states have taken concrete steps yet to design their budgets for human services according to community partnerships' comprehensive plans, although some are working hard to figure out how to do so.[22]

Funding: Core Dollars versus Project Dollars

The functioning of any human-services system depends substantially on how resources such as funding and staff are made available for service delivery and administration. The existing human-services system allocates resources according to centrally determined categories of need and benefits. Budgets depend on policy makers' willingness to commit resources to programs defined by general problems that children and families face. Federal and state funding for maternal and child health, for example, pays for specific programs and services that address the health needs of pregnant women and children. Federal and state funding for child welfare pays for specific programs and services that seek to prevent abuse and neglect, or that protect children from families who abuse or neglect them. Similar federal and state programs in other categories (e.g., child care, income maintenance, job training, juvenile justice, mental health, mental retardation, developmental disabilities, etc.) supply the core funding for the mainstream of the existing human-services system.

In contrast to the existing system, a system of collaborative adjustment would allocate resources to achieve specific improvements in children's and families' lives. In a fully operational system of collaborative adjustment, the allocation of core funding to support communities' efforts might occur through a process of "budgeting by outcomes," in contrast to the budgeting by programs that occurs in the existing system.[23] To budget by outcomes, the state collaborative and the community partnerships would agree on the outcomes they wish to achieve (e.g., more healthy births), as well as indicator data to measure the achievement of these outcomes (e.g., lower rates of underweight births, higher rates of prenatal care). Next, they would examine best practices in the field, community experiences, and research literature to identify effective techniques to achieve these indicators, including providing and publicizing direct services, restructuring program incentives to influence individual behavior, and increasing the availability of informal neighborhood supports. Each community partnership would develop a comprehensive community plan that included approaches to address each indicator. These plans would build on existing local resources, redeploy resources that might work more effectively in new ways (e.g., emphasizing the prevention of family problems instead of their remediation), and identify the staff and budget needed for implementation. By putting all the community partnerships' plans together, the state collaborative would compile an "agenda of actions and costs" to use in developing a multiyear budget plan to address the range of issues that the communities prioritized.

Initial Approaches

No state has achieved this ideal in practice, but innovating states have initiated two approaches to funding the comprehensive community plans and to improving the local capacity for planning and management. Some states have given their community partnerships special project funds from foundations, federal programs, or new state initiatives to support the implementation of specific service strategies.[24] A few states have block granted narrow portions of core human-services funding to their community partnerships to use flexibly to achieve very specific outcomes.[25]

Budgeting by outcomes ultimately requires that community partnerships' comprehensive plans allocate core funding to service strategies that will achieve specific outcomes for children and families. A number of innovating states envision using their communities' comprehensive plans as direct guides to budget core state and federal funding in the future, but are still working out the details of how to do so. Those states that now finance their community partnerships' efforts with project funds rather than core dollars run the risk that the community partnerships may remain the planners and administrators of a few integrated service strategies that operate parallel to the mainstream, existing human-services system. The states that have given their community partnerships direct control over narrow portions of core funds must avoid letting the community partnerships end up as enclaves with little impact on the mainstream human-services system.

Transition Strategies

States face challenges in trying to make the transition from a parallel or enclave operation to a mainstream one in which core human-services funds are budgeted according to the outcomes for children and families that communities prioritize in their comprehensive plans. Meeting this challenge requires building the capacity and extending the authority of the community partnerships to encompass a number of new responsibilities. The best approach is likely to vary, depending on state and local circumstances, so reformers must keep the end goal in mind and remain flexible about the best route to achieving it. States that now finance their community partnerships' efforts with project funds, for example, need to find a way for the communities to begin to handle core funds to support the implementation of their comprehensive plans. For example,

- Through its Family Connection Initiative, Georgia gives a small amount of special-project funding to informal local collaboratives throughout the state to support locally designed integrated service strategies. The Georgia Family Policy Council has also designated ten community partnerships, and given them specific, formal responsibilities for improving outcomes for children and families.[26] The impact of the partnerships' comprehensive plans on the state agencies' core budgets and practices remains unclear and indirect, however.

- Ohio has delegated responsibility for allocating a small portion of core funds to its community partnerships (County Family and Children First Councils) through a block grant that consolidates all funding for teen-pregnancy prevention. Once the county councils gained experience with the block-grant approach, the state created another one that consolidates and passes through funding to support services to prevent child abuse and neglect.

States that have already given their community partnerships control over narrow portions of core funds to achieve very specific outcomes need to find ways to extend these innovations to encompass a wider range of service strategies and outcomes. For example,

- Iowa's Innovation Zones build on the success of the state's narrower Decategorization Initiative by encouraging a variety of partners to collaborate at the community level to try to improve a wide range of outcomes for children and families.[27]

- Maryland is redefining its Systems Reform Initiative to address services and supports for children and families that go beyond avoiding out-of-home placements, which was the initial focus of the activities of its community partnerships (called Local Management Boards).[28]

Some states have had more difficulty defining the role of their community partnerships in relation to core human-services funding. For example,

- Policy makers' interpretations differ over whether the Oregon County Commissions on Children and Families ought to control their own (parallel) program funds, or develop plans that influence how state agencies allocate their human-services budgets. The county commissions handle some program funds of their own (e.g., Great Start), but also develop comprehensive plans. The plans rarely have a direct impact on the allocation of state agencies' core funds, however, and the commissions' role in relation to the state agencies and to service-provider organizations is still under debate.[29]
- Minnesota's community partnerships (Family Service Collaboratives) receive special-project funds from the state to implement their comprehensive plans. The state encourages them to connect their efforts to other public services and community resources, but has no explicit plans to give them formal power to allocate core human-services funding.[30]

As the community partnerships make the transition to allocating core funds, the state collaborative can play a critical role in supporting and reinforcing the requests of the community partnerships for changes in systemic operations by state agencies and service providers. Some state collaboratives have the authority to waive regulations and propose changes in agency operations in response to requests from individual community partnerships.[31] Some state collaboratives have identified community liaisons within each state agency who are responsible for coordinating the agencies' responses to communities' requests for assistance or resources.[32] Other state collaboratives function more informally as intermediaries between community partnerships and state agencies. In these cases, the agency heads—who are members of the state collaborative—may be able to exert authority within their respective agencies to ensure operational changes that address the concerns of the community partnerships.[33]

Advantages and Drawbacks

These initial approaches and transition strategies suggest a variety of prospects for states' attempts to move toward budgeting by outcomes. The success of Iowa's Decategorization Initiative—in terms of both improved outcomes and political support—indicates the virtues of giving community partnerships responsibility for allocating core funding from the very beginning. Even if the breadth of community responsibility is narrow, control over some core funding enables the communities to drive changes in the way that state agencies and service providers operate (even if only for a few types of services and for specific client populations). Iowa's and Maryland's current efforts to extend the reach of their community partnerships to address a wider range of outcomes for children and families via a broader set of service strategies will illuminate the challenges of starting communities off with responsibility for a narrow base of core funding.

Recent developments in Georgia and Ohio suggest that using special-project funds to build the capacity of community partnerships does not necessarily prevent later attempts to devolve responsibility to them for managing core funds. For the community partnerships to increase their role in allocating core dollars, however, key actors (including state agency staff) must change their expectations about the roles and responsibilities of the community partnerships.

Reformers in Minnesota and Oregon, finally, have not begun to adapt their emerging reforms to address the issue of core funding in a definitive way, and their community partnerships continue to receive only project funds. As the incremental developments in other states illustrate, however, reformers who keep the ultimate aim (fostering joint state and local responsibility for improving outcomes for children and families) clearly in mind can usually find ways to pursue it, regardless of their initial approaches to funding local efforts.

Communitywide Measurement of Outcomes Achieved

Formal or informal evaluation is critical to help policy makers decide whether to continue funding human-services programs, and to enable administrators and service providers to make changes to improve their effectiveness in serving children and families. Evaluations can be based on various criteria, ranging from programs' political popularity to their effects on their target populations.

Existing program evaluation techniques usually compare the effects of a single specific program (a service or intervention, or a package thereof) on one group of children or families with the experiences of a demographically similar control group that receives no intervention. This approach can identify programs that achieve their particular goals with their particular target populations well, but is difficult to use to determine the effectiveness of an array of strategies directed to many different subpopulations in an entire neighborhood or county.[34] Its impact on human-services policies, moreover, can be marginal, as policy decisions often respond to log rolling, political exigencies, and other concerns that have little to do with the measured impact of programs on the lives of children and families.

Policy making in a system of collaborative adjustment, in contrast, focuses explicitly on improving poor outcomes for children and families (such as dropping out of school, unemployment, teen pregnancy, or criminal or violent behavior). Most state collaboratives have identified a set of outcomes or "core results" for children and families that the new system is intended to improve. Core results play two critical roles in a system of collaborative adjustment. They serve as goals that community partnerships' comprehensive plans, and ultimately state budgets, are designed to achieve. Outcomes also serve as measures of communities', and ultimately the system's, performance, and hence as standards for evaluation.[35]

To measure the outcomes that community partnerships achieve, the state collaborative specifies indicators for which the community partnerships can collect annual data.[36] The state collaborative and the community partnerships can use these indicators to measure accomplishments over time in various ways:

- By setting a fixed indicator standard to be achieved (e.g., immunize all two-year-olds by 2000).
- By tracking the change in each indicator from one point in time to another (e.g., increase the percentage of two-year-olds immunized by 2000).
- By tracking the progress achieved on each indicator against a baseline forecast (e.g., increase the percentage of two-year-olds immunized by 10 percent by 2000, to improve on the 2-percent decrease that current trends predict).

The baseline approach is the most realistic and fair, since it takes into account predictions about how indicator data might change in the absence of new service strategies and comprehensive planning. Regular data reports of progress achieved against baselines can provide a continuous source of information to guide the work of community partners and state-level collaborators.[37]

The community partnerships, with assistance from the state collaborative, are generally responsible for tracking the indicator data over time, to enable state and local policy makers, clients, and citizens to monitor what their service strategies achieve. Tracking indicators can be more complicated than it might appear, since different state agencies and community-based organizations—if they track data on the relevant indicators at all—often track them in different ways that make comparisons difficult if not impossible (e.g., by census tract, zip code, school district, service delivery region, etc.). State evaluation plans therefore need to identify uniform indicators, data sources, and tracking methods.[38]

The design and ease of using indicator data to evaluate community performance depends largely on the types of services and families that communities' comprehensive plans address. Community partnerships whose service strategies and target families are extremely specific can measure their accomplishments relatively easily, both in terms of services offered and their fiscal impact.[39] Communities whose comprehensive plans address a variety of families and services face more difficulty determining their successes, their fiscal impact, and the revisions needed to make improvements in the future.

In particular, a communitywide, outcomes-based approach to evaluation has difficulty discerning the precise impact of particular service strategies or program components on the well-being of individual children and families. It nevertheless can offer a portrait of the combined impact of an array of service strategies on outcomes for children and families throughout an entire community. In its role as a central clearinghouse for best practices and good results, the state collaborative may be able to compare and contrast the effectiveness of different combinations of service strategies and implementation efforts in demographically similar counties.[40] While such a strategy could never prove definitively that one set of service strategies is superior to another, it can provide some guidance as to what works and what does not in different kinds of settings. No innovating state has developed its new system of outcome-based evaluation far enough yet to undertake these kinds of comparisons. Planning documents from a few states suggest that evaluators are at least considering trying to structure comparisons of the plans and implementation efforts of different community partnerships.[41] Developing techniques to address these challenges is critical to refining the evaluation component of a system of collaborative adjustment.

Since the ultimate goal of the new system is to improve the results that the community partnerships' service strategies achieve, the new evaluation approach eventually needs to include some consequences for local performance. Some states offer financial incentives to communities that achieve their core results, to encourage innovative efforts to design new service strategies and achieve efficiencies in management and administration. By providing additional resources for community partnerships to use for new service strategies, incentive schemes can make the work of successful community partnerships politically popular as well.[42] Some states also specify that communities that consistently fail to achieve their core results will face sanctions or receive enhanced technical assistance and scrutiny from the state (e.g., Washington), but most states have yet to identify actual penalties for poor performance.

State–Local Partnership Agreements

In addition to collaborating horizontally, neighborhood, county, and state actors can collaborate vertically to design, implement, and evaluate service strategies. Vertical collaboration creates policy-making arrangements that permit local variation in place of a one-size-fits-all system, while simultaneously facilitating cross-site learning, monitoring, and coordination by the state. Local actors are free to craft service strategies and delivery approaches that best suit their own local needs and capacities, supported and overseen by the state collaborative.

As the earlier descriptions of the responsibilities of state, county, and neighborhood collaboratives suggest, however, connections among the activities of the three levels of collaboration remain vague in many instances. To start resolving these ambiguities, some states have designated community partnerships as formal local governance entities, distinguishing them from the more informal collaboratives from which they developed.[43] The state collaborative and these community partnerships have begun to negotiate "partnership agreements" that identify explicit state and local responsibilities for improving outcomes for children and families, and clarify mutual expectations about carrying them out. Some of the issues that these partnership agreements encompass are the following:

Targeted Services and Population(s). The general concept of improving human services for children and families does not specify exactly which services and families the community partnerships will address in their comprehensive plans. Some states specify the types of services and families that community partnerships must address (e.g., children at risk of out-of-home placement in Iowa's Decategorization Project). Other states ask their community partnerships to offer a variety of services to all children and families in specific neighborhoods (e.g., Missouri). Still other states permit their community partnerships to specify which services and population(s) they will address in their comprehensive plans (e.g., Georgia). Instead of specifying which services and populations the community partnerships must address, some states specify that state agencies must retain explicit authority for delivering certain kinds of services (e.g., child protective services in Oregon). Communities then have the option of addressing all other types of services and supports in their comprehensive plans.

Implementation. Some states specify that their community partnerships are responsible for managing the delivery of services, either by deploying staff to a frontline collaborative or by contracting with service providers (e.g., Missouri, Ohio). The public-agency line staff and service providers in the existing system, however, may be loath to give up their current implementation roles, regardless of their (in)competence or (dis)comfort working in a system of collaborative adjustment. The expedient political solution—assigning service provision solely to existing public agencies and service providers—nevertheless leaves community partnerships as mere planning and advisory bodies, with no direct influence on final decisions about service design and delivery. In such a scenario, community partnerships and other policy tools of collaborative adjustment may remain outside the mainstream human-services system. Some states therefore specify that their community partnerships should not implement their comprehensive plans directly, but assign implementation to state agencies and service providers "in partnership with" the local collaboratives.[44] Here the formal role of community partnerships is restricted to planning, and the details of managing and administering their comprehensive plans for service delivery must be worked out with the relevant public agencies and service providers.

Fiscal Authority. The earlier section on flexible funding explored the critical question of which funds may be included in state–local partnership agreements. Regardless of the source of funding for local activities, partnership agreements must resolve the mechanics of flowing funds directly from the state to support local service priorities. The principle of local decision making implies that community partnerships ought to manage funds directly, but both the logistics and the politics of such arrangements cause problems when the funds involved comprise a large portion of the state human-services budget. A practical compromise is to allow community partnerships or the state collaborative to submit budget requests that determine the allocation of state-managed funds. Some states that make pooled funding available to communities, for example, retain fiscal authority at the state level, although community partnerships decide how to allocate the funds.[45] In addition, many states require community partnerships to designate fiscal agents or to establish new collaborative fiscal entities (e.g., the Youth Futures Authority in Savannah, Georgia) to process any funds that they receive from state agencies, private foundations, the federal government, or other sources.

Capacity Building and Training. Training and capacity building may or may not be an explicit component of a state–local partnership agreement, but they are nevertheless an important aspect of the state–local relationship. States usually designate mid-level state staff as liaisons to community partnerships. Some states have also established independent state-level technical-assistance and capacity-building organizations.[46] They offer workshops and networking opportunities for community partnerships, and occasional field trips to other states to learn more about alternative approaches to collaboration, community planning, and service delivery. In addition, some states offer their community partnerships modest funding for staff, planning, collaboration training, and other capacity-building efforts.[47] Many states also develop and document best practices for assessing local needs and delivering comprehensive services, and make them available to the community partnerships. Approaches include pulling together existing models from literature and from other states, as well as working jointly with community partnerships to pilot and refine new strategies specially suited to local conditions.[48]

Negotiation between the State and the Community Partnerships. A few states encourage community partnerships to develop and implement their service strategies independently from the state, as long as they achieve the outcomes the state has designated.[49] This approach threatens to leave community partnerships' activities without a clear structure, and may limit opportunities for cross-site learning, or engender other debilitating effects of local isolation. Other states envision a more substantive role for the state collaborative in working with community partnerships. In order to work together, the state and communities need a process for specifying and carrying out their responsibilities, as well as for revising their commitments and responsibilities when appropriate.

Some states have used a request for proposals (RFP) process to guide the community partnerships in designing and implementing local service strategies.[50] In this approach, communities develop and submit comprehensive plans on their own, in response to parameters that the state specifies in advance in an RFP. The state reviews each plan, and approves it, suggests revisions, or rejects it. Officials in other states maintain that the design and implementation of communities' comprehensive plans can be more effective if state and local partners review and revise the plans together, and then jointly marshal resources (e.g., funding, staff, waivers) for implementation. Holding formal meetings between the state collaborative and community partnerships to discuss the communities' comprehensive plans has been difficult in some states, however, as both parties are still accustomed to top-down processes such as state mandates or RFPs.[51]

To address this difficulty, a few states have begun to specify a process for state–local collaboration in the form of a protocol for negotiation between the state collaborative and community partnerships.[52] Using the protocol, the state collaborative will meet with community partnerships directly to discuss the specific responsibilities, consequences, and risks community partnerships will assume in their new roles as formal governance bodies.[53] The protocol is designed to help both parties work "to understand each other's underlying interests, jointly develop criteria for an acceptable agreement, jointly generate options, and together, build an agreement."[54] By specifying mutual expectations and behavior guidelines, such an explicit framework for negotiation can enable state and community actors who are not used to working as partners to do so more easily. Once established, the framework can provide a structure for regular meetings in which the state collaborative and each community partnership discuss the strengths and weaknesses of the design and the implementation of the community's comprehensive plan, and revise the details of their partnership agreement accordingly.

Iterative Revision: The Master Tool

The ways the various collaboratives work with one another in a system of collaborative adjustment (budgeting based on comprehensive local plans, evaluation using outcome measures, regularly renegotiating responsibilities) lend themselves to cyclical operations. Communities submit their comprehensive plans annually, and once states begin budgeting by outcomes they can do so when they review the community plans. The community partnerships and the state collaborative could also use these regular get-togethers to assess their recent accomplishments and to brainstorm about future plans. This section proposes a systematic way to capitalize on this cycle to improve the effectiveness of the policy tools of collaborative adjustment continuously.

Every year, when each community partnership submits its comprehensive plan, it could meet and negotiate with the state collaborative. The agenda could begin with a review of recent successes and failures, as measured by the outcomes the community partnership has achieved. The two parties could then review and approve a new comprehensive plan developed by the community partnership—including new outcomes to be achieved, revised service strategies, and a redistribution of responsibilities—based on the extent to which each has successfully met the terms of their previous partnership agreement.

By repeating these negotiations annually, the state collaborative and each community partnership could regularly adjust the distribution of responsibilities and authority between themselves according to the community's proven capacity to improve outcomes for children and families. The state collaborative's oversight role would enable it to check inadequate, excessive, or otherwise errant local practices (e.g., violations of civil rights or due process guarantees). By consistently tracking and comparing different communities' indicator data and service strategies, moreover, the state could conduct quasiexperimental evaluations to identify the most effective strategies in particular kinds of communities.[55] The state could then provide planning and management assistance—or coordinate resources and mentoring from neighboring sites—for communities whose comprehensive plans consistently performed poorly as measured by indicator data.[56] The extent of guidance and oversight the state collaborative provides could thus vary by community, depending on each one's track record in assisting children and families. The state collaborative and the community partnerships could specify in their "partnership agreements" what the consequences are if either one of them fails to keep its commitments. The annual occasions for periodic review would enable either the state or the community to take concrete steps to improve a troubled relationship, or to opt out of the agreement if necessary.[57]

Annual repetition of the sequence of community planning, state budgeting, and the negotiation of state and local responsibilities could ultimately form the basis for an iterative cycle of learning about past accomplishments and joint strategizing about how to achieve future improvements.[58] State and local stakeholders would have regular, structured opportunities to assess and revise the particular interventions being used to serve children and families, as well as their responsibilities for designing and managing implementation. This type of cycle would engage key human-services actors in an ongoing joint discussion about policy goals and means—about what they are trying to achieve and how they will achieve it. Such a discussion could help focus the attention of the actors involved on how to achieve measurable improvements in the lives of children and families, giving collaborative adjustment the potential to adapt and improve the effectiveness of human services continuously.

Most states have yet to establish such periodic discussions between the state collaborative and community partnerships, however, for two reasons. First, most community partnerships have only just begun to implement comprehensive plans and measure their results they achieve. Second, most state collaboratives and community partnerships are still unaccustomed to working together as partners.[59] A few local collaboratives have nevertheless used indicator data to inform the redesign of their service strategies. By scrutinizing the outcomes that past service strategies produce, collaborators have identified areas in which new approaches are needed. The Chatham–Savannah (Georgia) Youth Futures Authority, for example, was formed to improve the lives and school performance of at-risk youth and young adolescents. After several years of work, collaborators recognized that some of the bad outcomes they sought to prevent for junior high and high school students could only be addressed by intervening when the children were younger. The authority therefore added new service strategies focused on improving early childhood development and elementary education. Another local example of iterative learning from outcomes achieved comes from Ware County, Georgia. The Family Connection Collaborative there initially created a one-stop service center for youth (DAISY), to provide a range of services and supports, including efforts to prevent teen pregnancy. Despite some success in reducing the rates of teen pregnancy, collaborators recognized that they still needed to assist those teens that became pregnant and had children anyway. In response, they developed a new network of service provision for pregnant women and infants (DAFFODIL).[60]

These examples represent one-time uses of indicator data to refocus service strategies and collaborative efforts. They suggest the possibility that these communities, and eventually entire states, may begin using more structured, consistent approaches to learning iteratively from the outcomes they have achieved. At least some state and local practitioners intend to continue moving in this direction.[61]

THE PROMISE OF IMPROVED PERFORMANCE: SYNERGY AMONG THE POLICY TOOLS

Collaborative adjustment could help improve human-services performance in four ways:

1. Desired outcomes for children and families—rather than categories of need, programs, and funding—would guide community planning of services and state funding for implementation.
2. To achieve those outcomes, a range of responsive services would be available to families across agency lines through service-delivery strategies that customize packages of services and supports in response to the particular strengths and needs of individual families.
3. Interagency collaboratives at the neighborhood and county levels would design and implement these service strategies. State-level interagency

collaboration would support the customization of services by adjusting management practices and policies in response to local conditions as presented in comprehensive community plans.

4. Desired outcomes for children and families would also serve as the basis for evaluating local plans and implementation. State and county collaborators would meet regularly to examine the outcomes they have achieved, and revise local service strategies as well as the distribution of state and local responsibilities. As a result, state support and oversight of local efforts would be customized to the capacity and limitations of each county collaborative, just as the service strategies themselves would be customized to the strengths and needs of individual families.

In this portrait of collaborative adjustment, local actors direct key aspects of the policy-making process—including the design, funding, and delivery of services—to achieve specific improvements in outcomes for children and families. At the same time, they do not work in isolation. They receive hands-on assistance and oversight from the state collaborative to help them learn from one another and from other states about best practices, and to hold them accountable for achieving specific results. The measurement and comparison of the results that different communities achieve, along with the broad base of stakeholders and lay participants involved in local decision making, can create pressures and foster new ideas to improve performance.

As with any system of human services, the success of collaborative adjustment depends on its implementation, which is by no means assured. The changes in work habits and organizational cultures that the new fiscal arrangements, service strategies, and daily work of collaboration entail are unfamiliar at best, and threatening to many. The line staff of most state agencies, for example, are not involved yet in most of the new system's operations. Collaborative adjustment can only move beyond being an idea and a set of emerging practices and become a new way of making human-services policies if line staff commit to it, or if state-level proponents can find alternative local partners with whom to collaborate.

Three effects of the new system nevertheless may counteract these obstacles to successful implementation. Two are "disciplining" effects built into the system's design: planning and evaluating by outcomes, and iteratively assessing and revising service strategies and actors' responsibilities. The third may result from the process of implementation: The joint, pragmatic efforts of committed practitioners may become self-reinforcing over time.

Disciplining Effects. Outcomes provide a focal point on which all actors can (most likely) agree. Prioritizing outcomes when funding is scarce, or deciding how best to achieve them, may provoke disagreement, but collaborators are still likely to be able to agree on what generic results they want to achieve for children and families. As shared goals, outcomes can inspire actors to restart negotiations or collaborative processes that have faltered or run into difficulty. The very process of identifying shared goals, moreover, may begin to turn distant bureaucratic enemies into collaborative partners by creating a joint interest and willingness to work together on other tasks (e.g., to design service strategies, negotiate responsibilities, or allocate funding). As evaluation measures, indicators provide a relatively objective means of assessing progress. Collaborators may disagree in interpreting and reacting to their accomplishments, but they at least have common reference points that measure their achievements.

The goal of improving outcomes can also foster local cooperation instead of obstructionism: Since the state is monitoring whether they achieve specific results, actors may choose to collaborate to try to succeed if the alternative is to fail separately. In this context, pragmatic attempts to work together may have an advantage over finger pointing, blame shifting, and other destructive behavior.

The iterative master tool of collaborative adjustment forces state and local collaborators to convene periodically to discuss what they have done and where they want to go. Such discussions offer opportunities for flexibility in redesigning services and in reallocating responsibilities for planning, funding, delivering, and evaluating them. This flexibility, in turn, gives collaborative adjustment the potential to adapt, both to the successes and failures of particular service strategies in communities, and to limits or breakdowns in the capacity of individual community partnerships or state agencies to carry out the responsibilities to which they have agreed.

The possibility of adaptation over time in response to diverging developments in different localities sets collaborative adjustment in stark contrast to the existing system of human services, in which legislation and administrative rules centrally designate categories of human need and services to address them. Under these circumstances, if adaptation occurs at all, it must happen via a one-size-fits-all redesignation that may not accommodate differences in the situations of individual families or the capacities of local service providers. A key virtue of the existing centralized system, however, is its uniform standards for service delivery and procedural guarantees for recipients. Collaborative adjustment's monitoring and evaluation approach nevertheless permits the state to promote equitable treatment for individual children and families, while also recognizing local differences and fostering systemic adaptation.

Self-Reinforcing Effects. The processes of implementing the policy tools of collaborative adjustment may, over time, reinforce collaborators' willingness to work together. The experience of working together to craft local plans and negotiate agreements about outcomes and budgets may gradually improve actors' familiarity and comfort level with one another and with the collaborative process in general. Collaborators who achieve some success, moreover—whether by submitting a well-crafted comprehensive community plan, or actually improving outcomes for children and families—may develop a camaraderie that helps them continue collaborating during hard times. The final appeal of the tools of collaborative adjustment is personal: Working creatively with others to improve outcomes for particular children and families seems inherently more pleasant and interesting than working separately to implement a program that distant policy makers have designed to address generic human needs.

CONCLUSION: BUILDING AND INSTITUTIONALIZING SYSTEM CAPACITY AND POPULARITY

The policy tools of collaborative adjustment distinguish it from the existing system of human services in the United States in fundamental ways. Under collaborative adjustment, state policy makers essentially grant local actors more authority over state resources in exchange for a promise to measure and improve the results they achieve with their newfound flexibility. This chapter has offered promising examples, but documented only limited progress toward a fully operational system of collaborative adjustment. States, it seems, are adopting the policy tools of collaborative adjustment piecemeal, and even the foremost pioneers still face the daunting prospect of going to scale and institutionalizing them.

Which tools a state adopts, and in what order, affect the likely success of its reform efforts, as the discussions of advantages and drawbacks indicate. While there may be no one best path to collaborative adjustment, the approaches and timing with which a state puts various tools in place influence the possibilities for successfully adopting additional ones in the future. The experience of Iowa's Innovation Zones, for example, may differ from that of the block grants that Ohio has made to its County Family and Children First Councils. Iowa is attempting to extend the responsibilities of "enclave" local collaboratives that are responsible for a small set of core human-services funds. Ohio is seeking to build on the efforts of collaborative county councils that have been operating comprehensive service programs parallel to the existing mainstream human-services system. Both approaches to building local capacity are viable, but the two are worth comparing to see if early choices about system design have path-dependent effects on later efforts to expand systemic change.

Regardless of the sequence of the change process, conflicts among collaborators are likely at various points. Disputes may arise over general policy directions, or over the priority given to different service strategies to achieve a given policy direction. For example, state legislatures and agencies may seek to conserve public resources by requiring community partnerships to place welfare recipients in jobs, or to reduce out-of-home placements of children in troubled families. Community partnerships, however, may be more interested in developing an array of family-centered services and supports that may cost more (at least in the short run) than the services that some families already receive from the existing system. Debates over these types of issues by a broad base of state and community stakeholders who agree to try to achieve a set of outcome goals for children and families nevertheless have constructive potential, because they entail discussions about the best means to achieve concrete goals.

The policy tools of collaborative adjustment can structure policy discussions and implementation in productive ways. The process of implementing the tools may also increase stakeholders' support for the new system, and increase the political popularity of human services, through citizen participation in improving their effectiveness. A system of collaborative adjustment, in consequence, just might offer human services that are more effective and politically popular than they are under the existing system.

NOTES

Many thanks to the state and local officials who provided so much of the information contained in this chapter. Thanks for comments on earlier drafts to Gene Bardach, Frank Farrow, Mark Friedman, Michael Lipsky, Chuck Sabel, and Tom Sample. Any errors of fact or misinterpretation are mine, and I welcome comments or corrections.

1. This chapter is based on detailed research in six states (Georgia, Iowa, Minnesota, Missouri, Ohio, and Oregon), and more cursory research in a few others (e.g., Maryland, Washington). The research involved reviewing state planning documents, reports, and evaluation studies, as well as interviewing state and local policy makers and staff.

2. Portions of this section draw directly on S. Page, "State and Local Governance Structures for Comprehensive, Integrated Services: Options and Strategic Rationales," draft paper prepared under contract for the Missouri Family Investment Trust, St. Louis, Missouri, July 1996. Thanks to the Family Investment Trust for permission to use the material.

3. L. Schorr, *Within Our Reach* (New York: Anchor, 1988); J. Kinney, K. Strand, M. Hagerup, and C. Bruner, *Beyond the Buzzwords* (resource brief) (Falls Church, Va.: National Center for Service Integration, 1994).

4. Interview by author with Georgia state official, 1996.

5. Child Protective Services (CPS) in Jacksonville, Florida, for example, asks families it serves to identify supportive friends or neighbors, and develops an agreement that specifies what they will do to support the family and under what circumstances they will recontact the CPS agency. Housing managers may keep an eye on families, or a neighbor may visit daily to ensure that parents are taking care of their children. The Patch Project in Iowa integrates informal supports with formal services for families, using neighborhood offices that operate as part of the community. See J. Waldfogel, "Rethinking the Paradigm for Child Protection," *The Future of Children* 8 (1998).

6. Examples include Missouri Caring Communities (school-linked services) and Ohio's Family Resource Centers.

7. Georgia's Family Connection is an example. The Service Strategy Team of the Georgia Family Policy Council assists state agencies and communities in designing and implementing various service strategies. See Georgia Policy Council, "How We Are Organized for Implementing *The Framework for Improving Results*" (Atlanta, 13 February 1997, mimeographed), 7. The team recently completed piloting, revising, and disseminating a new preventive-service strategy for communities to implement, called universal contact at birth. Once the team refined the new service strategy, the legislature provided funding to serve every newborn child in the state. Interviews by author with state officials, 1996, 1997.

8. Examples include Oregon's Community Partnership initiative and Minnesota's Family Service Collaboratives.

9. Examples include Iowa's Decategorization Initiative and Maryland's Local Management Boards. The Decategorization Initiative brings together local Department of Human Services staff, the juvenile court, and the Board of Supervisors in each county and lets them use various child-welfare funding streams to offer a flexible array of preventive and treatment services to families to reduce the need for restrictive, institutional, out-of-home services.

10. Iowa's Decategorization Initiative, for example, started in only two counties, took ten years to expand around the state, and still only targets a very specific population and range of services (alternatives to out-of-home placement).

11. For examples and details, see Center for the Study of Social Policy, *Systems Change at the Neighborhood Level: Creating Better Futures for Children, Youth, and Families* (Washington, D.C.: Author, 1996).

12. In Missouri, for example, "The community partnerships are ... more than advisory, planning, or coordinating bodies. They are making strategic decisions using good community assessments, more reliable data, and a collaborative process. These decisions are about how services are organized and funded for children and families in their communities. Community partnerships are moving toward sharing the responsibility and the

risk for their decisions with state agencies." P. Rozansky, *Navigating the River of Change: The Course of Missouri's Community Partnerships* (St. Louis: Family Investment Trust, 1997), 19.

13. In Georgia, for example, each community partnership's comprehensive plan features objectives, a target population, service strategies, and intermediate performance standards for each core result (or outcome) to be achieved. The Dawson County Family Connection Partnership, for example, seeks to achieve the outcome of preventing teenage pregnancy by "reduc[ing] the five-year average rate of pregnancies for 15–17 year old girls from 42.1 to 30.0 within five years." Their target group is "families of: children living in poverty in female-headed families, children who experience early school failure, children who are abused/neglected." Service strategies consist of "economic development, school referral and resource system for high risk youth, preventive health and delinquency programs." Intermediate performance standards include getting partners to cooperate on the referral and resource system, economic development, and prevention programs. See Georgia Policy Council for Children and Families, "Summary of Community Partnership Comprehensive Plans" (Atlanta, 28 March 1997, mimeographed), 4.

14. Examples include Georgia and Ohio, among others. In Iowa, county Boards of Supervisors are members of the county Decategorization Boards.

15. Washington state legislation, for example, specifies that thirteen of the twenty-three members of each Community Health and Safety Network board must be "non-fiduciary" members, and that the others must be fiduciary. The aim is to have both lay participants and service providers at the table to generate innovative and sensitive responses to local issues. Provider-only planning can help coordinate services, but rarely transcends existing programs and systems. Citizen participation, in contrast, can move the discussion beyond how to design programs in a way that splits existing funds among current providers. Disputes may continue among providers over which program strategies are best and how to allocate funds, but the providers ultimately need at least a portion of the citizen majorities to make binding decisions. The citizen–provider split helps focus the dialogue on designing service strategies and using data to evaluate activities, and can prevent outright log-rolling among providers. Interviews by author with Washington state official, 1995, 1997. For similar reasons, the Deschutes County (Oregon) Commission on Children and Families and the Local Investment Commission (LINC) in Kansas City (Jackson County), Missouri, have established boards comprised entirely of lay citizens.

16. Interview by author with Frank Farrow, Center for the Study of Social Policy, 1997.

17. Membership in Children's Cabinets is usually restricted to participants in the executive branch of state government: the directors of state agencies that serve children and families, a representative from the governor's office, and sometimes the director of the state department of budget, finance, or administration (e.g., Maryland, Minnesota, Ohio). State Policy Councils or Commissions on Children and Families are usually more inclusive (e.g., Georgia, Oregon, Washington). They often include state

agency heads as ex-officio members, as well as state legislators, business representatives, civic and religious leaders, community representatives (sometimes at large, sometimes from the community partnerships), local government representatives, service providers, policy analysts, advocates, and consumers. Depending on the state, these members are appointed by the governor, the lieutenant governor, members of the legislature (e.g., the speaker, president, or committee chairs), and/or the groups to be represented themselves.

18. States using this approach include Maryland and Ohio.

19. Examples include the Georgia Academy and the Missouri Family Investment Trust.

20. Georgia, for example, has a state team responsible for developing and disseminating new service strategies (see note 7), as well as a Management Team that establishes ad hoc teams (nicknamed "Barrier Busters") as needed to address policy barriers that communities have identified. Georgia Policy Council, "How We Are Organized," 8.

21. See Georgia's web page, for example: http://www.pccf.state.ga.us/ results (last visited March 1999).

22. A number of states (e.g., Minnesota, Oklahoma) currently have Children's Budgets, which identify the public funds spent on different programs for children and families. These differ from budgets that are actually based on outcomes in response to community partnerships' comprehensive plans.

23. This term and the following paragraph draw directly on the Center for the Study of Social Policy, *From Outcomes to Budgets* (draft) (Washington, D.C.: Author, 1995), 12–18. For further details and examples of the process of budgeting by outcomes, see M. Friedman, *A Strategy Map for Results-Based Budgeting* (Washington, D.C.: Finance Project, 1996). For examples and a discussion of outcomes and their use in evaluating community partnerships' efforts, see the next section.

24. For example, Minnesota, Missouri, Ohio's Family Resource Centers.

25. For example, Iowa's Decategorization Initiative and Maryland's Systems Reform Initiative both seek to reduce out-of-home placements. Ohio's Wellness Block Grant seeks to prevent teen pregnancy. For a more detailed discussion of the issues involved in using project funds or core funds to support communities' service strategies, see the Center for the Study of Social Policy, *Trading Outcome Accountability for Fund Flexibility* (Washington, D.C.: Author, 1995), especially pp. 22–23.

26. "Each community partnership is created . . . to achieve a core set of results defined jointly by the community partnership and the [state] Policy Council; to develop, adopt, submit to the Policy Council for approval, and from time to time amend, a comprehensive plan for public and private agencies to deal effectively with the problems of children, youth, and families . . . ; to coordinate, evaluate, and provide services and assistance in implementing and carrying out the comprehensive plan . . . ; and to contract with public and private agencies . . . to provide programs and services . . . to carry out the provisions of the comprehensive plan." Georgia Senate Bill 256, Section 49-5-260.

27. In accordance with legislation enacted in 1996, "a new equal partnership will be developed between the Innovation Zones and the State to provide technical assistance, negotiate local flexibility, and share the risk and the responsibility for improving results for children and families." *Bold Steps . . . Breakthrough Results* (Des Moines, Iowa, mimeographed), 36.

28. In the words of one state official, systems reform "is a way of looking at how we provide all kinds of services that affect families (economic development, health care, transportation, job training, child care, etc.), rather than being a particular program or set of services for particular populations." Interview by author with Maryland state official, 1997.

29. Exacerbating the confusion, the state Department of Human Resources recently established a separate "Community Partnerships Team" initiative, in which local collaboratives—some centered around county Commissions on Children and Families—design and implement local service plans, and the state agency adapts its operations to support them. Interviews by author with state and county officials in Oregon, 1996, 1997.

30. Interviews by author with Minnesota state officials, 1996.

31. For example, Georgia's "Barrier Busters" team. See note 20.

32. For example, Missouri's Caring Communities Coordinators.

33. The members of Ohio's Children's Cabinet play this role, for example. Interview by author with Ohio state official, 1996.

34. On the limits of using control sites to evaluate comprehensive initiatives, see R. Hollister and J. Hill, "Problems in the Evaluation of Community-Wide Initiatives," in *New Approaches to the Evaluation of Comprehensive Community Initiatives*, ed. J. Connell, A. Kubisch, L. Schorr, and C. Weiss (Washington, D.C.: Aspen Institute, 1995).

35. Georgia Policy Council, "How We Are Organized," 5.

36. Georgia's Core Results, for example, are healthy children, children ready for school, children succeeding in school, strong families, and economically self-sufficient families. The state policy council has specified indicators to measure progress on each result (e.g., healthy children will be measured by, among other indicators, the percentage of children immunized by age two). See Georgia Policy Council, *On Behalf of Our Children: A Framework for Improving Results* (Atlanta: Author, 1996). For other state outcomes and indicators, see Center for the Study of Social Policy, *Trading Outcome Accountability*, Appendix A.

37. This paragraph draws directly on Friedman, *Strategy Map for Results-Based Budgeting*, 20–23. Also see Center for the Study of Social Policy, *Trading Outcome Accountability*, 10–11.

38. Missouri's evaluation plan, for example, specifies that data will be tracked by zip code, using school-wide averages for students enrolled in Caring Communities (school-linked services) schools, and individually for "core clients" identified by each school. The schools and relevant state departments are responsible for tracking specific indicators that they have the data to measure. The findings will show state and local collaborators "how the benchmarks [indicators] are changing for Caring Communities' neighborhoods, schools, and core clients," as well as "how these changes compare to similar neighborhoods, schools, and individuals." Philliber

Research Associates, *Using Benchmarks to Chart the Progress in Caring Communities* (St. Louis: Author, 1997), 4–5.

39. Iowa's and Maryland's efforts, for example, focus explicitly on families at risk of out-of-home placement. Not only is the target population clearly defined, but the outcome—avoiding out-of-home placements—is easy to measure.

40. This observation is inspired by C. Sabel, "Learning by Monitoring," in *The Handbook of Economic Sociology*, ed. N. Smelser and R. Swedberg (Princeton: Princeton University Press, 1994); C. Sabel, "A Measure of Federalism," paper prepared for the workshop Manufacturing Modernization: Evaluation Practices, Methods, and Results, Atlanta, Georgia, 18–20 September, 1994.

41. For example, Georgia and Missouri. See Georgia Policy Council for Children and Families, *Aiming for Results: A Guide to Georgia's Benchmarks for Children and Families* (Atlanta: Author, 1996); Philliber Research Associates, *Using Benchmarks*.

42. Iowa's Decategorization Initiative, for example, permits counties to apply the savings they achieve through service improvements to new, preventive-service strategies. The initiative has reduced out-of-home foster placements, and proven popular in participating counties. See Human Services Research Institute, *Iowa Decategorization and Statewide Child Welfare Reform: An Outcome Evaluation*, prepared for the Iowa Department of Human Services, August 1995.

43. Leading examples include Georgia, Maryland, Missouri, Vermont, and Washington.

44. For example, Oregon. Oregon nevertheless permits their community partnerships (called County Commissions on Children and Families) to implement a few specific services (e.g., Great Start, which offers preventive services for families with children ages birth to six), even though the communities' comprehensive plans themselves are supposed to guide the work of existing public agencies and service providers. Whether the county commissions should implement services directly or function solely as planning and coordinating bodies has engendered significant confusion and contention since their inception. Interviews by author with state and county officials in Oregon, 1996, 1997.

45. Iowa's Decategorization Initiative uses this approach.

46. For example, Georgia and Missouri. See note 19.

47. Examples include Minnesota, Ohio, and Oregon. Georgia's Family Connection secured outside foundation funding for these purposes at first, which the legislature later supplemented and eventually replaced.

48. Georgia has developed an effective approach to the latter. See note 7.

49. The state's role in this case is that of an "outside monitor." See C. Bruner, *Legislating Devolution* (draft occasional paper no. 21) (Des Moines, Iowa: Child and Family Policy Center, 1996). This "hands-off" approach characterizes a number of brand new attempts at state-initiated, community-driven planning for human services in states such as Arkansas and Maine. Interviews by author with state officials in Arkansas and Maine, 1997.

50. Examples include Minnesota's Family Service Collaboratives and West Virginia's Family Resource Networks.

51. In some instances, members of the state collaborative have expected the community partnerships to request funding or waivers for new services, while the community partnerships were waiting for the state collaborative to suggest approaches to them. This mismatch in expectations stems from long-standing patterns of doing business, and from a game of "chicken": Communities worry that the state will not live up to its promise to support innovative local proposals, but instead will resist them. The state, however, cannot proceed without community initiative, since the basis of the new system is bottom-up planning. Interviews by author with officials in Georgia, 1995, and Missouri, 1996.

52. States currently developing protocols for state–local negotiations include Georgia, Illinois, Maryland, and Vermont.

53. See the Center for the Study of Social Policy, *Trading Outcome Accountability*, 5–18.

54. "Rather than mandates from the state or leaving communities to struggle on their own, this effort is based upon a clear desire to develop a mutually acceptable framework, supported by an effective working relationship, to . . . reform the human service system." W. Potapchuk, *Managing the State–Local Negotiations on "Vision to Scale" in the State of Maryland* (Baltimore: Governor's Office of Children, Youth, and Families, 1997), 1, 4.

55. On the potential for improving system performance through quasiexperimental comparisons among comparable geographic regions, see Sabel, "A Measure of Federalism."

56. Several of my interviews suggest that state reformers are currently puzzling over how to operationalize such an approach. Interviews by author with state officials in Georgia and Missouri, 1996.

57. See Center for the Study of Social Policy, *Trading Outcomes Accountability*, 17–18.

58. This idea draws on Sabel, "Learning by Monitoring." On the concept of a human-services learning organization, see S. Gardner, "Afterword," in *The Politics of Linking Schools and Social Services*, ed. L. Adler and S. Gardner (Washington, D.C.: Falmer Press, 1994).

59. Interviews by author with state officials in Georgia, 1996, and Missouri, 1997. The game of "chicken" between state and local collaborators illustrates this problem nicely (see note 51).

60. Interviews by author with staff of the Chatham–Savannah Youth Futures Authority and the Ware County Children's Initiative, 1996.

61. Interviews by author with Georgia officials, 1996; Philliber Research Associates, *Using Benchmarks*.

Bibliography

Albo, Gregory, David Langille, and Leo Panitch, eds. *A Different Kind of State? Popular Power and Democratic Administration*. Toronto: Oxford University Press, 1993.

Ashford, Douglas E. *British Dogmatism and French Pragmatism*. London: Allen and Unwin, 1982.

Aucoin, Peter, and Herman Bakvis. *The Centralization–Decentralization Conundrum: Organization and Management in the Canadian Government*. Halifax, Nova Scotia: Institute for Research on Public Policy, 1988.

Ball, Terrence, James Farr, and Russell L. Hanson. *Political Innovation and Conceptual Change*. New York: Cambridge University Press, 1989.

Barber, Benjamin. *Jihad vs. McWorld: How Globalism and Tribalism Are Reshaping the World*. New York: Ballantine Books, 1996.

Bates, Robert, and Anne O. Krueger. *Political and Economic Interaction in Economic Policy Reform*. Oxford: Basil Blackwell, 1993.

Bennett, Robert, ed. *Local Government and Market Decentralization: Experiences in Industrialized, Developing, and Former Eastern Bloc Countries*. Tokyo: United Nations University Press, 1994.

Boston, Jonathan, John Martin, June Pallot, and Pat Walsh. *Public Management: The New Zealand Model*. Auckland: Oxford University Press, 1996.

Bryson, John M. *Strategic Planning for Nonprofit Organizations: A Guide to Strengthening and Sustaining Organizational Achievement*. San Francisco: Jossey-Bass, 1995.

Burlingame, Dwight, ed. *Capacity for Change: The Nonprofit World in the Age of Devolution*. Indianapolis: Indiana University Center on Philanthropy, 1996.

Collier, David. *The New Authoritarianism in Latin America*. Princeton: Princeton University Press, 1979.

Conlan, Timothy. *New Federalism: Intergovernmental Reform from Nixon to Reagan*. Washington, D.C.: The Brookings Institution, 1988.

Diamond, Larry, Juan J. Linz, and Seymour Martin Lipset, eds. *Democracy in Developing Countries*. Boulder, Colo.: Lynne Rienner, 1989.

Drucker, Peter F. *Managing the Non-Profit Organization: Principles and Practices*. New York: HarperCollins, 1992.

Falk, Richard A., S. S. Kim, and S. H. Mendlovitx, eds. *Toward a Just World Order*. Boulder, Colo.: Westview Press, 1982.

Fox, Jonathan, and Josefina Aranda. *Decentralization and Rural Development in Mexico: Community Participation in Oaxaca's Municipal Funds Program*. San Diego: Center for U.S.–Mexico Studies, 1996.

Frank, Andre G. *Critique and Anti-Critique: Essays on Dependency and Reformism*. Westport, Conn.: Praeger, 1984.

Freedom House. *Freedom in the World: The Annual Survey of Political Rights and Civil Liberties, 1995–1996*. New York: Freedom House, 1996.

Fukuyama, Francis. *The End of History and the Last Man*. New York: Penguin, 1992.

Graham, Carol. *Safety Nets, Politics, and the Poor: Transitions to Market Economies*. Washington, D.C.: The Brookings Institution, 1994.

Grey, Robert D. *Democratic Theory and Post-Communist Change*. Englewood Cliffs, N.J.: Prentice Hall, 1997.

Gwartney, James, Robert Lawson, and Walter Block, eds. *Economic Freedom of the World, 1975–1995*. Vancouver: Fraser Institute, 1996.

Haggard, Stephan, and Steven B. Webb, eds. *Voting for Reforms: Democracy, Political Liberalisation and Economic Adjustment*. New York: World Bank, Oxford University Press, 1994.

Henig, Jeffrey R. *Public Policy and Federalism: Issues in State and Local Politics*. New York: St. Martin's Press, 1985.

Herman, Robert D., ed. *The Jossey-Bass Handbook of Nonprofit Leadership and Management*. San Francisco: Jossey-Bass, 1994.

Huntington, Samuel, Myron Weiner, and Gabriel Almond. *Understanding Political Development: An Analytic Study*. New York: HarperCollins; and Boston: Little, Brown, 1987.

Inter-American Development Bank IDB. *Economic and Social Progress in Latin America*. Baltimore: Johns Hopkins University Press, 1997.

Johnson, Bryan T., and Thomas P. Sheehy. *1996 Index of Economic Freedom*. Washington, D.C.: Heritage Foundation, 1996.

Kettl, Donald F. *The Regulation of American Federalism: With a New Epilogue*. Baltimore: Johns Hopkins University Press, 1987.

Kofman, Eleonoe, and Gillian Youngs, eds. *Globalization: Theory and Practices*. New York: Pinter, 1996.

König, Klaus. *Public Administration: Post-Industrial, Post-Modern, Post-Bureaucratic*. Budapest: EGPA, 1996.

Kuper, Adam, and Jessica Kuper, eds. *The Social Science Encyclopedia*. 2d ed. London: Routledge, 1996.

Lane, Jan Erik. *Constitutions and Political Theory.* New York: Manchester University Press, 1996.

Lipson, Leslie. *The Great Issues of Politics: An Introduction to Political Science.* Englewood Cliffs, N.J.: Prentice Hall, 1989.

Liu, Shao-qi. *Selected Works of Liu Shao-qi.* Beijing: People's Press, 1985.

Luo, Rong-qu. *The Quest for the Process of China's Modernization.* Beijing: Beijing University Press, 1992.

Mainwaring, Scott, and Timothy R. Scully, eds. *Building Democratic Institutions: Party Systems in Latin America.* Stanford, Calif.: Stanford University Press, 1995.

Mao, Ze-dong. *Selected Works of Mao Ze-dong.* Beijing: People's Press, 1977.

Marin, Bernd, ed. *Governance and Generalized Exchange: Self-Organizing Policy Networks in Action.* Boulder, Colo.: Westview Press, 1990.

Massey, Andrew. *Managing the Public Sector: A Comparative Analysis of the United Kingdom and the United States.* Aldershot, England: Edward Elgar, 1993.

Messick, Richard, ed. *World Survey of Economic Freedom, 1995–96: A Freedom House Study.* New Brunswick, N.J.: Transaction Publishers, 1996.

Metcalfe, Les, and Sue Richards. *Improving Public Management.* London: Sage, 1990.

Meyer, John W., and W. Richard Scott, eds. *Organizational Environments: Ritual and Rationality.* Beverly Hills: Sage, 1983.

Mintzberg, Henry. *The Structuring of Organizations: A Synthesis of the Research.* Englewood Cliffs, N.J.: Prentice Hall, 1979.

Montanheiro, Luiz, Robert Haigh, and David Morris, eds. *Understanding Public and Private Sector Parternships.* Sheffield, England: Hallam University Press, 1997.

Nutt, Paul C., and R. Backhoff. *Strategic Management of Public and Third-Sector Organizations: A Handbook for Leaders.* San Francisco: Jossey-Bass, 1992.

Oates, Wallace E., ed. *The Political Economy of Fiscal Federalism.* Lexington, Mass.: Lexington Books, 1977.

O'Donnell, Guillermo A. *Modernization and Bureaucratic–Authoritarianism: Studies in South American Politics.* Berkeley: Institute of International Studies, University of California, 1973.

Olasky, Marvin N. *The Tragedy of American Compassion.* Washington, D.C.: Regency Press, 1992.

Organization for Economic Cooperation and Development (OECD). *Integrating People Management into Public Service Reform.* Washington, D.C.: OECD, 1996.

Ostrom, Vincent. *The Meaning of Democracy and the Vulnerability of Democracies.* Ann Arbor: University of Michigan Press, 1997.

O'Toole, Barry J., and A. G. Jordan. *Next Steps: Improving Management in Government.* Dartmouth: Aldershot, 1995.

Owens, Edgar. *The Future of Freedom in the Developing World: Economic Development as Political Reform.* New York: Pergamon Press, 1987.

Payne, Leigh A. *Brazilian Industrialists and Democratic Change.* Baltimore: Johns Hopkins University Press, 1994.

Peterson, George E. *Decentralization in Latin America: Learning through Experience.* Washington, D.C.: World Bank, 1997.

Pinkney, Robert. *Democracy in the Third World.* Boulder, Colo.: Lynne Rienner, 1994.

Rothgeb, John M. *Foreign Investment and Political Conflict in Developing Countries.* Westport, Conn.: Praeger, 1996.

Safran, W. *The French Polity.* White Plains, N.Y.: Longman, 1991.

Salamon, Lester M. *America's Nonprofit Sector: A Primer.* New York: Foundation Center, 1992.

Saxena, Pradeep. *Public Policy, Administration and Development.* Jaipur: Rupa Books, 1988.

Sbragia, Albert M. *Debt Wish: Entrepreneurial Cities, U.S. Federalism, and Economic Development.* Pittsburgh: University of Pittsburgh Press, 1996.

Schmalensee, Richard, and Robert Willig, eds. *Handbook of Industrial Organization.* Amsterdam: Elsevier, 1989.

Seligson, Mitchell A., and John T. Passé-Smith, eds. *Development and Underdevelopment: The Political Economy of Inequality.* Boulder, Colo.: Lynne Rienner, 1993.

Silva, Eduardo. *The State and Capital in Chile: Business Elites, Technocrats, and Market Economics.* Boulder, Colo.: Westview Press, 1966.

Slater, Robert R., Barry Schutz, and Steven Dorr, eds. *Global Transformation and the Third World.* Boulder, Colo.: Lynne Rienner, 1993.

Smith, Steven R., and Michael Lipsky. *Nonprofits for Hire: The Welfare State in the Age of Contracting.* Cambridge: Harvard University Press, 1993.

Wang, Bang-zhuo, and Li Hui-kang. *Socio-Ecological Analysis on the Western Political Party's System.* Shanghai: XueLin Press, 1997.

Waterbury, John. *Exposed to Innumerable Delusions: Public Enterprises and State Power in Egypt, India, Mexico, and Turkey.* Cambridge: Cambridge University Press, 1993.

United Nations Development Program (UNDP). *Human Development Report.* New York: Oxford University Press, 1994.

Vanhanen, Tatu. *Prospects of Democracy: A Study of 172 Countries.* London: Routledge, 1997.

Wiarda, Howard J. *Latin American Politics: A New World of Possibility.* Belmont, Calif.: Wadsworth, 1995.

Wiarda, Howard J., and Harvey F. Kline, eds. *Latin American Politics and Development.* 4th ed. Boulder, Colo.: Westview Press, 1996.

World Bank. *World Development Report, 1996.* Washington, D.C.: World Bank, 1996.

Young, Dennis, Robert M. Hollister, and Virginia Ann Hodgkinson, eds. *Governing, Leading and Managing Nonprofit Organizations.* San Francisco: Jossey-Bass, 1993.

Zhao, Zhen-jiang. *The Forty Years of China's Legal Institutions.* Beijing: Beijing University Press, 1990.

Zifcak, Spencer. *New Manageralism: Administrative Reform in Whitehall and Canberra.* Buckingham, England: Open University Press, 1994.

Index

About the Editor
and Contributors

Neelima Deshmukh is Head of the Post Graduate Teaching Department of Public Administration and Local Self-Government at Nagpur University. She is Chairperson of Nagpur University Employee's Credit Cooperative Society. She worked with the late Prime Minister Shri Rajeev Gandhi in drafting the 73rd Amendment Bill. She is Chief Managing Trustee of the Shirish Memorial Education and Cultural Trust and is active in the training of elected women public representatives of local government organizations.

Sherry J. Fontaine has served on the faculty of public-administration programs at Marywood University and Memphis University. She has taught in the areas of nonprofit management and health management. Her research interests are in health and human services strategic planning and marketing, and in the interactions between the nonprofit, public, and private sectors. She is currently on the administrative staff at Indiana University–Purdue University of Indianapolis.

John W. Harbeson is Professor of Political Science in the Graduate Center and Chairman of the Department of Political Science at the City College in the City University of New York. His books include *The Ethiopian Transformation: The Quest for the Post-Imperial State, Civil Society and the State in Africa* (ed. with Donald Rothchild and Naomi Chazan), and *Africa in World Politics* (ed. with

Donald Rothchild, now in its 3d edition). In 1998–1999, he was a Jennings Randolph Senior Fellow at the United States Institute of Peace.

Douglas N. Jones is currently Professor of Regulatory Economics at the School of Public Policy and Management at Ohio State University and is Director Emeritus of the National Regulatory Research Institute at Ohio State. He taught economics at the U.S. Air Force Academy and has been a lecturer in public-utility economics at several universities, including the University of Colorado and Alaska Methodist University. He has held research and policy positions in the Johnson administration, served on the U.S. Senate staff, and worked for the Congressional Research Service, Library of Congress. His publications have appeared in various professional and academic journals, conference proceedings, and committee prints. Professor Jones has advised the governments of Argentina, Bolivia, Brazil, Canada, Costa Rica, and Egypt in recent years as these countries have moved toward regulatory reform and privatization of previously state-owned utilities.

Sushil Kumar is a Professor of International Politics in the School of International Studies, Jawaharlal Nehru University, New Delhi, India. His recent publications are *Gorbachev's Reforms and International Change* (1993) and *New Globalism and the State* (1999).

He Li is an Associate Professor of Political Science at Merrimack College. He is the author of *Sino–Latin American Economic Relations* (Praeger, 1991) and several articles on Latin American and Chinese politics.

Stuart S. Nagel is Professor Emeritus of Political Science at the University of Illinois at Urbana–Champaign. He is secretary–treasurer and publications coordinator of the Policy Studies Organization and coordinator of the Dirksen–Stevenson Institute and MKM Research Center. He holds a Ph.D. in political science and a J.D. in law, both from Northwestern University. His major awards include fellowships and grants from the Ford Foundation, Rockefeller Foundation, National Science Foundation, National Social Science Council, East–West Center, and the Center for Advanced Study in the Behavioral Sciences. His previous positions include being an attorney to the U.S. Senate Judicial Committee, the National Labor Relations Board, and the Legal Services Corporation. He has been a professor at the University of Arizona and Penn State.

Dora Orlansky is a sociologist and full professor at the Department of Political Science and in charge of a research program on "Public Sector and State Reform" at the Instituto de Investigaciones Gino Germani, University of Buenos Aires. She has conducted various projects at different research centers in Argentina and elsewhere and has been a consultant for several international agencies and a visiting research fellow (Fulbright, René Thalmann–UBA, etc.) at the Department of Political Science, University of Pittsburgh. She has held different positions as an advisor for the Argentine government. Her contributions on the public sector have been published in journals and compilations in Argentina and elsewhere.

Stephen Page is an Assistant Professor at the Evans School of Public Affairs at the University of Washington, and consults to state and local governments and nonprofit organizations regarding social policies that affect children and families. He received his Ph.D. in Political Science from MIT in 1999; his dissertation is entitled "Reform in Progress: The Emergence of Collaborative Adjustment for Human Services in the 1990s." He is also the coauthor, with Jane Knitzer, of *Map and Track: State Initiatives for Young Children and Families* (New York: National Center for Children in Poverty, Columbia University School of Public Health, 1998 and 1996 editions).

Pradeep K. Saxena is Assistant Professor of Public Administration at the University of Rajasthan, Jaipur, India. He is a writer in the field of public policy and public administration and has published more than a dozen books and several articles in national and international journals.

Stanka Setnikar-Cankar is an Associate Professor of Economics and Public Sector Economics at the School of Public Administration, University of Ljubljana. She is Head Chair of Public Sector Economics, Vice President of the Slovenian Association of Public Administration, former Vice Dean at the School of Public Administration, and from 1999, Dean at the School of Public Administration, University of Ljubljana. Her research and publishing work consists of approximately forty items, most of them articles, published in national scientific and expert periodicals, or presented at national and international meetings and conferences. She has published in the fields of public-sector economics, public finance, local-government economics, and local-government finance. She has participated in research and consultative work at the Ministry of Science, the Ministry of International Affairs, and the Institute of

Regional Economics and Development. She also takes an active part in the in-service training of civil servants in Slovenia. Her professional interests are directed toward integrating concepts drawn from the theoretical macroeconomics field with the needs of the practical transformation process taking place in the economy and in the public sector.

Bonu N. Swami is currently working at the University of Botswana, Gaborone, Botswana. He has forty years of professional experience, seven years of which were administrative, and the remainder of which dealt with academic matters in various capacities. He has published four books, five chapters, and thirty papers in journals of international repute. He has presented eighteen papers at international conferences.

Bradford H. Tuck is former Dean of the School of Business and Public Affairs and Professor of Economics at the University of Alaska, Anchorage. His considerable research product has focused on resource development in Alaska and quantitative analysis useful to policy makers in understanding, measuring, and forecasting the Alaskan economy. He joined Methodist University in 1965.

Xunda Yu is Chairman of the Department of Political Science and Public Administration, Zhejiang University, Hangzhou, People's Republic of China. His main research fields include modernization, political development, and comparative studies.

ISBN 1-56720-299-3

HARDCOVER BAR CODE